THE LIVING TORCH

THE LIVING TORCH

A. E.

EDITED BY

MONK GIBBON

WITH AN INTRODUCTORY ESSAY

CORACLE PRESS

San Rafael, Ca

Second, Facsimile edition,
Coracle Press, 2008
First edition, Macmillan and Co., 1938

For information, address:
Coracle Press, P.O. Box 151011
San Rafael, California 94915, USA

Library of Congress Cataloging-in-Publication Data

AE, 1867–1935.
The living torch / A.E.; edited by Monk Gibbon;
with an introductory essay.—2nd facsimile ed.
p. cm.
ISBN 978-1-59731-319-3 (pbk.: alk. paper)
ISBN 978-1-59731-324-7 (hardback: alk. paper)
I. Gibbon, Monk, 1896- II. Title.

PR6035.U7L5 2008
823'.912—dc22   2008021931

"He shook out ideas as from a torch in dazzling improvisation, and each one carried away a spark to light his own fire."

SIMONE TÉRY, of A.E.'s conversation.

EDITOR'S NOTE

I owe a big debt of gratitude to my wife for assistance in the selection and arrangement of this book, to Mr and Mrs Curran and Mr and Mrs Norman for many talks about A.E. and much helpful criticism and suggestion, to Mrs E. Hickson for a similar service, and to my friend Rupert Hart-Davis for the infinite patience and care with which he has read the proofs.

CONTENTS

CONTENTS

CONTENTS

CONTENTS

MORE CRITICISM

CONTENTS

CONTENTS

A.E.

.

A.E.

IT WAS JOHN EGLINTON who provided Moore with the word "maieutic" to describe A.E., an epithet Moore would have liked people to think given him by heaven. It is a good word, even though it should be necessary to consult the dictionary to ascertain what it means: "maieutic, ma-yu-tik, delivering, as in childbirth; a term applied to the probing method, by which Socrates made people bring forth for themselves the truths they disputed and which he sought to teach them".

A good word, but not quite good enough; a little misleading also, because, though A.E. acted as midwife to the thoughts of others, it is doubtful if he ever deliberately strove to teach. He had spent his own life learning and the most he attempted was to impart a little of what he had learnt. He was a mystic, indifferent to most of the things that other men think important. Indifferent to obscurity; for years a cashier at a small salary in a Dublin business-house, spending his evenings studying the Upanishads and the Vedas, and practising those mental disciplines which were to be for him the road to enlightenment. Indifferent to poverty, for even later, as the apostle of co-operation to the Irish farmer, he remained in the estimation of the world a poor man. Indifferent to fame, or rather only pleased by it in so far as it meant the achievement of an ideal or the approval of a friend. And a mystic not of one talent but of many, a poet, a painter, a master of philosophic prose, who could have pursued a dozen different roads to success but who held with a steady purpose to the path he had chosen. To pursue virtue armed with a number of talents is an even higher achievement than to pursue it with only a few. There are some who seek to enter the kingdom of heaven with their intellect shackled or their will tamed and emasculated. They are afraid that these servants, if they once got out of hand, might rob them of salvation. But in A.E. virtue shared house with an intellect passionate and fiercely speculative and with a will which had been disciplined but not by fear. Dunsany speaks of dreams as the hardest of all materials for labour, and the artificer in ideas as 'the chief of workers, who out of nothing will make a piece of work that may stop a child from crying or lead nations to higher things'. It might be said that there is a material even harder still—the individual soul. In that intractable domain few of us feel the satisfaction of the victorious artist. It was here that A.E. had laboured. He never withdrew from life; indeed he was continually being drawn into an ever closer contact with men, their thoughts and actions. But like all true mystics the deeper he penetrated into reality the more he was disposed to accept it with patience. He hated error and imperfection as much as any man, but he kept steadily before him the concept, and those occasional glimpses that life affords us, of perfection. Hearing of his death one of his friends was to cry:

> Give back to earth the ear that strained
> Out to the beat of hidden wings,

Sensing in imperfection still
Shadow of perfect things.

Shake off the last of body's chains.
Shall not that spirit now be free
Which such immortal longings brought
To its mortality?

'How conscious he is of his own eternity', wrote Moore, who seems to have realised more clearly than anyone else that A.E.'s life had a single objective, and that the objective was not supremacy in a particular craft but as complete a perfecting of the self as was possible in the circumstances which destiny had decreed. Never completely his own master, his spirit remained, notwithstanding, infinitely freer than that of many men whose time is wholly their own. He might have said with Epictetus—'Material things are indifferent, but how we handle them is not indifferent. Counters and dice are indifferent. How do I know what is going to turn up? My business is to use what does turn up with diligence and skill'.

He brought with him a unique flavour both of goodness and greatness. It is doubtful if anyone ever heard A.E. say an arrogant or unfair thing. The most I have ever known him show was a slight petulance or irritation at some stupidity, or the grave ironic anger of a man who knows that what he condemns is without justification and must one day purge its offence in the course of the divine justice which orders the world. I think of his remark to Seán O'Faoláin, "It is part of my philosophy that things that are evil are to be got rid of by thinking of their opposites. We become what we contemplate." Of the many things said of A.E. after his death perhaps the best was said by his friend Con Curran, who had known him for thirty years—"He was a tribunal before which the ignoble dwindles".

It is the custom to praise a man when he is dead, but it was A.E.'s fate that his friends were constantly saying such things about him while he was still alive. As early as 1909 Clifford Bax had written:

> I know that one may easily injure whatever one most loves by speaking of it in superlative praise to those who as yet remain aloof with interest unaroused, but for me it is hard to refrain from an expression of that admiration, and I would fain say also that affection which burns up within me when I read the writings of A.E. For they cause me to think of him as one of those rare spirits who bring to men the realisation of their own divinity, who make the spiritual life seem adventurous, attractive and vivid, so that we go forth into the world with a new interest and a new joy at heart. The life of such a man makes beautiful the generation with which it coincides.

I remember myself how in Italy, at a time when my mind was preoccupied with other things, his image for no reason flashed into my thoughts and I wrote:

> I have known one great man,
> One man alone to rise
> Shoulder and head above
> All his contemporaries.
>
> Greater than any now,
> Equal indeed it seemed
> Of those dead few of whom
> Reverent youth had dreamed.
>
> Holding that ancient path,
> Lofty in speech as they,
> Turning to nobler gold
> The dross of every day.
>
> Now when a sick world seems
> Late to be put to school,
> Blind still directing blind,
> Fool still exhorting fool,

A. E.

I would remind myself,
This thing is not the whole,
I too can boast in time
I have known one great soul.

Katharine Tynan could say:

> I have known in my time some few undoubted
> geniuses—three certainly in literature—W. B. Yeats,
> Francis Thompson and George Russell (A.E.) to which
> I believe I have a fourth in James Stephens. In none of
> these have I found the beauty of genius as I find it in
> George Russell. His flame has always burnt upward
> clearly. When I am struck cold, remembering that such
> and such an one, something uniquely precious of God's
> making, is no longer of this world, I turn to think of
> George Russell, that untroublesome genius. I am glad
> that in all probability he will survive me, for of him
> more than of anyone else I have known I would say,
> "We shall never look on his like again".

Praise of this kind would have spoilt some men but A.E.
remained unspoilt by it. He preferred the affection of his
friends to their adulation. He could poke fun at hero-
worship, implying, with a twinkle in his eye, that eulogy was
an art to be practised posthumously, if at all. To the most
successful of his panegyrists he complained that he had made
him 'the hero of a young girl's novel'. "Why have you found
no fault with me? If you wish to create human beings you
must discover their faults"—an accusation which so terrified
the literary artist in George Moore that he began to search
frenziedly for faults, but had to be content with A.E.'s
inability to distinguish between turbot and halibut, and his
indifference to money. If it is a fault to despise your meals
A.E. was guilty. Mrs. Kingsley Porter notes his scorn of food
as the rival of good conversation, but says that he allowed

himself to be led meekly to the dinner-table provided he could
still continue to talk. Nothing would be more false than to
imagine him as self-consciously ascetic. He ate absent-mindedly
only because ideas interested him so much. Conversely, he
smoked freely because a pipe is a good background to conversation. In writing about him it is easy to stress the nobility of his mind—self-evident from his writings and which
might therefore be left to adduce itself—but it is much
harder to convey the gaiety and geniality of the man. I remember how St John Ervine called him the most lovable of
Anglo-Irish writers, not the greatest in that list but the
most lovable, 'more lovable even than Goldsmith'. Impishness and fun, never ill-natured, irradiated his talk and made
him not merely the sage moving in spheres of lofty contemplation, but the most delightful, homely and human of companions as well. "Simple, extraordinarily open and generous,
doing his best to meet all comers on the level at which he
would be most helpful to them", is how one friend describes
him. It is perhaps a pity that his writings, which are concerned
with deeper issues, contain hardly a hint of this spirit of innocent fun.[1] He could for instance parody his own verse with
immense zest, a feat of which anyone who takes himself too
seriously is incapable. Indeed it was his humanity which immediately impressed those who met him, before either his
spirituality or his force of intellect had had time to do so.
The truth is that he resembled one of those characters which
both Anatole France and James Stephens have introduced
into fiction, a demiurge or being from another world who,
while retaining memory of the hierarchy from which they
have sprung, are at the same time capable of identifying
themselves completely with the human scene.

[1] The Dietician who was betrayed into spiritual pride and boasting, is a
slight example, though it may seem incongruous in the context in which I
have placed it in this book.

2

Until a full-length biography appears, it is in the pages of
Hail and Farewell that we are most likely to find A.E. Neither
Darrell Figgis, whose little book was published before the
war, nor William Clyde, who is concerned mainly with the
poetry, has the literary skill of Moore. Moore understood
his man. It is true that when his trilogy first appeared a certain number of people thought that he had caricatured A.E.,
especially in that passage where he describes the unsuccessful invocation of the gods at Newgrange. It is true also that
later years were to see a breach for a time between the two,
a breach which I may have helped to heal by carrying a
kindly message from Moore to A.E. in Dublin, hoping that
the latter would visit him if he came to London.[1] There
must always have been one aspect of Moore which appealed
little to A.E., and in one of his later books he refers to him—
indirectly but with great severity—placing the words used
in the mouth of those to whom ribaldry would have been
especially distasteful. But, if he disliked this side of Moore,
he was alive also to the latter's kindliness, and to his skill
and conscience as a writer. Indeed he has held him up to me
as a model of pertinacity, describing how he has seen Moore's
face pale with anguish after a morning's unsuccessful wrestling
with his work.

Moore on the other hand, as an anonymous reviewer has
recently pointed out, was drawn to 'men of innate goodness,
such as George Russell, John Eglinton, Degas and Tonks'.
There can be no question of his affection for A.E. It trans-
pires continually. He says, "It was to meet this man that
I had come to Ireland as much as to see the plays". Worried

[1] Amongst my letters I find one, of about the same time, from A.E.,
expressing pleasure but surprise that Moore should have approved what he
had recently written about the censorship.

about A.E.'s health and trying to persuade T. P. Gill to have him sent to Italy, he cries, "For you know A.E. is the most important person in Ireland". Elsewhere he says, "There never was anybody like him. While we strive after happiness he holds it in his hands. A.E. forgets what he gives . . . my feet taking me instinctively to A.E., who settles everybody's difficulties and consoles the afflicted . . . when he left me a certain mental sweetness seemed to have gone out of the air."

Moore does not describe A.E., rather he evokes him in the same way that he evokes his writings:

> I remembered the delight and wonder which his verse and prose had awakened in me. It was just as if somebody had put his hand into mine, and led me away into a young world which I recognised as the fabled Arcady that had flourished before man discovered gold, and forged the gold into a ring which gave him power to enslave. White mist curled along the edge of the woods, and the trees were all in blossom. There were tall flowers in the grass, and gossamer threads glittered in the rays of the rising sun, and it seemed to me that the man must live always in this hour, and that he not only believed in Arcady, but that Arcady was always in him.

By a succession of intimate touches he conveys the man as surely as an impressionist painter does a landscape. We feel as it were the emanation of his spirit. It is Moore too who sees A.E.'s activities in the cause of co-operation in their true light. They formed what St. Paul might have called his salvation by works.

> They gave him a bicycle and he rode through Ireland preaching the doctrine of co-operation and dairy-farming from village to village, winning friends to the movement by the personal magnetism which he exer-

cises wherever he goes, and the eloquence of his belief in Plunkett. As soon as he arrived in a village everybody's heart became a little warmer, a little friendlier; the sensation of isolation and loneliness, which all human beings feel, thawed a little; everybody must have felt happier the night that kindly man mounted a platform, threw back his long hair and began to talk to them, giving them shrewd advice, and making them feel that he loved them and that they were not unworthy of his love. The only house in the poor village in which he could lodge would be the priest's house, and the lonely village priest, who does not meet a friend with whom he can exchange an idea once every three months, would spend a memorable evening with A.E. The priests in those villages have little bookshelves along their rooms, and A.E. would go to these shelves and find a book that had not interested the priest since the enthusiasm of his youth had died down; he would open this book, and read passages, and awaken the heart of the priest. In the morning the old bicycle would be brought out, and away A.E. would go, and the priest, I am sure, looked after him, sorry that he was going. Protestants, Catholics, Presbyterians, Methodists—all united in loving A.E.

This is perhaps the moment to refer very briefly to A.E.'s activities in the cause of co-operation. The poet became an economist but the economist always remained a poet. One can trace the story in the files of the agricultural journal of which he presently became editor.[1] As the travelling propagandist of the movement he must have visited every county in the land. He rode through Ireland and he rode with his eyes open. His humanity was enriched by contact with all classes of people, and if theosophy hitherto

[1] *The Irish Homestead*

had encouraged him to live too much in a world of mystifica-
tion, he had ample opportunity now to become acquainted
with the world which ordinary men inhabit. It meant a new
unfolding of personality. Dr. Best of the National Library
tells me that his first recollection of A.E. is of a shy, vague
young man, bearded and dreamy, offering pamphlets for
sale at some theosophic function yet utterly ignorant of
their price. This was the man who was to harangue farmers,
hold meetings, found creameries and banks, give evidence
upon finance before a royal commission, have his writings
upon rural economy translated into a number of languages,
and even be summoned to Washington to advise the American Government upon a rural economy for that country.

Both he and H. F. Norman, who worked with him in the
cause of co-operation, are a complete vindication of the
mystic when he turns his hand to practical affairs. During
these years he was fighting like a modern Don Quixote on
behalf of the small farmer against the gombeen man and
the higgler, "monstrous people, bloated out like tropical
spiders who are filled with the life-blood of their people".
So he described them.

He condemned a system by which the gombeen man, the
local storekeeper, both bought from and sold to the small
farmer at his own price, till, wound in the toils of loans and
mortgages, he was no longer his own master. Against this
tyranny A.E. waged fierce war. It has been said of him that
he could never be angry with men, only with actions; he
had only to meet the man for his anger to vanish, filled with
a vast tolerance for his kind. But this is an exaggeration. In
the struggle against selfish interests he could strike hard
when he wished, giving quite as good as he received. Writing
for an audience of country folk and small farmers, he used
his gift of irony and did not always make that irony too
subtle. As Lincoln had said of slavery, "I made up my mind
that, if I ever got the chance, I would hit that thing, and

that I would hit it hard". It was this struggle which may have developed his gift for invective. As one friend put it, "When he condemns it is overwhelming coming from his immense and almost boundless tolerance". Yeats, speaking of him to me, has said, "His invective could be terrific"; and it was Desmond MacCarthy who wrote, "He had at command, like many serious men, a gift for vituperation. But he refrained from using it. Only twice to my knowledge did he use words to wound and not to persuade. Then he was tremendous."

How many of the gombeen men, 'the only survivors of the cave tiger, the plesiosaurus and other primaeval monsters . . . . picking the bones of their victims', knew that their opponent who scourged them so savagely was a poet and a mystic? He used ridicule, he said, because he found it the most effective weapon. "Ireland has grown so solemn and pompous from standing so long on its hind legs on platforms, that it dreads nothing more than a jest; and indeed, it would hardly be an exaggeration to say that most Irishmen dread being laughed at by their neighbours while alive more than they fear being damned after they die." It is doubtful if many of his readers knew who their editor was. His name is not mentioned. Only once, in the notes for the week, does he half draw aside the curtain.

> We have always tried to steer by the stars, to endeavour to make our readers remember . . . that in the midst of all these immediate matters, these needs of the week or the day, humanity, a strange cavalcade, was journeying on to divine events and awful and august climaxes and judgements. It is not the business of an economic journal to preach these things; but it is, all the same, an urgent duty laid on us not to forget them, or in what fields we will camp when our journey is over. . . . The fashion of the day is to keep the needs of the soul and the needs of the body in

watertight compartments, and it is a fashion we hate. We hope in the next generation the then editor of the *Homestead* will find it possible to print along with the instructions what seeds should be sown in the earth, the songs which the farmer might sing at his work. . . . A friend once described to us how in Poland she heard hundreds of people singing as they came home from the steppes. Song and labour, the soul and the body, are far apart in Ireland; but they may be brought closer, and a more light-hearted life made possible, if we can get our rural population . . . to realise what they came to earth for, to live together and work together, and that they will attain to and enjoy their Heavenly Paradise just in the proportion they have contributed to an earthly Paradise here.

In a passage like this we get a glimpse of another man besides the one who bludgeoned his enemies with the heavy club of ridicule. It is to Moore's credit that though his own interests were chiefly literary, and literature was the common ground on which he and A.E. met, he has yet managed to give us other facets as well—the mystic and the economist, both largely alien to Moore's own temperament, yet faithfully rendered. A.E. emerges from his pages as a whole, and it is the more wonderful in that, though in his account of him cycling through Ireland and elsewhere we see A.E. so clearly, Moore has no direct description of him—"he exists rather in one's imagination, dreams, sentiments, feelings, than in one's ordinary sight and hearing, and try as I will to catch the fleeting outlines they escape me; and all I remember are the long, grey, pantheistic eyes that have looked so often into my soul and with such a kindly gaze".

Only one other writer rivals Moore's success. Not less tenderly but with perhaps a more Gallic wit Simone Téry has drawn for us the A.E. of later years. The fifty pages devoted to him in *L'Île des bardes* are so good that it is a pity they have not found a translator. Simone Téry came to Dublin for the purpose of writing a book about its literary celebrities, but the incense which she burns at the different shrines is not allowed to blind her, as it does some votaries, to the distinctive features of her divinities. Nothing passes her notice and all is set down wittily, truthfully and without pedantry. She gives us A.E.'s appearance, his mannerisms, his views on life, his conversation, the very effluvia of his personality. As he talks to her the coils of smoke from his pipe mingle with the convolutions of his beard and she re-echoes what Katharine Tynan had already said, that this beard "le fait ressembler à Dieu le Père", in an Italian primitive. She tells us how,

> "toute la vie est rassemblée dans les yeux d'un bleu-gris tendre, lumineux, pacifié, le bleu du ciel après la pluie. Derrière les lunettes, on dirait que ces yeux clairs rient, et une tendre malice les éclaire. Lorsqu'il se penche vers un interlocuteur pour l'écouter ou lui parler, ses yeux avec une douceur aiguë le pénètrent jusqu'au fond. Il semble appuyer les yeux sur ce qu'il observe, et son regard prolongé ne quitte pas celui à qui il s'adresse."

How many must remember the sweetness and the tender malice of A.E.'s eyes. And it is not only in noticing externals that she is so successful. She is equally good when it comes to penetrating and assessing the secret of his greatness.

> Qu'est-ce qui peut donc inspirer une si tendre admiration à tous ceux qui ont rencontré A.E.? C'est d'abord sans doute le merveilleux exemple qu'est sa vie. Avec son intelligence diverse et hardie, son activité prodigieuse, sa puissance de travail, le monde pouvait

lui donner, comme à la plupart de ses amis, honneurs et fortune. A.E., pourtant, a su réaliser ce tour de force de rester, à cinquante-sept ans, pauvre et solitaire. Non seulement il n'a rien sollicité de la vie, mais il a refusé doucement tout ce qu'elle venait lui apporter. Il a repoussé la richesse, les consécrations officielles; il a préféré conserver sa liberté, se dévouer au bien public, obscurément, attendre, au lieu de forcer la renommée par une réclame tapageuse, la gloire qui lui viendrait d'elle-même. . . . Il est des êtres choisis d'où émane un rayonnement mystérieux; lorsque les passants croisent l'un d'eux dans la rue, ils le suivent des yeux; ceux qui rencontrent son regard deviennent tout joyeux; ceux à qui il adresse la parole se sentent réchauffés. Tous les visages se tournent instinctivement vers lui, comme les fleurs vers le soleil. Par sa seule présence il crée autour de lui une zone bienfaisante; ceux-là mêmes qui d'ordinaire sont moroses ou mesquins deviennent soudain devant lui, comme par miracle, joyeux et bons. Il a le pouvoir singulier de susciter ce qu'il y a de meilleur dans les hommes et de refouler le pire. Walt Whitman, Tolstoi, Tagore sont de ces âmes puissantes et douces. A.E. en est une autre. Ces hommes-là sont les bons génies de l'humanité; ils ont quelque chose de plus qu'humain, c'est leur force tranquille qui fait avancer le monde.

With one of those flashes of insight which show her to have had a wisdom beyond her years, she says:

> Ce qu'on aime le mieux dans Yeats, ce sont ses vers. Mais le chef-d'œuvre d'A.E., qui est un grand artiste, c'est encore lui-même.

Is it a reproach to a man to say that he was his own masterpiece? It was the same feeling probably which prompted Moore to remark to Mrs. Murray Robertson one evening as they walked back across the streets of Dublin, "You know, I think that A.E. is too great a man to be a great artist". He meant that whereas a Rossetti, a Swinburne or a Baudelaire had always sacrificed the man to the artist, in the case of A.E. the talents were only an accidental revelation of the soul that had given them birth. I am interested in this remark, told me by Mrs. Murray Robertson herself, because it proves that Moore's praise of A.E. was not merely part of a literary programme, a device to enhance his book by striking a note of eulogy where so much was censure; it was sincere.

3

If only Simone Téry and George Moore had sketched A.E. it would still be possible to envisage him from their words. But actually a number of portraits and at least three busts of him exist. Between the gentle boy with the heavy quiff of hair and the dreamy expression, in Hughes' bust,[1] and the marble head by Oliver Sheppard, now in the National Gallery of Ireland, lay who knows what ardours and endurances of the soul. We are fortunate to have this earlier record by Hughes, which used for years to stand above the mantelshelf of the outer sitting-room in A.E.'s home at Rathgar Avenue. The mouth is large and good-humoured, but something in the expression of the eyes suggests that this youth, glancing broodingly downwards, has already set forth on those adventures of the spirit which were to take him so far. Sheppard's bust is by far the best rendering of the man in maturity. It conveys with splendid success the intentness of the knit brows, as he leant forward in his chair to interrogate some visitor, or to listen, with a gaze of penetrating sympathy, to what they had

[1] Dublin Municipal Gallery, Charlemont House.

to say to him. It is the head of a thinker, meditating upon profound destinies, but at the same time it has a Greek serenity and detachment. He used to refer to it himself, mockingly, as "Sheppard's Olympian Zeus". The pointed beard as the chin sinks forward into the marble, the heavy eyebrows twisted at the corner and faintly suggestive of the faun or satyr, the gravity and almost mystical calm of expression, all convey the man and are a tribute to the sculptor's skill. The original version was lost, when the Hibernian Academy was burnt in 1916, but Sheppard had still the plaster cast, and getting A.E. to sit to him again made a second, and, it is believed, better version in white marble.

Sarah Purser and Count Markiewicz both painted him, and F. R. Higgins possesses an excellent pastel of him in his early forties by a foreign visitor to Dublin. It belongs to the period Moore had in mind when he wrote, "He has the kindly mind of a shepherd and ten years ago he was thin, lithe, active, shaggy, and I can see him leaning on his crook meditating". I have not seen the portrait by Yeats' father, which was at one time in the possession of John Quin of New York, but both the Gilbert bronze and the dry-point by Walter Tittle seem to me to make him too gross and heavy. Neither is characteristic, though it is true that he grew stouter about five or six years before his death. It is probably of this time that MacCarthy is thinking when he says, "a large, shabby, stooping, bearded man, of a rather flabby habit of body, with a glint in his eye that might have suggested slyness in another but of the kind that I have come to associate with genius". This emphasis on his heaviness is a little exaggerated and at most is only true of a short period in his life. A.E. in his thirties had been lean and wiry. As he approached fifty his appearance became more majestic. A series of photographs taken in New York at the time of his first visit[1] emphasise the

[1] I think by P. Macdonald.

poetic grandeur of his head. It was at this time, in his early
sixties, that he was probably nearest in aspect to that conception of the sage which one might form of him from his
writings.

4

My mind goes back to the time of my own first contact
with him. I had sent him a copy of verses for an opinion. His
literary weekly had not yet been founded, but his kindness
to young writers was already proverbial. He was the oracle
towards which, sooner or later, every literary aspirant in
Dublin gravitated, and there is an amusing cartoon by
"Mac" of a devotee, a youth, prostrating himself before the
shrine, while A.E., like some bearded sphinx, looks im-
passively over his head. The humility of that approach may
have been true but its reception was far different. There was
hardly a young writer in Ireland who did not owe to A.E.
his initial encouragement in literature. How generous and
how helpful that encouragement could be I was to experience for myself.

I was unknown to him. I had no claim upon him and no
introduction, but within a few days I received a long letter
in his own hand. Telling me he had read the poems with
interest, he went on to say:

> I would like to encourage you to write but only on
> the understanding that you take writing as seriously, let
> us say, as an engineer, chemist or biologist ardently
> desirous of complete mastery over his profession. I do
> not think it is worth while trying to write poetry unless
> one feels it is the highest expression of the human
> spirit, and the quality of thought, sincerity and feeling
> must be the highest of which the writer is capable. . . .
> I do not think poetry is the expression of thought. It
> would be didactic and without illumination. But I

think all writing of poetry should be preceded by a passionate desire for truth, and when the poet is writing he should continually ask himself, "Do I really believe this? Is this truly what I felt? Is that the true expression of my imagination?" Style is truth-telling. . . . I believe every human being has in him the roots of genius if he digs deep enough. Keats said in a letter, "there is a kind of ancestral wisdom in man and we can, if we turn inward, drink that old wine of heaven". . . . I remember talking to a great artist who told me that he acquired his facility by always thinking of his art. His pencil was rarely out of his hand. Everything he saw he thought of as material for his art. When he was not working he was dreaming or imagining intensely. He was obsessed by his art. I think that is true of the best poetry, that the writers were obsessed by their art and their imaginations and clung to the idea of perfection. My friend Yeats broods and broods over single lines, letting nothing pass until it is as perfect as he can make it. . . . "In painting", said Corot, "one must go a little beyond oneself." That is true of poetry.

In the same letter came an invitation to visit him at Plunkett House, in Merrion Square, where he carried on his activities in the cause of co-operation. F. R. Higgins has a vivid description of his sanctum there:

A.E.'s office, a room at the top of that building, seemed like an opening in fairy woods. He had painted each wall, from roof to floor, and there you looked on trees, and, beyond them, on beings rarely seen on land or sea, but always seen in the woods of vision and the air of dream. And there in the painted wood A.E. sat. His shaggy head—with its bright and heavily-cleft brow, its blue eyes bespectacled above a strong nose and rugged beard—looked at you from behind a barricade

of papers and books. And from the first sound of his
voice, with its wooing gentleness, the visitor was made
at home. Were you interested in economics, in the
mystics, in new brands of politics? Maybe you preferred
opinions on poetry, or better agricultural methods, or
on paintings? The range of your enquiries was never
met with a stare. It was always enlightened by the
illumination of A.E.'s mind. And for the first time in
your life you felt that you had truly met with a wonderful man. You were only one of many minds who questioned A.E. and left his presence in peace. You differed
from him but you were drawn towards him. Indeed his
immense humanism attracted opposites.

I remember my own emotions as I climbed the successive
flights of stairs on that first occasion. At last we arrived on
the top landing, the door was pushed open by the boy who
had been showing me the way, and I saw a great bearded
man rising from his desk by the window and lumbering
forward rather like a bear. Stooping slightly, for he was
short-sighted, he shook hands with that shy abrupt deprecation of manner which Dublin adopts towards such amenities.
And yet there was nothing but goodwill in that greeting, and
presently a great benevolence beamed at you from behind
the spectacles, while he talked of poetry as though it were
for him and for you the most important subject in the
world. Susan Mitchell made tea for us and still A.E. talked,
pouring out his wisdom with a prodigality which amazed
a visitor new to him.

I carried away on that occasion an impression of profound
sincerity, and of the great width and range of his thought,
a giant of the intellect but not an intellectual, a seer yet
without any wish to impress. One left feeling that there
were still heroes upon earth.

Before I went he invited me to visit him in his home in

Rathgar Avenue any Sunday evening I cared to come, but for some reason I did not avail myself of this invitation for nearly a year.

There must be people all over the world who remember A.E.'s salon. On Sunday evenings from seven-thirty onwards he was at home to every caller. Norah Hoult has described those evenings well, "the modest two-storied house, the long narrow room divided by folding doors, which was one part studio and one part study and sitting-room", and A.E.'s phrase—"We were just discussing", which was his method of linking up the newcomer with the symposium in progress at the moment when he arrived. That phrase, which I had forgotten but which returns to me now, brings with it vividly my own memories of visits to 17 Rathgar Avenue.

One had gone prepared for this symposium. In winter in the tiny garden a single tree threw faintly its stark shadow from a distant street lamp. One mounted the steps and rang the bell. There were slow footsteps in the hall and the door was thrown back with a grating sound to show A.E., pipe in hand, in the half-opened doorway. The bland soft northern accent would greet you, "Oh, it's you, come in", and you would follow him into the first room, where his pictures were kept, many of them still unframed and stacked against the wall, and from there into the room at the back which opened out of it, where there were more pictures hung on the walls and where his books stood on three low shelves that ran the length of the room. Sometimes there would be a number of guests and the room would already have split into groups and factions, each discussing whatever topic interested them; but when the party consisted of half a dozen or so conversation would generally revolve round some central theme, of which A.E. held the threads and to which each guest was encouraged to contribute something.

My first visit was a prelude to many others. I have come when the room was so crowded that an odd guest was quite content to sit on the floor, or I have come and found him talking to a single poet, entering to hear him say, "You will not write poetry merely by wanting to write poetry. Have you anything to say?"

He had few mannerisms. The curious, chanting voice, with its broad flat tones, in which he read his own and the verse of others as if he were a priest occupied with litany or prayer, though some liked it, was not always particularly pleasing from the point of view of poetry; and may have seemed an affectation to many who did not know him well. But it was part of the man, and to him it was the way poetry should be read. He would chant passages from the Bhagavad-gita, or, crossing the room, he would grope in the book-case for some book, find it and then, holding it close to his eyes, read slowly aloud the passage he wanted, the page almost touching his face, so that one wondered how he could focus on it. When I read that Ouspensky, lecturing, did the same, I thought that the act might have some occult significance, a mannerism of intense concentration perhaps, until a friend assured me that in A.E.'s case it was short-sightedness and nothing else. Sometimes he would look at the book in this way, almost touching his eyes, and then hold it away when actually reading, perhaps because the passage was in the main known to him. Over the question of the esoteric meaning of some phrase in the gospels I have known him take down a Greek testament and, though he said he had forgotten most of the Greek of his schooling, read it slowly aloud with very careful deliberation. As the evening progressed and he talked more and more, a gentle dew of perspiration would break out on his face, one would notice the light shining on his gold spectacles, his blue tie, his loosely-laced boots, the ruffled brown hair and the golden beard turning grey; while all the time the caressing, soothing voice focused attention on the thought quite as much as the man, for though it seemed too melodic almost for a poem, it was the most persuasive of all voices when it came to an argument or a theory.

Knees crossed, pipe in hand, he would sit in his chair in the centre of the room, conversing perhaps with some guest who was then meeting him for the first time. "Even the shallow", says Norah Hoult, "could hardly fail to be struck by the instantaneous impression of goodness—there is no other word—which he made. People who had not met him made jokes about the weak tea, often made by himself, and plum-cake served out at these Sunday gatherings, and suggested that here was another poseur. When they had met him they were silenced. A great natural simplicity and dignity expressed the integrity of one who never in his whole life could have done or thought a mean or a petty thing."

Presently if the guest expressed a wish to see them he would get up and take him into the next room to show his pictures. This was part of the ritual of a visit, and just as in the case of the handshake there was an abrupt shyness and some slight deprecation of manner in the way in which he would substitute one unframed canvas for another upon the easel. Looking at the succession of landscapes his visitors felt, as one of them has put it, that they could hardly have been painted outside the borders of Ireland. In the artist's meditation locality counted for little, accidentals had fallen away and little trace of human activity remained. And yet "their harmony and gracious line built up a place of refreshment and peace in correspondence with the painter's mood. His figures, irradiated in sunshine, became ethereal, and there was disengaged from mountain and flowing water, from the recollection of evening skies, from the fugitive play of children and lovers, a Virgilian beauty in which the transitory neighboured the eternal."[1]

[1] C. P. Curran, in a note on A.E.'s painting.

The best of his painting was done on holiday in the summer, but it was his habit also for a long time to paint during the week-ends. Professor Osborn Bergin tells me a story of a friend who watched A.E. counting his canvases at the end of the year. "Forty-eight. Forty-nine. Fifty. Fifty-one. —Fifty-one?—There is one picture missing." So great was the regularity with which the weekly canvas was produced. It was to Bergin he said that if he had been entirely free he would undoubtedly have been a painter. The latter replied, "You would have done nothing of the sort. You would have gone to India and sat cross-legged at the feet of some guru. You are essentially the sage."

A.E. painted many pictures that were bad, but he painted others that were unquestionably beautiful, and that could have been the work of no one but himself. Orpen, who was no advocate for his painting, remarked at one of the exhibitions, "The strange thing is that the intention is always right".

Unquestionably it was the artist which first awakened in him. At school he amused and delighted his schoolmates by the humour and talent of his pencil. We get a glimpse of him in his sketches, many of them playful in intention, kept by one of these school friends—the Rev. H. C. Browne. They give the impression of a temperament ardent, enthusiastic and refreshingly gay. He brought to life all the spirits of the normal boy. Though he was not distinctive as a scholar his friends nicknamed him "the genius". Yeats, speaking of his youth, says, "I used to listen to him at that time, mostly walking through the streets at night, for the sake of some sentence, beautiful and profound amid many words which seemed without meaning," and he goes on to say, "We derided each other, told tales to one another's discredit, but we never derided him or told tales to his discredit".

There is a coloured sketch by the same friend who kept his juvenilia in which he depicts A.E. as a boy being run into by a passer-by as he gazes ecstatically into the window of an art shop at a cast of the Dancing Faun. Some of his early work exists. Hughes told Moore that A.E. was by far his most talented contemporary in the Dublin School of Art. In later years A.E., either from forgetfulness or from modesty, would imply that painting was only his hobby, that owing to the circumstances of his life he had taken it up too late for his pretensions to be taken seriously, yet at the same time he could write to a friend, in a different mood, "Painting is the only thing I have any real delight in doing. Nature intended me to be a painter." Actually he had taken it up in youth and abandoned it again. Moore says, "Yet in spite of an extraordinary fluency of expression, abundant inspiration and the belief of the whole school that a great artist was in him, A.E. laid aside his brushes, determined not to pick them up again until he had mastered the besetting temptation that art presented at that moment. He feared it as a sort of self-indulgence which, if yielded to, would stint his life; art with him is a means rather than an end; it should be sought, for by its help we can live more purely, more intensely, but we must never forget that to live as fully as possible is after all our main concern. . . . He could have been a painter if he had wished it, and possibly a great painter; but a man's whole life is seldom long enough for him to acquire the craft of the painter; and, setting life above craftmanship, A.E. denied himself the beautiful touch that separates the artist from the amateur, and he did well."

Yeats tells us the same but draws a different conclusion. "I remember that I was ironic and indignant when he left the Art Schools because his 'will was weak, and must grow weaker if he followed any emotional pursuit'."[1]

A.E. never abandoned painting completely. Even in his

---

[1] I agree with Norman that this statement is relative, that A.E. was intensely self-critical and that his will was infinitely stronger than that of most men.

earlier theosophic days he made use of the talent. The poet
Seumas O'Sullivan has shown me the beautiful little water-
colour drawings with which A.E. illuminated his copy of
Homeward, Songs by the Way, and though these may have been
done at a later date, there are a number of semi-mystical
paintings which belong to that period.

5

It was Clive Bell, I think, who once referred to the 'Dicky
Doyle' fairies in A.E.'s paintings. He was probably thinking
not of the fairies at all but of the maidens who frolic in some
of the forest scenes, and who may vaguely suggest Doyle's
work. The "fairies" which A.E. painted were not the diminu-
tive, conventional kind at all but were tall heroic figures,
"people of the Siodhe". Darrell Figgis has an interesting
point to make in this connection. He writes:

> We feel in these paintings that the artist was in
> labour to communicate a part of his assurance with
> regard to the spiritual beings we ourselves are; how-
> ever fantastic his designs may at first sight seem to us
> that certitude of ours is the first thing we have. A.E.'s
> colours even while achieving, it may be, a gorgeous or
> very pure symphony of colour are marked by a very
> earnest attempt at fidelity to psychic vision . . . they
> may almost by adepts be accepted as mystical charts,
> because these pictures are directly related to his
> mystical experience. Looking at them we begin to
> understand that when old warriors decked themselves
> with helmets and feathers suggesting plumes of light
> above the spinal cord or wings branching from the
> temples, they were not merely fanciful; we remember
> that they lived in a day when vision and the psychic
> powers were not slighted in the world.

Equally interesting is what St. John Ervine says:

> I have a picture by A.E. of an ascending road on the
> side of a mountain. There is rain in the air and the road
> has a lonely unfrequented look. Yet, though there is no
> living creature visible in the picture, Life fills it. I feel
> sometimes when I sit back in my chair and look at "The
> Mountain Road" that there are divine beings behind the
> bushes, that if I could only climb up that road and turn
> the corner of the mountain, I should come upon the
> Golden Age. Is it not ungracious to make complaint,
> even if the complaint be a slight one, of a man who can
> make the invisible world so powerfully felt as that?
> And if he persuades me, by nature sceptical, almost to
> believe in the Shining Ones, how much more strong
> must his influence be on those who are eager to believe.

These paintings raise the whole question of the visionary
element in A.E.'s life. Its implications are too far-reaching to
be discussed adequately here. Men are still quarrelling over
the precise nature of Blake's visions, and to A.E.—who wrote
with extreme honesty and simplicity of the matter—the
nature of his own vision was still largely a mystery. Whether
they were earth memories retained in some etheric substance
so that they became visible at certain times, or whether
they were sudden glimpses into an interpenetrating spiritual
world, or whether, as a friend has suggested to me in relation
to Blake, they were in the nature of waking dream, a projection of the mind of the same mysterious kind as we experience
in sleep, need not be argued here. They may have been an
extension of the ordinary artistic faculty by which the painter
visualises almost objectively what he has seen in the imagination previously, or—and I myself lean to this opinion—
they may have been in the nature of a real experience, such
as St. Paul hints at when he quotes the psalmist's "who
maketh his angels spirits and his ministers a flame of fire".

A.E.

I find in my journal an account of how I walked back with
A.E. as far as Harcourt Street, after an evening spent with
Yeats, where I had listened to a discussion between them of
certain visions each had had. With the tenacity of youth and
the scepticism of one who had known no such experience, I
cross-examined him as to the nature of these visions. Were
they subjective or objective? He disliked the terms, for he
contended rightly that all vision is a mystery, even normal
waking vision, and in a sense subjective. "I do not know
what you mean by subjective and objective", he said a little
angrily. "I really see them. And another witness at the same
moment has corroborated what I have reported, correcting
me in this detail or in that. I am convinced that there is
another world about this world, more beautiful in every
way and possessed by more beautiful men and women, far
above us"—and he went on to tell me of his seven years of
mystic culture, abandoned only on the score of health. This
was entered in my journal some weeks later, but is a faithful
transcript, I believe, of what was said.[1]

In his mystical paintings the figures are often rearrange-
ments or reconstructions of what he had seen thus, either in
mental vision or perhaps even with the open eye. Occasion-

[1] Turning to Yeats' *Trembling of the Veil* I find he has a good deal to say on
the subject of these visions. "At the time I write of him he was the religious
teacher, and that alone—his painting, his poetry, and his conversation all
subservient to that one end. Men watched him with awe or with bewilderment; it was known that he saw visions continually, perhaps more continually
than any modern man since Swedenborg; and when he painted and drew in
pastel what he had seen, some accepted the record without hesitation, others,
like myself, noticing the academic Graeco-Roman forms, and remembering
his early admiration for the works of Gustave Moreau, divined a subjective
element, but no one doubted his word. One might not think him a good
observer, but no one could doubt that he reported with the most scrupulous
care what he believed himself to have seen; nor did he lack occasional objective
corroboration. Walking with some man in his park—his demesne, as we say
in Ireland—he had seen a visionary church at a particular spot, and the man
had dug and discovered its foundations. . . . He and I often quarrelled, because I wanted him to examine and question his visions, and write them out as
they occurred; and still more because I thought symbolic what he thought

ally they may be pure fantasy; in a very beautiful painting
which Mrs. Perry has, the winged figure is, I believe, her
niece, one of the Law children. But others record or seem
to indicate a definite experience. Mrs. Curran tells me how
once in the Pine Forest in the Dublin mountains he remarked, "There is a figure over by that tree", and taking out
his materials began to sketch it. She has shown me a painting
which he did later from this very sketch, a figure like a
dryad embodied in the trunk of a tree. Such a picture may
have been in some sort a mental projection of thoughts
existent in his own mind. It is possible to regard all visions
as objectifications of thoughts or images in the individual
mind. This is Shaw's attitude to Saint Joan. This too is the
explanation offered by Tatham of Blake's visions. The validity
of a purely subjective explanation is weakened if the same
vision can appear to two people. F. R. Higgins has an interesting story which was told him by A.E. himself. In a lonely
country district he met a farmer who claimed to have seen the
same noble and stately figures upon the hill which he himself
had seen. A.E. determined to test the man and, taking out
his notebook, drew certain figures which he knew to be false,
asking if what he had seen were like these. The man said
"No". Whereupon A.E. made other drawings, true to his own
vision, to which the man replied, "Yes, they were like that".

To Moore he said that if he were to tell people that all
his drawings were done from sittings given him by the gods
it would be easy for him to sell every stroke he put on
canvas, and to pass himself off as a very wonderful person.
But he had no wish to do so.

"But your drawings are done from sittings given to you

real, like the men and women that had passed him on the road. Were they so
much a part of his subconscious life that they would have vanished had he sub-
mitted them to question; were they like those voices that only speak, those
strange sights that only show themselves for an instant, when the attention
has been withdrawn; that phantasmagoria of which I had learned something in
London; and had his verse and his painting a like origin?"

by the gods. I remember your telling me that three stood at the end of your bed looking at you one morning."

"Three great beings came to my bedside, but I cannot tell you if I saw them directly, as I see you (if I see you directly), or whether I saw them reflected as in a mirror. In either case they came from a spiritual world." A vision, he explained, was the personal concern of the visionary: there the matter must be allowed to rest.

Katharine Tynan in her memoirs tells how he related to her one of his visions, which seems to have belonged to a different state of consciousness and to have been definitely symbolic in character. These are his words as she gives them: "Many years ago I was sitting in my room in a house in Grantham Street, when suddenly the walls opened before me and I saw a great mountain of very peculiar shape. At the time I did not know what mountain it could be but I knew it later as Ben Bulben in Sligo, which you remember in the story of Dermod and Grania. I sat in a valley below the mountain, and as I gazed about me there appeared the figure of a young man. His countenance was most remarkable. He had brown eyes and hair, and his face was of the Napoleonic type, with broad straight brows, and his expression was determined and persistent. Then he vanished and there appeared the figure of a woman with a blue cloak over her head and she carrying a child in her arms, and rays seemed to come from all parts of Ireland, and they rested on the child's head so that he was in the midst of a halo of light. This vision, in its turn, vanished, and there came a picture of what appeared to be a queen upon her throne, and while I looked the throne fell and she with it. That too vanished, and I saw a man of gigantic stature striding up and down Ireland beating a drum, and as he walked smoke and flames sprang up in his path. Then he too vanished and I saw nothing but rays coming from every part of Ireland, so that I could not tell whence they came or where they ended. And while I looked the walls closed and I was sitting in my room alone."

A.E., as has been said, never placed great emphasis upon his visions. If he speaks of them in his books he does so with great simplicity and straightforwardness. He does not stress them at all. He was equally if not more interested in the nature of ordinary dream, though he realised that in all probability we dream at different levels at different times. Where Freud discusses the symbolism of dreams, A.E. studies them as part of the mystery of consciousness and its functioning. Like Dunne he pushes the problem back into the domain of metaphysics. What is the explanation of this faculty, this dramatic sundering of consciousness in which we seem at once to create the drama and to play a part? In the first of his books to attract really wide attention he discusses the source of dream and vision in a spirit of detached and patient and, one might say, scientific curiosity, conscious that this gift of creating living and moving forms beyond anything we could possibly achieve in waking effort, is in truth one of the great mysteries of the brain, and of our lives, which in a sense are dream also.

In regard to the visions, St. John Ervine is wrong, I think, when he implies that these were merely the little figures the mind sometimes summons up when we close our eyes. A certain number may have been of this order, evoked with closed eyes after intense concentration, but others, it is clear, were of a different nature. In his preface to *The Avatars*, A.E. wrote: "There is no imagination of mine about Avatars in this book. No more than an artist could paint the sun at noon could I imagine so great beings. But as a painter may suggest the light on hill and wood, so in this fantasy I tried to imagine the spiritual excitement created by two people who pass dimly through the narrative, spoken of by others but not speaking themselves. I have, I fear, delayed too long the writing of this, for as I grow old the moon of fantasy begins to set confusedly with me. *The Avatars* has not the spiritual gaiety I desired for it. The friends with whom I once spoke of these things are dead or gone far from me. If they were with me, out of dream, vision and intuition shared between us I might have made the narrative to glow. As it is I have only been able to light my way with my own flickering lantern." Much depends here on the precise meaning which we give to the words imagination, fantasy, vision and intuition.

To certain people all this side of the man will be distasteful and will seem mere moonshine. And yet it was part of one who, later in life at least, was most practically-minded. If his visions were self-created they certainly led him into a country of strange beauty, and left him with a mind to which the keynote is nobility. My own view is that the matter remained largely a mystery even to A.E. himself, and must remain so to others. Like Montaigne, there are some of us who can accept all of Socrates except his daimon. But to those who are unduly sceptical I would recall Goethe's words, Goethe whose mind shrank instinctively from all that seemed merely superstitious in the affirmations of his fellow men, "No one is more inclined than I am to believe in another world beside the visible one; and I have imagination enough to feel that even my own limited ego can embrace a Swedenborgian conception of the spirit sphere".

6

The mystical paintings are only one side of his art and not necessarily the most important. Anyone who knows his work cannot fail at once to identify them. They are the gods and demi-gods, the heroes and dryads, the plumed riders upon fiery horses which came to him in some form of mental vision or out of that earth memory in which he believed.

But as well as these he painted at least two other styles of

33

pictures. There are the forest scenes in which children and maidens play in some open glade shafted with light in the middle of a leafy wood. He describes these pictures very well in a passage in *The Avatars*, where he speaks of the artist Paul going on painting, "intoxicated with the beauty he saw and the beauty he imagined. The forest depths before him were a dazzle of green and starry scintillations. Branches were suⅼdenly burnished with vivid colour, as suddenly vanishing. Patches of orange flame awoke, blazed on the russet floor, then darkened to purple. There was incessant birth and death of light. Through it all went the dance of lovely shapes. Then into the figures of imagination a living figure raced, a girl running down the glade, the sunlight on her blue dress flecking it with a glow rich as the bloom on a peacock's tail." It is interesting to find an early unpublished poem in a notebook which he gave to Browne, soon after he left school, which reveals just this disposition of mind towards a particular type of scenery, and bears out his contention that it is in childhood that our innate preferences are determined.

The best of these woodland scenes, influenced a little perhaps by the Monticellis which Lane brought to Dublin, can be very beautiful, but I would not say that they were the most beautiful or the most typical examples of his work. Far more lovely to my mind are certain landscapes and seascapes into which he introduced an occasional figure. It has been said that his figure-drawing was weak, but in these pictures he conveys with amazing impressionistic faithfulness the value of certain poses, children playing, swinging from a ledge of rock, wading or running races—the nonchalant and dreamy abandon of their movements silhouetted against the sunset or on a wide beach beneath rose-tinted clouds. He delighted always in the mauve shadows which the clouds cast on the sand, in the shimmering light-irradiated surface of the water itself, the gleam of bare limbs or of white dresses under an azure sky. The eye is dazzled by the warmth and colour of summer, the very day seems to vibrate with sunlight, and the material world becomes every whit as beautiful as any visionary world into which his imagination gave him entry. Small wonder that he affixed as the motto to one of his books Monet's dictum, "The light is the real person in the picture". In these paintings he has captured all the translucency of the Irish scene, that mysterious quality by which the earth itself seems alive, radiating its own vitality. The air is living, the sea is living, they are essences as it were breathed from the vital soul of the world. I find him using these very phrases in a conversation which Simone Téry reports. "L'air est vivant," she makes him say, "la terre est vivante, l'eau est vivante et la vie qui les pénètre coule de l'âme du monde." Yet in the same pictures he can capture some of the still serenity of the human moment, that moment when man seems part and not the whole, and when a child, stooping in the foreground of some hushed sun-spilt lagoon, is only one aspect of the mysterious panorama which is life.

At his best A.E. was a great painter and there is an excuse for those who, like A. G. B. Russell, the authority on Blake, think that painting was his true vocation if he had cared to follow it exclusively.

His poetry and painting are often closely allied. He is at Dunfanaghy, watching some children run and play on a lonely beach. Hearing their voices, as they pursue one another shouting and laughing, he might begin to speculate on what great artificer was responsible for this magic of energy and delight. Taking pencil he would write:

> On this fawn-coloured shore,
> All delicately strewn,
> Gold dust and gleaming shell,
> White stone and blue stone,
> Lie sweetly together whether
> Eye be to see them or none.

35

The air is gay with voices
Of children. The sun
Casts flowers of purple shadow
Before them as they run;
Blows clouds and blooms of shadow
Where the swift feet may run.

Onward the children race
To leap into the sea
That bubbles silver bright
In the lovely revelry
Of foam and limbs together
In a white revelry.

How grew that airy tumult
On shores that were so still,
That wind of flowers and shadows?
What art invisible
Made all that airy wonder,
At what enchanter's will?

Or out of the same experience might come a picture, for there are many which might almost be a transcript of this very scene. It was moments like these which he liked to paint, as though wishing to weave the sunlight, the opalescence of day, the dreamy landscape and the breathless arrest of time, into some pattern where his friends, to whom the pictures would be given, might long afterwards hold them.

7

These were the canvases which hung round the walls or which he would place one after the other upon the easel to show the visitor to Rathgar Avenue. I have digressed at some length upon the artist, but it was an integral part of the man, one aspect of his many-sided talent. Returning to the other room when the pictures had been viewed, he would soon be caught into the current of one or other of the discussions in progress then and, drawing the threads together, he would begin to discover some principle or unity in the debate, which before seemed absent.

If he had any frailty it was the one which MacCarthy suggests. "He was not without the vanity of the improvisatore . . . though about his poetry and practical ability he was not vain. As long as what he produced, or did, came from, so to speak, the right place—out of himself, he was content. He left it at that. But to create an answering glow of sympathy, to astonish in discourse by an effortless flow of imagery and quotation, was dear to him; these surprising feats and the impression they created soothed him." "He awakened as a conversationalist and he conversed mightily until he slept again", says Stephens.

Those who knew A.E. in later life will smile incredulously when they find a contemporary of his youth writing, naïvely, but probably with perfect truth, "He was so shy and unassuming when I knew him first that he said little, only beamed, when he was of a party".

For it is true that as he grew older he liked perhaps to dominate the conversation, and there were times even when to strangers it seemed that he was trifling with ideas, when he might have allowed others to give their opinion, or tell their story. Margaret Cunningham, a friend of long standing, remembers at least one such occasion, when a traveller from some foreign country was silenced for a whole evening by A.E.'s pertinacious irrelevancy. As a young man and in middle life, she tells me, he was a good listener and would sit silent for long periods hearing the opinions of others and reserving his own. Once when a friend was being attacked he broke in and quickly silenced those who were abusing him. I myself can testify to having often seen him as an older man listening patiently while others spoke. At Yeats' in the evening, when the Alcibiades of Dublin was present, or some wit from among the professors at the university, and the talk took a light or ribald turn, he would become silent, and I can see him now, withdrawn into himself, detached, aloof, neither amused nor condemnatory, a brooding sweetness in his eyes, as though his thoughts chose other pastures.

There is no doubt that his conversation had an astonishing range and that he had the gift of evoking whatever was most interesting in others simply by the prodigality with which he gave himself. Whatever the topic, he brought to it a certain quality of spiritual insight which lifted comment on to a higher plane. The talkers against whom he matched himself were of every kind and description. As well as the strangers who might come, they included Yeats, James Stephens, whose fancy can range more playfully in conversation than that of almost any man in the world, MacKenna, the translator of Plotinus, by all opinion the most brilliant talker of his time in Dublin, Gogarty, Padraic Colum, Austin Clarke and many others. Often in conversation he would throw out an idea as airy speculation which he hoped might presently be accepted as truth. Norman has suggested to me that this was done partly because he did not feel justified in postulating something not yet completely proved, but partly also to evoke a response from his listeners so that they also might contribute their testimony to the issue.

And yet the best moment of all was possibly when one found A.E. alone. By going early one could sometimes do this, for Osborn Bergin, the most faithful of his visitors, seldom came before nine o'clock. To find him alone was often more interesting and more profitable than when the room was packed. One could question him and cross-examine him upon his beliefs. He was fond of telling the number of different "good lives" which Patanjali outlines, for the soldier, for the cultivator of the soil, for the philosopher and so on. He never despised a truth because it had already been stated. The continual reappearance of certain favourite quotations in his writing is explained when we realise that he regarded Truth not as a plaything for the dialectician but as a sacred achievement. If, therefore, a sage seemed to have captured it in a phrase he was not afraid to quote and requote him. In the same way he had certain favourite quotations, for instance Lao-Tse's "One cannot remain for ever standing on tiptoe"; or a passage from a Upanishad (many will remember the curious drawn-out pronunciation of the word "chaaryot" for "chariot")—"There are no chariots there, nor steeds for chariots, nor roadways. The Spirit of Man makes himself chariots, steeds for chariots and roadways"; as well as a kindred passage from Gaelic myth, "Whenever we desire the fields to be sown they are sown, when reaped they are reaped". He loved to discover similarities between the sacred writ of different nations, holding that this similarity strengthened their validity rather than weakened it. Other phrases that often recurred in his talk were: "What a man thinks, that he is, that is the old secret"; "Let him approach it by saying, 'He is pure,' he becomes filled with purity"; "All lost hearts burn in the oil of the lamp of the King".

Of all the occasions when I found him alone at Rathgar Avenue, one stands out most vividly in memory. This was the night when, soon after the first volume of MacKenna's wonderful translation of Plotinus had appeared, he took it from the bookshelf, and read to me slowly this passage from the *Tractate on Beauty*:

> He that has strength, let him arise and withdraw into himself, forgoing all that is known by the eyes, turning away for ever from the material beauty that once made his joy. When he perceives those shapes of grace that show in body let him not pursue: he must know them for copies, vestiges, shadows, and hasten away towards that they tell of. . . .

And this inner vision, what is its operation?

Newly awakened it is all too feeble to bear the ultimate splendour. Therefore the Soul must be trained —to the habit of remarking, first, all noble pursuits, then the works of beauty produced not by the labour of the arts but by the virtue of men known for their goodness: lastly you must search the souls of those that have shaped these beautiful forms.

But how are you to see into a virtuous soul and know its loveliness?

Withdraw into yourself and look. And if you do not find yourself beautiful yet, act as does the creator of a statue that is to be made beautiful: he cuts away here, he smoothes there, he makes this line lighter, this other purer, until a lovely face has grown upon his work. So do you also: cut away all that is excessive, straighten all that is crooked, bring light to all that is overcast, labour to make all one glow of beauty and never cease chiselling your statue, until there shall shine out on you from it the godlike splendour of virtue, until you shall see the perfect goodness surely established in the stainless shrine.

It is a privilege to think that I heard these words for the first time on the lips of one who came nearer than any other man I have met to exemplifying them in his own life.

8

He tended in conversation of this nature to revert to certain themes: the paramount need for concentration and meditation; the Eastern thought that every ascent of the soul implies the power and willingness to accept a corresponding descent—Christ's three days in Hades being this condescension of goodness to evil; the Pauline doctrine of the triple nature of man, "body, soul and spirit", the latter being perhaps the psyche which in sleep is able to return whence it came, perhaps, "those angels which do ever behold my Father's face in heaven". He held that men had forgotten the meaning of their own sacred books, that all these things were not fantasy but had been spoken originally out of knowledge and experience and were open to verification now by those who were strong enough to pursue the path. In one of his books he writes, "Our religions make promises to be fulfilled beyond the grave because they have no knowledge now to be put to the test, but the ancients spake of a divine vision to be attained while we are yet in the body. The religion which does not cry out: 'I am to-day verifiable as that water wets or that fire burns. Test me that ye can become as gods'—mistrust it. Its messengers are prophets of darkness."

He made no claim to great knowledge himself. Even as a student of occult science he fell far short, he contended, of certain of his contemporaries, bringing only a greater literary talent, not greater knowledge, to the subject. He consistently practised what Steiner calls the golden rule of occultism—"For every step that you take in the pursuit of the hidden knowledge take three steps in the perfecting of your own character". He would have agreed too with the latter when he says, "It is right that a person should learn of the secrets of nature only so much as corresponds to his own degree of development". At the Hermetic, I am told, he never encouraged students to dabble in the occult but dwelt rather upon the paramount need for the practice of meditation and concentration, and the value which all such discipline has for the soul. He could write in *Song and Its Fountains*:

I am a far exile from that great glory which inhabits

41

the universe, and can but peer through some momentary
dusky transparency in my nature to a greater light than
the light of day. I know the royal road is by practice
of the great virtues. But I cannot speak that language
nor urge those obligations, I who have been angry and
sensual. I can only speak where I have been faithful. I
have never ceased from the inward search, and might
by that faithfulness have gone far if I had not a rabble of
desires tugging me by the skirts to travel alluring roads
in the world of illusion. I could only peer a little way,
apprehending behind form the Creator, behind thought
the Thinker, behind intuition the Seeker, behind conscience the Love, and in fallen life some still unfallen
majesty, and even in the basest of desires could find
signs of their spiritual ancestry.

He hints continually at a darker side to his own nature. I
remember his telling me how in early life when he lived
in a community with several friends he had great difficulty in
overcoming the irritability which certain natures arouse in
others, and how it was only by the conscious exercise of his
will that he had done this.

In a rather extravagantly worded document, written while
he was still a young man, with reference to a dissension which
had arisen in theosophic circles, he says to his colleagues
who were threatening one of their number with expulsion,
"I confess to greater sins than he is charged with; to years
smothered with sensuality, lurid with anger, wrinkled with
meanness, dark with fear. Why should I try to pose among
the elect?"

What is interesting in this is his own humility and self-
deprecation—"smothered with sensuality, lurid with anger,
wrinkled with meanness, dark with fear", true perhaps of
the recalcitrant heart, yet said by one of whom it has been
written, "He captivated by honesty and entire absence of

arrogance, but most of all by the conspicuous purity and unselfishness of his spirit".[1]

All his life he was exceptionally modest. If ever he gave the impression of vanity, as happened in a few rare instances, it was the reaction of a man who, thinking very poorly of himself, is surprised into boasting. He annoyed one visitor to Plunkett House by waving his hand towards the frescoes upon the walls and saying airily, "They were thrown off in four days of frenzied activity".[2] Great and simple men are occasionally betrayed like this into the appearance of boasting by a sort of naïve surprise at their own achievements. Danes of to-day sneer at Hans Andersen because, when you met him in the street, he would say with childish delight, "Did you hear? My latest volume has been translated into Spanish." And yet neither Hans Andersen nor A.E. were vain men. No one knew better than A.E. that the real assessor of the soul is the soul itself. Replying to a letter of appreciation written to him just before he sailed for America he says, "It is pleasant to know that one's soul in transit through this world has seemed to others to have some kind of glow. Praise and blame really spring from within, but the voices of friendship outside are soothing voices. I wish I could believe them, but if I did I might develop egomania, the worst of all the psychic diseases." To Lorraine Meredith he said, "Someone has been praising my pictures, but if ever Satan wants to lay a trap for my soul he will have to choose a more cunning bait than flattery". And when Clyde, shortly before his death, sent him his ardent and enthusiastic essay and asked him if he would kindly amend whatever seemed to him inaccurate he replied, "I could not amend anything of what you have written without seeming to approve of all the praises left unaltered. If I really amended out of the depths

[1] Gogarty.
[2] Norman, who was his colleague, points out to me that this probably referred not to his painting at all but to other work done on those same days.

of intuition and conscience I would take all the praise
away. . . ."

9

He was essentially religious. It is wrong to regard A.E. as
the pagan enemy of Christian values. He could attack savagely
what he believed to be priestcraft but this does not mean that
he decried faith. One or two of his later letters might suggest
that the attacks, to which he himself was subjected, had begun
to embitter him and make him misunderstand those by whom
he was often misunderstood; but these are not characteristic.
His passionate belief in liberty made him the declared enemy
of any form of compulsion in religion. The soul must turn
to truth of its own volition. But his differences in matters of
creed with the majority of his countrymen have, I imagine,
been emphasised by a few who liked to foment them, when
he was living, and to lay stress on them, now that he is dead.
The presence at his funeral of so many whose faith differed
from his, shows the respect in which he was held, even in
those circles where he was supposed to be anathema. Two
of his closest friends, Katharine Tynan and C. P. Curran,
were devout Catholics, and his friend and colleague for years
in the co-operative movement a priest, Father Tom Finlay.
It was a Catholic who could say of him, "He is of the world
unworldly—the world's stain has never touched him.
Without religion, yet profoundly religious; the peace of
God which passeth understanding lies all about him," and
then add—"he finds gods in the earth and air—rather I
would say he finds God; and his life unconsciously has cast
incense on the altars of the Unknown God". After his
death, one of the leading journals of the country was to
write in the same spirit, "He was never orthodox and his
views on religion hardly would be acceptable to any of the
Churches. Yet if ever Ireland bred a man whose life ex-

emplified the teaching of the Sermon on the Mount that man was A.E. He had a depth of soul and a saintliness of character that are found all too seldom in our time."

He would have resisted any claim which makes Christianity the sole and exclusive revelation. For him, as Norman puts it, *essential* Christianity was a path already trodden by the pre-Christian mystic. He was fond of saying that, as a religion, it possessed no cosmogony, no psychology, only a most perfect ethic, overlooking perhaps the profound psychology behind many of the parables. He sought always for a universal element in religion and he carried this even into personal practice, for as Higgins puts it, "his virtues arose not from the preserves of one religion but from the fruits of all, and who can name his vices according to any moral law?" To Simone Téry he said, "I have read all the sacred books which I could find, those of China, of Egypt, of India, of Persia, of Judæa, as well as the mystic philosophers like Plato, Plotinus and Sankara; and I have found truth in all and a singular identity of belief; I have found however that the sacred books of Judæa are the least interesting of all and contain less spiritual truth than the Bhagavad-gita or the Upanishads for example. The Old Testament is a collection of poems and legends far more than a collection of sacred texts which are profound."

It is possible that he had had too much of the God of the Old Testament as a child. Moore describes how walking along a road in Armagh as a boy the thought suddenly came to him that God had no right to punish him for something he had not promised not to do. In that moment a spiritual rebel was born. A friend tells me that A.E.'s parents, though North of Ireland Protestants, were very far from being dour and unsympathetic. They belonged to the evangelical tradition, a tradition which, as Inge points out, contains a vein of pure and genuine mysticism. The imagery of its hymns, many of them beautiful and ardent, is full of just that symbolism, that reference to the invisible world, the river "where bright angel feet have trod", the white robes and the hierarchy of heaven which is perfectly consistent with a belief in the immanence of another world. Did A.E. owe more to this influence than he realised? Much of his beauty of character and consistent purity of moral outlook came too, perhaps, from that early faith from whose narrower tenets and harsher and darker standpoint he later broke away.

His interest in Pauline mysticism may have had its origin in the same source. He would refer often to St. Paul's mystical experiences, "such an one caught up to the third heaven . . . whether in the body I cannot tell; or whether out of the body I cannot tell . . . how that he was caught up into paradise and heard unspeakable words which it is not lawful for a man to utter". I remember his telling me of the pleasure with which he had received a series of letters from an old clergyman, after the publication of *The Candle of Vision*, discussing certain issues raised there, in relation to some of the visions described in the Apocalypse.

10

The hardest task before A.E.'s biographer will be to determine his precise debt to theosophy. There can be no question that he owed much to the original movement and to the contacts to which it introduced him, and that he remained sympathetic to his friends of those days to the end. He might even have said that all which was deepest in his nature had been learnt on that path on which he had first set foot in their company. But men of his spiritual calibre will always outgrow movements, especially when these display their inevitable tendency to split into sects and to quarrel among themselves. Theosophy did one thing, it enabled him to adopt the Celtic mythology and make use of it for his own purpose. Presently Angus and Lir and Nuatha were to replace Ananda and Valmihar and Kedar in his writings. What values he attached to these titles is not clear. It is possible that he regarded the names of all gods as merely the symbols given to certain divine beings or hier-archs, by men in different parts of the world. Or he may at times have thought of them as embodiments of the highest aspirations in man, so that the names were really an irrele-vancy, what mattered being the inner significance of the legends attached to them. Shelley, another visionary but also a sceptic, makes a similar use of myth. It is significant that A.E. avoids the use of the word theosophy in his published works. That he does not use it is probably because it had acquired too specialised a meaning and had even come to be associated with charlatanry.[1]

[1] Simone Téry is fairly explicit on this question and I believe that her memory can be trusted, if she does not write from actual notes supplied her by A.E.

— Vous êtes bien un théosophe?

— Un certain Apollonius de Tyane a été le premier, je crois, à déclarer qu'il y avait une vérité divine dans tous les livres sacrés, et cette vérité qui leur est commune à tous, il l'a appelée la Divine Sagesse; je suppose que je suis à sa manière un théosophe. Une grande part de ce qui est appelé théo-sophie dans les temps modernes est, je crois, charlatanerie pure. Certains théosophes s'adonnent à des pratiques qui peuvent être très dangereuses pour la raison; ils cultivent en eux une sorte d'hystérie mystique qui est fort loin de la vraie sagesse, de la contemplation divine. . . . Je crois qu'il est possible de *vérifier* la religion comme de vérifier que le feu brûle ou que l'eau mouille, mais les prêtres ne nous enseignent pas à vérifier l'Esprit. Le plus sage des anciens dit qu'on y arrive par une intense concentration d'esprit et une volonté jamais relâchée: par cette intensité nous dégageons les éléments les plus déliés et les plus subtils dans notre être, de même que la chaleur appliquée à la glace la transforme en eau ou en vapeur. J'ai constaté qu'en effet une concentration ardente de la volonté et de l'esprit peut progressivement rendre le cerveau lumineux, si bien que l'on ferme les yeux sur de la lumière plutôt que sur de l'obscurité. On peut alors voir toutes les formes de l'esprit, tous les habitants de l'âme dans la plus claire des lumières internes, de même qu'on peut voir les gens qui se trouvent dans une pièce illuminée. Les mé-thodes précises de concentration et de méditation qui permettent d'illuminer l'esprit sont à peu près inconnues en Europe. Mais il est assez dangereux de les pratiquer sans une longue initiation préalable, sans avoir compris la

On the other hand he would always acknowledge his gratitude to those who turned his attention to the sacred books of the East, to the Bhagavad-gita, to Patanjali and the Upanishads. His deepest intuitions date back undoubtedly to the period of this introduction. It was the time of his spiritual discipleship. And though, later, his sympathies might widen and his intellect seem more critical and acute, he himself could speak of "a thickening of the walls of the psyche", as though he had failed to achieve the full enlightenment which had once seemed within his grasp, and as though there had been atrophy as well as growth.

Unlike the minds of some students who venture out of their depth and pay the penalty, his managed to remain simple and strong and to keep its essential sanity. Dabblers in magic and persons of uncontrolled esoteric enthusiasm seem often, by the very tension of their lives and their fanatic ardour, to refute the serene heights to which they would fain have us aspire. They shake confidence in their system because they shake confidence in themselves. A.E., if he had ever known this phase, outgrew it. His mysticism, like that of Plato, never deserted earth completely, though he speaks deprecatingly in a letter in old age of himself gathering "the rootless flowers of meditation". Like Plato he was not afraid to admit his doubts. After the death of Susan Mitchell he told Lily Yeats that his faith in immortality had momentarily faltered. "But it will come back, I know". To another friend he said that this faith had been shaken twice in his life, but—so the friend understood him to imply—it had only faltered, because he had had experience of the immortal worlds and *knew*. It is perhaps good for the mystic to experience doubt; indeed it is almost as though he needed a strong mingling of scepticism to pre-

théorie. Je ne pense pas d'ailleurs que ces méthodes soient pour tout le monde, et je crois qu'il suffit, pour vivre bien, de désirer rendre le monde heureux, d'aimer la beauté et la joie, les arts et la nature. . . ."

serve his balance. When John Eglinton, speaking of A.E.'s youth,[1] refers to "his moments of illumination alternating with disconcerting avowals of doubt", we realise that even then he was bringing the salt of reason to the banquet of credulity.

Later in life he was to condemn extravagances—"The soul of the modern mystic is becoming a mere hoarding-place for uncomely theories. He creates an uncouth symbolism, and obscures his soul within with names drawn from the Kabala or ancient Sanskrit, and makes alien to himself the intimate powers of his spirit, things which in truth are more his than the intimate beatings of his heart."

He may have turned eventually from much that held the more callow enthusiasm of his youth. As he grew older he tended more and more to test every speculation of the imagination in the crucible of reason and moral truth. But his transcendental studies and experiences, whatever validity they had in themselves, did one thing for him. They were a means of inducing that mood through which, as Bax says, "we may see the world once more in its primal beauty, may recover a sense of the long forgotten and inextinguishable grandeur of the soul."

And while they were doing this his work in the cause of rural economy, as we have seen, was bringing him into close and personal contact with men and affairs. The Platonic world in which his spirit lived was not allowed to tempt him to avert his eyes from the reality of its material, if distorted, counterpart here. For twenty-five years he worked for, wrote for, and travelled for co-operation, a practical and quite mundane ideal. All this was bound to have its effect upon his character, saving him from becoming the mere dreamer, and from isolation from his fellow men. Lastly, saving him from the same fate, was the essential goodness of the man himself, that goodness which Yeats

[1] *Irish Literary Portraits*, 1935.

indicates when he draws a picture of his life with several other students in the house of Mr. and Mrs. Dicks in Ely Place—"it was I think his benevolence that gave him his lucidity of speech and, perhaps, of writing. If he convinced himself that any particular activity was desirable in the public interest or in that of his friends, he had at once the ardour that came to another from personal ambition. He was always surrounded with a little group of infirm or un-lucky persons, whom he explained to themselves and to others, turning cat to griffin, goose to swan."

II

Best has suggested to me that theosophy did for A.E. what the classics do for other men, that it stood for a background of culture in his life as well as representing much hard work and mental discipline. "He read the sacred texts as another man would study Aristotle." There is probably a measure of truth in this but at the same time it would be a mistake to think that A.E. had not come under the influence of the classics as a boy with Dr. Benson or that his knowledge of literature—helped by his phenomenal memory, which would allow him to recite hundreds of lines of verse from a poem he had not seen for years—did not extend to that field. He had always read Plato, but as he grew older Greek thought, I imagine, began to influence him more. He outgrew much that was colourful and extravagant in his earlier prose. He himself has spoken of the "flaming rhetoric" to which anger could move him in those days, until he discovered that every passionate energy evokes its contrary and that real wisdom lies in the reconcilement of opposites. There is a touch of melodrama even in his much-praised letter of rebuke to a fellow author.

Theosophy unquestionably developed and disciplined his

mind, but its influence upon his style was bad, and some of
his worst and vaguest writing belongs to the days when he
regarded himself as the apostle of a cause. At that time he
adopted the semi-mystical jargon, a mixture of colourful
metaphor and highly abstract thought, which was popular
then among a branch of esoteric students. He never surrendered completely to the shibboleths or enthusiasms of a
particular circle. But whereas the form of his later prose is
often flawless, serene, lucid, persuasive, clothing an idea or
image with the inevitable word and with an almost Greek
precision, his earlier is often wordy and rhetorical.

Compare this passage from the early essay *The Hero in
Man*, an essay which contains so much that is good:

> And this is part of the plan of the Great Alchemist,
> whereby the red ruby of the heart is transmuted into
> the tenderer light of the opal; for the beholding of love
> made bare acts like the flame of the furnace; and the
> dissolving passions through an anguish of remorse, and
> through an adoring pity, are changed into the image
> they contemplate, and melt in the ecstasy of self-forgetful
> love, the spirit which lit the thorn-crowned brows,
> which perceived only in its last agony the retribution
> due to its tormentors and cried out, "Father, forgive
> them, for they know not what they do"—

with this, taken at random, from *The Interpreters*:

> Even those lost and hopeless who pursue their de-
> sires to spiritual death are still seeking spiritual life.
> They follow a gleam mistakenly as we may imagine
> light-demented moths dashing themselves at a moon in
> water. As in their private lusts men still follow some-
> thing in its essence universal, so too in their imagina-
> tions about society are they allured by images and
> shadows of their own hidden divinity.

Language is more concrete here, metaphor is more restrained, there is a harder, more chiselled quality not only about the words but in the thought itself, as though the man had grown in the meanwhile and was speaking now out of a wider spiritual experience. It is only fair to add, however, that if theosophy had this effect on his early prose it inspired some of his finest verses.

Curran has thrown out the suggestion that A.E.'s original mystical experience took place as a youth, before he had encountered theosophy at all, and that he was drawn to theosophy because he sought there a scheme into which to fit these phenomena. This may be the case. In one of his books he speaks of a meditation or day-dream when he was fifteen 'or thereabouts'. The memory of this returned to him in later life when he was practising a form of retrospective contemplation enjoined by certain teachers. He goes on to say, "In that retrospect too, I regained memory of the greatest of all wonders in my boyhood, when I lay on the hill of Kilmashogue and Earth revealed itself to me as a living being, and rock and clay were made transparent so that I saw lovelier and lordlier beings than I had known before, and was made partner in memory of mighty things, happenings in ages long sunken behind time. Though the walls about the psyche have thickened with age and there are many heavinesses piled about it, I still know that the golden age is all about us and that we can, if we will, dispel that opacity and have vision once more of the ancient Beauty." His chronology was not always correct, as we have seen in the case of his painting, but if this experience really belonged to his early boyhood, then it is likely that Curran's contention is right.

12

Whether he was born or became a mystic is not so

material. Certainly his poetry began as that of a mystic and remained so to the end. Hunt Grubb says well that the key to the whole of it might be found in a text taken from one of the most ancient records available, an Assyrian inscription transcribed by a Chaldean priest in Greek:

> Explore the river of the Soul, whence or in what order you have come, so that although you have become a servant to the body, you may again rise to the Order from which you descended, joining works to sacred reason.

When he published his first small book of verse A.E. called it *Homeward, Songs by the Way,* and, in the briefest of prefaces, wrote:

> I moved among men and places, and in living I learned the truth at last. I know I am a spirit, and that I went forth in old time from the Self-ancestral to labours yet unaccomplished, but filled ever and again with homesickness I made these songs by the way.

I hesitate to dogmatise about his verse. He wrote no poem in which there was not beauty of thought and sincerity of utterance but he wrote many poems in which the form seems inadequate and the imagery a little vague. Here again we need to beware that the fault is not sometimes our own. The mystical poets demand to be read almost a single poem at a time. Otherwise we cannot keep pace with the wheeling of systems in their metaphysical universe. The implications of his verse take us too far. Every poem really needs separate acceptance, a separate meditation; the crust of the ascetic rather than the rich and varied banquet before which appetite presently fails. As with his prose they should be read at a time when our mood is already in some measure attuned to them. Then a poem that seemed to mean little before will unlock its heart to us, speaking direct to that spiritual ear which, when it hears at all, seems to hear certainties. The journey which A.E. asks the mind to take is often a far one. It is not the surface meaning of his words which matters but their profound inner content and implication. We should be careful before we agree with the opinion of one critic that A.E. "will be remembered for his life and talk, for the personal manifestations of his gentle and radiant spirit, rather than for his poetry".

For that spirit reveals much of itself to us in the poems. His poetry is nearly always an attempt to plumb some mystery of the soul or to reveal some moment of illumination in consciousness. There is a deeper and more profound mysticism than much which goes by that name in Wordsworth in these three verses from his poem *Continuity*:

> No sign is made while empires pass.
> The flowers and stars are still His care,
> The constellations hid in grass,
> The golden miracles in air.
>
> In that wild orchid that your feet
> In their next falling shall destroy,
> Minute and passionate and sweet
> The Mighty Master holds His joy.
>
> Though the crushed jewels droop and fade
> The Artist's labours will not cease,
> And of the ruins shall be made
> Some yet more lovely masterpiece.

Something of the same thought is in that other lovely poem which Santayana chose as prefix to one of his books.

> Who is that goddess to whom men should pray,
> But her from whom their hearts have turned away,
> Out of whose virgin being they were born,
> Whose mother nature they have named with scorn
> Calling its holy substance common clay.

Yet from this so despised earth was made
The milky whiteness of those queens who swayed
Their generations with a light caress,
And from some image of whose loveliness
The heart built up high heaven when it prayed.

Lover, your heart, the heart on which it lies,
Your eyes that gaze and those alluring eyes,
Your lips, the lips they kiss, alike had birth
Within that dark divinity of earth,
Within that mother being you despise.

Ah, when I think this earth on which I tread
Hath borne these blossoms of the lovely dead,
And makes the living heart I love to beat,
I look with sudden awe beneath my feet
As you with erring reverence overhead.

Poetry for him was never purely an art. I remember his telling me that he had once written the line, "Truth, a fantasy which flies", but realising that this was false and that he had maligned truth, he altered it later to "Truth and fantasy which flies". It is a small matter, but it is illustrative of his attitude to his craft. In an early letter to his great contemporary A.E. writes, "I deny altogether that beauty is the sole end and law of poetry. I think the true and the good, using them in the old Hermetic sense, are equally the subject of verse, and demand an equal share in the guidance of the writer." Or, as Curran puts it, "his conception of the poet was not as the artisan of beauty but as seer and prophet deriving a special authority from communion with arcane ancestral wisdom".

The soul into itself withdraws, thinking on all
The gay, heroical ardours it forsook; the years
That were made over-sweet with passion; the tears
Love wept, dying of its own fulness; and the fall
Into the pit, where seven unholy spirits conspire
Against the Holy Ones, turning the sky-born fire

Unto infernal uses, feeding beauty to the beast.
Remembering the dark joys that were born of the feast,
It dreads the everlasting fire, the torment of sense.
Oh, unhappy, the judge is not without thee but within,
Who shall condemn thee, as retribution for thy sin
To the consuming fire of thine own penitence.

In a poem like this, in the *Farewell to Pan*, in *Germinal*,
or in the lovely *Recollection*, the voice is wholly his own,
recognisable among a hundred others. No other poet has
struck quite the same note. He wrote only when the spirit
moved him. He told Lewis Chase that when his second
book of verse was published the reviews and talk which
followed made him self-conscious, and, finding he was in
danger of approaching poetry from a false angle, he imposed
slience on himself and published nothing more for seven
years.

Ernest Boyd has written with great insight and considerable appreciation of the earlier poems up to the time of the
war. There could hardly be a better introduction to them
than what he says in his book, *Ireland's Literary Renaissance*.
This earlier poetry is best read not in selection but in its
original context and in relation to the period that produced it, and it is well to be reminded of its importance by a
critic of high standing. At the same time it is true that some
of A.E.'s best poetry was written late in life. Though he
philosophises in these poems (he was fond of quoting Plato's
"the gods never philosophise"), there is less pure abstraction
than in earlier ones, and image and thought are more intimately allied.

13

"He was a mystic with astonishing aptitudes, and whatever
he set his hand to he achieved with odd facility—except, of
course, the task of making his contemporaries more reason-

able, practical and kind, at which he laboured steadily, serenely and in vain." So says MacCarthy, speaking of the period immediately after the war. This time of the troubles in Ireland was the only time when bitterness seems to have invaded his heart. He saw the work of years of his life being destroyed, his creameries being burnt down by temporarily-enlisted forces as a reprisal for other acts of violence. His heart hardened against a ruthlessness which seemed to strike still more against the innocent than the guilty, and for a time he refused to visit the country which he held responsible. His faith both in men and movements must have been dashed, but nothing could overthrow that central serenity and stability of soul. Even in those days MacCarthy got from him, "something I should have expected not a few in Dublin to have stood in need of during recent years: reassurance, calm . . . it was good to be reminded of something beyond the struggle; this relief was precisely what A.E.'s talk provided. Hot frantic feelings subsided under it, and a more patient sense of justice, and some sort of pattern in the confusion, emerged."

The pattern was to emerge still more clearly in the book which he was writing at this very time—*The Interpreters*—and which was to appear before the troubles were over. In it his mastery of philosophic prose probably reached its highest level. It was an attempt to reconcile or at least to give adequate expression to the different ideals which govern the body politic. In answer to a letter of mine about the book, he wrote:

> I think the spirit of kindness reconciles things which are otherwise incompatible and that almost any political theory would endure if its administration was pervaded by that spirit. . . . I have always envied that statement by Pericles about the Athenians, "We listen gladly to the opinions of others and do not turn sour faces on

those who disagree with us". I would like that as an illuminated text to be hung somewhere in every Irish home.

The Interpreters is the contribution of a poet and a sage to political science. In this profound book A.E. tries to plumb the motives which decide men's actions in times of chaos and disturbance, and to discuss the different ideals of government for which they are willing to die. He was always the philosopher of politics rather than the politician. To use the phrase which he was so fond of employing, he saw it as his business, to relate "the politics of time to the politics of eternity". He held that men, even in their politics, whether they realise it or not, are governed by the ideals and images which they set before themselves. The philosopher is as necessary to them as the politician, perhaps even more necessary. He could be witty at the expense of the latter. Asked, during the Home Rule controversy, about a certain political question, he replied that he would give what he considered the main arguments both for and against it. These were "the intolerable stupidity of the politicians on one side and the stupid intolerance of the politicians on the other". But he could go deeper than this and write, years later, "I have an intuition that the true way of writing history which some poet-historian in the future may discover is for the historian to reveal causes rather than to chronicle results. Things take place in the soul before they take place in the body."

He never forgot this. When he considered men's actions he always remembered those secret springs in which they have their source. As well, he possessed a genuine faculty for understanding and giving expression to opposites. Yeats could say of him while he was still living, "He had and still has the capacity beyond that of any man I have known to put with entire justice not only the thoughts but the emotions of the most opposite parties and personalities, as it were dissolving some public or private uproar into drama by Corneille or Racine; and men who have hated each other must sometimes have been reconciled, because each heard his enemy's argument put into better words than his own; and this gift was in later years to give him political influence, and win him respect from Irish Nationalist and Unionist alike".

All his vast tolerance, his width of understanding and ability to express diverse points of view, while keeping the level of argument upon a high philosophic plane, is shown in *The Interpreters*. He is not a difficult writer. His style in these later books is always simple. He never labours his point and the note which he strikes is lyrical but not fervid. What is needed most in the reader is a kindred insight or illumination which will enable him to follow the thought behind these apparently simple phrases, which nevertheless open up endless vistas before the mind.

In his last prose work, written ten years after *The Interpreters*, he returned to other speculations, perhaps nearer his heart. Though he said that he had delayed writing it too long it is doubtful if he need have felt this regret. All his life he had been a lover of beauty in its many forms and at sixty-five the springs from which his lyric inspiration was drawn had not dried up. The whole book shines with an inner light derived from that purity of spirit out of which it was written. It reveals his love of his own country, especially of that district in it where he was accustomed to do his painting; his delight in the colour and beauty of the two worlds, the seen world of nature and that other unseen world of dream and vision; his joy in discussion and in the exchange of ideas with friends, as well as that abiding youthfulness of outlook which is the heritage of certain poets and which a few unique souls share with them. Anyone who wishes to taste again the flavour of A.E.'s mind, its crystalline purity and the transparency of vision with which he viewed this earth of ours, as though all formal and visual beauty were only an elusive reminder of something further and more permanent, should read the earlier pages of *The Avatars*. Poet, artist, visionary, all are there. This work written in old age, when his journalistic activities had been abandoned and he had leisure to give to it, contains something so quintessential of his nature that to pick it up is to find oneself for a little space once more in his company.

It is in these pages too that he reviews our modern civilisation and foresees its dangers. Great progress seems to him nevertheless to be accompanied by a strange and growing spiritual blindness. We conquer the material but we are also conquered by it. That which should have been the slave becomes the master. Certain passages strike almost a note of pessimism, as when he makes one of his characters say that the world has become too old in spirit to create a new civilisation. Energy which had birth and once functioned in innocence has grown self-conscious; all its aspirations are fulfilled: "the immaterial soul has cast substantial shadows of itself everywhere in brick and mortar . . . we are past the high noon of time and are drawing to its twilight".

Though he called his tale "a futurist fantasy", it was not solely the imaginative faculty which made him write of the cities of that new age:

> These cities are the last trap set for the spirit of man to draw him from nature and himself. The people who live in them are kind, but, oh, so unhappy. . . . They cannot bear to be still or alone. They are thirsty for beauty but cannot create it within themselves. . . . They were born into the mechanistic maze and do not know the way out. There was never anything in the world so pitiful as their souls. They are rich inconceivably

without, but paupers within, supplicating alms from any stray genius. They have become aliens to nature, the ancient Mother. In its silences and lonelinesses they might meet the outcast majesty of spirit; and to the poor soul that outcast majesty would be a thing of terror. They would not recognise it as themselves.

From this terrible emptiness he foresees eventually a return to the spiritual, to nature and to the secret springs of man's own being. Those who looked outward will begin again to look inward. The spiritual will come into its own and the veil may even be lifted between seen and unseen. Men will glimpse once more the ancient beauty, will ponder once more on the margin of the Great Deep. It will be said that this is the mere hope of a poet, as vague as anything in Shelley. Yet it is from the aspirations of poets and the intuitions of seers that civilisations have been built up in the past and that cultures have flourished. A.E. may even be one of the forerunners of a new culture in which mankind will find its spiritual rebirth.

14

His literary life falls roughly into three periods: the earlier and predominantly theosophic period; the middle period when Moore knew him and when much of his time was taken up as the propagandist of co-operation; and the third and last period when literature and journalism were his main concern.

After the war journalism claimed him almost wholly for a time. For seven years he edited the only literary journal which his country possessed. It is wrong to think that he is adequately described—as has been done—by the phrase "a great journalist". As well refer to Blake as "that most competent engraver". Journalism was the accidental overplus of his genius. Norman tells me that it was with difficulty that he was persuaded in the first instance to undertake the work and then only from a sense of duty.

But he gave himself freely here as in all things. Following the Treaty, Plunkett, helped generously by certain Americans, founded, or rather re-founded, *The Irish Statesman*, to give voice to the aspirations of the nation in politics, literature and art. A.E. was asked to edit it. He remained in his room at the top of 84 Merrion Square,[1] for the new venture had absorbed its more modest predecessor, the little paper dealing with rural and agricultural affairs. *The Irish Statesman* gave him greater freedom and far greater scope than he had possessed before. He was no longer tied to one country and to a single topic. He could range over the whole field of men's thoughts and activities. During these years all of what Yeats calls his impassioned versatility could find expression. He was a poet. He could write of poets now, discuss their methods and appraise their work. He was a painter. He could review books on art, visit contemporary exhibitions, study new tendencies and see what the younger men were about. The economist could follow world movements, the politician comment upon events, the philosopher direct all the wisdom, which self-discipline and meditation had brought him, to the actual problems of his own and other countries.

As an editor he had one fault. Reasons of economy forced him to write too much of his own paper. Finances only permitted so many outside contributions. He paid generously for these, from the funds at his disposal. But what he wrote himself was given freely, without stint, in his capacity of editor. There was therefore a double tempta-

[1] Yeats then lived at 83 and 'Mac' has commemorated a Dublin legend of the time by her drawing in which we see Yeats, the ribbon of his pince-nez floating in the breeze, his hands behind his back, gazing aloft at the sky as he goes to visit A.E.; while the latter, buried in his beard, his head sunk on his chest, passes only a few feet off in profound meditation on his way to visit Yeats.

tion—his talent being prodigal and his pen nearly as dis-
cursive as his conversation—to fill the gaps himself. The
paper had the further handicap of being half the price of
the other literary weeklies. It could only do this because
of the Promethean energy of A.E. himself. He laboured
like any Titan. "There were times when he had to write
at the speed at which other men fly", said a colleague. But
this had its disadvantage. If occasionally he repeated himself or seemed to contradict what he had said elsewhere,
no man as a whole could have been so consistent, or written
out of such a profound insight. He reminded a correspond-
ent, who had detected one of these apparent inconsistencies,
of Whitman's "Do I contradict myself? Very well, I contradict myself. I contain multitudes", and went on to say (he
was writing to a dramatist):

> You yourself have created, in masterly fashion,
> characters who are full of contradictions, who now
> barge like angry fishwives and the next minute are kind
> and generous. You recognise so much complexity in
> human nature. Well, if you meditate more you will
> find that many contraries are balanced in the soul, as
> they are in nature. One part of our complex being may
> thirst after the spirit sincerely and another may delight
> in bodily things. The spirit in us may believe, while
> another part of our nature—intellectual—may be
> sceptic. At one time we may desire solitude, at another
> moment multitude. At one moment we may like to
> surrender ourselves to the magic of a particular picture
> or poem and dream into it. At another time we may
> like to range over twenty or thirty drawings or poems,
> criticising and contrasting them, and there is no evil in
> this; and the person who yields to these contrary im-
> pulses is not a person of feeble mind, as you suppose,
> but quite wise.

And he recalls to him Emerson's "A foolish consistency is the hobgoblin of little minds".

The most gentle and good-natured of editors, his good-nature never betrayed him into publishing work which was shoddy. If there are any who doubt this they need only consult the files. Apart from his more illustrious contributors like Yeats, Bernard Shaw and others, he discovered and encouraged a great deal of new talent. And though his own note might tend sometimes to echo itself he took care to introduce variety into what he accepted from others. He had no prejudices. His journal was open to contributors of any nationality, of any point of view, from any school, provided only their work was good. Nor were any allowed to dominate the paper or monopolise it to the point of wearying the reader. No hobby-horses were allowed to be ridden too long—unless perhaps those wonderful coursers, the winged hobby-horses of A.E. himself.

At this time his salon on Sunday evenings was crowded, for the work made many contacts for him and brought him many friends. After his death one paper was to reproach him with being too much at the mercy of fools, but it is doubtful if anyone ever remained a fool for long in his company. "His influence on young writers derived from the complete freedom, hospitality and simplicity of his mind. He was not a propagandist of his own ideas amongst them, in the sense that he never tried to impose them on others nor required the least acceptance of them from his associates. He was the most magnanimous, the most generous of contemporary artists, and with this magnanimity went a simplicity of spirit which flung open his whole mind to all comers. There was no rancour in his judgements, nor did he willingly permit it in others; a kindly wisdom throned over debate, comprehending and all-forgiving."[1] Animosities breed all too readily in both literary and political circles,

[1] C. P. Curran.

and it was A.E.'s peculiar gift that even when there was hostility latent it never burst into flame. It was as though all who accepted his hospitality were under *geisa* not to break the law of friendliness which as host he laid upon them.

His attitude to poetry was probably unique. Dr. Best, speaking of a time before A.E. was editor at all, tells me that he must have been the only man in existence who when he took up a literary weekly always looked first in the column where poetry was published to see if he could discover a new voice there; or, as Stephen Gwynn puts it, when he opened a provincial paper he turned to the poets' corner as other men to the racing news. Years before, Yeats was supposed to have damped a project of Dunsany's to found a literary monthly, which A.E. should edit, with the remark, "I hear, Lord Dunsany, that you are going to supply groundsel for A.E.'s canaries". The story may be apocryphal, but in any case A.E.'s canaries compared favourably with those of any rival bird-fancier. Long before they were known to the world he encouraged and helped Padraic Colum, James Stephens, Seumas O'Sullivan, Austin Clarke, F. R. Higgins, D. L. Kelleher, Frank O'Connor and many others. "A.E. was born with a beautiful mind," says Moore, "and can pass a criticism on a copy of bad verses and send the poet home unwounded in his self-respect." It is doubtful if he ever praised anything in which he could not discover some merit. He could be severe on occasions. Sometimes he was noncommittal, uncertain whether to encourage or not. Of one who had worked with him and who was publishing her first book of verse, he wrote, "We see different eternities. This is not the heaven I would enter. These saints, these divinities are not those I worship. . . . But I remember the year she was a literary colleague, how natural, kind and good she was, and if any word of mine could draw attention to the natural charm of her verses, I gladly give it."

The verse he published showed considerable range and variety. If he used verse of a modernist tendency he took care that it should be of a high quality. A number of his own poems appeared in the paper, some under pseudonyms because, as he once explained to me, this gave him a greater freedom for experiment. The fact that he later acknowledged and republished some of them gave me the clue to the pen-names, for, though he had revealed to me those used for his prose, he never told me his pen-names as poet.

Though he used his own poems from time to time, by far the greater portion of the verse that appeared was the work of younger men. When at the end of seven years the paper came to an end, he was proud to remember this fact. Writing his valediction, he told his readers that he had tried to keep the promise made in the first number, that as far as lay within his power he would keep its pages free from bitter personalities. He has few regrets at abandoning his task. He counts himself among the elderly "whose minds have lost flexibility and who have come to a kind of spiritual deafness." But he can still, like George Herbert, relish versing and he would like to be remembered for one thing, that he was "the friend of the Irish poets, those who make the soul of the nation".

15

In his last letter to his son Diarmuid, written a few days before his death, A.E. suggested that if a portion of his enormous contribution to journalism were published after his death, I might be a suitable person to make the selection. Practically everything in this present book has been drawn from *The Irish Statesman*, and in reading it we will do well to remember its period—post-war Europe and post-treaty Ireland—and also the circumstances under which it was produced, in haste, with little revision and often while the

printer's devil waited. We must not judge it in the same way
that we would judge his finished work. To use the material,
it has been necessary to select, to extract, to amalgamate
and to re-arrange. Practically nothing has been changed
except the order of sentences or paragraphs, but a great deal,
of only passing interest, has been left out and most of the
titles have been added. It makes no claim to be more than
a sort of conspectus of A.E.'s thoughts at a certain period.
It should be dipped into in the same way that we dip into an
anthology. It is A.E.'s table-talk, a note-book of his ideas
and ideals, almost as informal as his conversation and spread
over as wide a diversity of topic.

And yet even in his journalism we find traces of the heroic
stature of the man. He distilled something of himself into all
he wrote. He saw things in their eternal procession. Again
and again some profundity would drop from his lips as it
were by chance. He was always on the look-out for the liberating thought, something which would release the spirit and
start it on a voyage of its own.

Stephen Gwynn speaks of "the philosophy which radiated
through his nature—in part a love of beauty, but more truly
a love of humanity, of the divine in human nature". It is the
calibre of a mind that counts. The great mind can reveal
itself by the way. When Goethe says, "Nothing is more
terrible than ignorance with spurs on", we detect at once the
quality of his mind. So A.E. could reveal himself in a phrase.
"In the long run the things which come out of the spirit are as
powerful as the deeds done upon earth." "Nothing is more
important than the images which haunt the mind of the
people, for by these they will be led to act. If they are images
of violence they will inevitably be led to act with violence.
If they are images of beauty they will create beauty." "The
people who do wicked things are always fools. Wickedness
and folly are both forms of stupidity." "There can be no
profound spiritual certitude except for those who have been

tested; who have consciously chosen between the dark and the light."

As often as not these are the asides in some book review or commentary of the week. At any moment his mind might jet forth something which was beautiful or striking. In the torrent which poured from his pen there were continually being thrown out these precious stones, crystal clear, proof against time, as well as the rainbow effects of airy fancy, formed as it were by the spray as it fell. His passionate interest in ideas gave him zeal for almost any topic. Some of the best things are of course his literary criticisms, especially what he has to say about poetry, and about other poets. All that he writes about Yeats is good and will be intensely interesting to students of that poet, for here is someone who had known Yeats since boyhood, writing of him in maturity but with a vivid memory of his own early impressions of the verse. Innovations of form interested him. "Poet and artist are always trying to enlarge their technique. As a girl becomes a little unhappy if she has to wear last year's fashions, so the poet becomes a little unhappy if he is confined to metrical tradition." He enjoyed discussing free verse, though he thought that few were capable of giving it an adequate musical quality. His verdicts on other writers, both on his contemporaries and on the classics, are always interesting, not merely as considered judgments but for the light they cast on A.E.'s own mind. It will be seen by those who read the book that in it A.E. looks at life from a more intellectual angle, that he has become the sage rather than the seer, and that he pours out his wisdom in relation to other men's thoughts and beliefs, subjecting even his own faith to a critical analysis. To many this philosophic attitude will make a stronger appeal than the ardencies of the earlier visionary, but behind the philosopher we can detect again and again the seer, the man who wrote the poetry and prose, and though there may be nothing here which rises to the height of *The Interpreters* or *Song and Its Fountains*, yet there are many passages which throw an interesting sidelight on topics discussed there.

16

It has been suggested that his last years at Rathgar Avenue were lonely ones, and MacCarthy draws a picture of the deserted sage which is pathetic but not wholly accurate.

> I am not surprised that as years went on fewer young men and women should have come of an evening to drink at A.E.'s fountain, that the battered chairs in the dusty studio should have proved in the long run more than sufficient to accommodate arguers and listeners. . . . During the years after the Civil War in Ireland when I sometimes enquired of Dublin friends visiting England, I was told, "A.E.? I haven't seen him. Nobody goes"; and a vision of him sitting there at night would rise before me; of A.E. painting—artificial light was never a deterrent (he knew his simple palette of dove-grey, light blue and pink by heart) painting and re-painting dusky visions of children leaping and dancing beside vague turquoise seas, or tall, boneless Spiritual Beings of mild authority crowned with white stars. And with what an ache of disappointment in him he must have sat there, unless he could step into regions of meditation where nothing matters and events are only symbols. Instead of a blossoming there had been a withering; instead of expansion, a bitter contraction. Many of his countrymen had learnt to live on hatred, and now they hated and shot each other. . . . Now no-one would listen.

MacCarthy exaggerates. A.E. was not the man to "slip into

regions of meditation where nothing matters" merely because some of his work seemed to have failed. All his life he had been a realist as well as an idealist. He could accept disappointment with greater fortitude than most men. Twenty years before, he had written in his little agricultural weekly for an audience of small farmers: "We don't expect any millennium. We hand that plaything of our youth on to the next generation hoping that they will enjoy it as much as we did, and hand it on untarnished to their children and to their children's children. We think that to work for a thing is better than to get the thing itself and we would rather see one man heroically struggling with difficulties than ten fat men whose millennium has arrived."

Nor is the suggestion that he was completely deserted by the younger men right. J. P. O'Reilly points out that there was not a single young writer in recent years in Ireland whose name has since come before the world whom he had not met from time to time at A.E.'s in the post-war period. It is true that after the Treaty there seemed for a time to be a greater influx of foreign visitors to the country, and the gatherings at Rathgar Avenue were probably larger on that account, people coming from abroad to visit an Ireland that had been for a time anything but salubrious for either native or stranger. Presently, when the Free State had settled down to respectability, fewer seemed to come. It is also true that a number of writers who were originally part of the circle were now no longer in Dublin. James Stephens had left Ireland, Colum was in America, O'Casey in London, Joyce in Paris, Yeats wintered upon the Riviera. It is hardly surprising that literary intercourse should have become more constricted, and that A.E.'s "salon" should have suffered like the rest. But that the younger men despised or deliberately avoided A.E. now that his paper was no longer there to publish their poems, or to voice their views, is saying too much.

There has grown up too the rumour that A.E. left Ireland because of opposition in this quarter or that, and that he died in exile, a disillusioned and disappointed man. This is completely wrong. He left Ireland soon after his wife's death for a number of reasons. One of these was probably loneliness consequent on his loss. His work was for the moment finished; one of his sons was in India, the other had just gone to America. He wished to renew acquaintance with certain early friends of his youth who were living in London, and he had also the thought of going upon a world cruise, which he had discovered could be done as cheaply as the occupying of a house alone in Dublin. He had crossed the Atlantic several times already, was a good sailor and could enjoy a storm and big seas, an experience at which he hints in one of his later poems. He gave these reasons to Curran before he left Dublin and again to me when I met him in England a few months later. But though he had sold his house and distributed his pictures and his possessions among his friends, there was no suggestion that he had broken the connection with Ireland permanently; during the next two or three years he returned each summer to paint there, and if the end had not come there is no doubt that he contemplated returning permanently, although his son was urging him strongly to join him in America.

I myself was living in England at this time, and though I saw A.E. each summer, when I returned to Ireland, the days when I had been a frequent visitor at Rathgar Avenue already seemed far off. It was a pleasure then when A. G. B. Russell[1] invited him to Swanage. Russell had known him years before and possessed some of his drawings, but they had not met for a considerable time.

A.E. came, and I saw much of him during the three days which followed. Russell brought him to tea, and I can see my small son aged three standing on a stool behind the sage's

[1] Lancaster Herald of Arms. Not a relation of A.E.

chair, looking at him with curious interest as he talks, and spreading his arms wide, as though he were some attendant spirit giving his blessing to this Olympian who was soon to depart.

Later in the evening when we joined him again at Russell's we were to taste fully the wit and universality of his mind. When we arrived he was outlining his theory of spiritual gravitation. He believed in it seriously, but he could jest about it too. He told us of an eccentric friend of his youth who, preoccupied with the doctrine of reincarnation, confided to him one day his discovery that the Second Coming had already taken place and that Shakespeare was its manifestation. When they next met intuition had taken him even further. He had learnt that the eleven apostles were now on earth and that he himself was Peter. He was now searching for the other ten. He believed that he would be led to them by spiritual gravitation. Looking earnestly at A.E. he said, "You are one of them". "If that is so, then I must be Thomas", was A.E.'s reply. But the law was to vindicate itself after all. Years later at a meeting in London Yeats referred to this man. "I do not know what has become of him", he said. At that instant a tall gaunt figure rose at the back of the hall and a voice announced, "He is here".

Conversation that night ranged over a wide field and continued till a late hour. I remember we showed him a book of criticism of poetry written in a modern and extremely analytic vein. He glanced at it for a few minutes and then put it down, saying quietly, "They break the enchantment". At two in the morning we were embarked on a heated discussion of the Greek mystery cults and the extent to which it is possible they may have revealed true mysteries, a topic veiled in such obscurity that everyone felt free to hold his own opinion.

Russell said to me afterwards that he was amazed at the development in A.E. since the days when he had first known him. "He had shed all that was fantastic and a little unreal in the interval. I realised in a moment or two that I was talking to a very great man. In the three days which he spent with us we listened as it were to a torrent of wise and profound observation."

A.E. returned to London early next day. In London he seemed content with the simplest quarters. He had kept a few paintings, a few books, and he took these with him when he moved his lodging. Some months later I visited him in Gloucester Terrace, where he had two small rooms at the top of the house. I had been asked by Derek Verschoyle to get a poem from him for the paper of which he is literary editor, but when I mentioned this to A.E. he shook his head, saying jestingly that he was an extinct volcano and would write no more. And then, in contradiction to this assertion that the last of his poetry was written, he told me how he was work-ing on a long poem which he had begun many years before, and taking up a sheet of paper he read me a long extract from *The House of the Titans*, that passage where Lugh the Sun-god comes on a winged horse over the waters offering help to the imprisoned Danaans in their cave. Outlining the story, and then chanting his lines slowly and melodiously in a caressing voice, he was able on this occasion to make the myth more real to me than any subsequent re-reading has ever made it. It was as though he evoked the visual image by his words at the same time that he uttered them. The tale became the parable of the soul and was yet intensely real in itself. Later, when he dedicated this same poem to Osborn Bergin, he was to write, in lines which may fall short of his best, but which completely express his meaning,

> I bring this poem, half dream, half vision, to you.
> I know, incredulous scholar, you will lift
> Ironic eye-brows as you read the tale.
> But being poet yourself you will forgive
> Unto the poet things unpardonable

Done by the scholar. Yet I would defend
My telling of the tale. These myths were born
Out of the spirit of man and drew their meaning
From that unplumbed profundity. I think
In after ages they will speak to us
With deeper voices and meanings. In one age
Men turn to the world about them and forget
Their old descent from heaven. In another
They storm the heavens with supplication. Some
Have found the glittering gates to open. I
Beat many times upon the gates, but was not
Like those who kept them mightily apart
Until they entered. Yet from fleeting voices
And visionary lights a meaning came
That made my myth contemporary. And those
Who read may find titans and king within
Themselves.

And then, remembering that the value of all myth or
heroic legend, true or untrue, for the individual is the
power it exercises over his imagination to change him to its
likeness, he remembered also that universal rhythm which
exists apart from any humanly-related tale, and he added:

And, if they ponder further, they may,
Not in my story, but on the shining heights
Of their own spirit, hear those lordlier voices,
The ageless shepherds of the starry flocks,
They whose majestic meditation is
The music of being; unto those who hear it
Sweeter than bells upon a darkening plain
When the dim fleeces move unto the fold.

17

He must have remained in London nearly two years,
though he spent the summer months in Ireland. Edith
Lyttelton describes a visit to him:

. . . at the very top of a house in Cambridge Terrace, divided up into little suites of one or two rooms, each with their own front door. A.E.'s sitting-room window looked on to one of those strange stone and stucco balustrades which topped houses of a certain period and darkened the second housemaid's room. But somehow it gave, as he said, character to A.E.'s lodging: beyond the balustrade was sky and nothing else, not a chimney pot, not a branch. It suited. Hither he had permitted me to climb one afternoon by appointment and I walked into his room with some nervousness. The floor was littered with books and papers, the walls were hung with his own pictures. It was the room of a king, glowing with colour. He did not remember my pictures but I told him about the misty one and that set him talking and he murmured on and on for more than an hour. It was enchanting to listen to him and to feel how near he lived to a world of light and beauty and to the great and small beings of his imagination, or perhaps his vision. I wish I could reproduce his talk—the heart of it can be found in his prose as well as his poetry.

He believed certain places to be more favourable to vision than others and she longed to ask him why. "At last I put the question into words. He leant forward and looked at me for a moment through his great spectacles: I could not guess whether he thought I was foolish or pitiful not to know the answer. 'Well,' he said in a kindly voice, 'the earth is a person—a goddess and we are part of her—in her. Now just as in our bodies there are certain parts which are more in contact with impressions than others, like the eyes, or perhaps the ears, so it is with the earth. There are certain places in her body which are sensitive, and beings, strangers to us, can manifest more easily in those places.'"

Some months later I saw him in London again myself, lunching with him and Paul Brunton, the writer on Indian mysticism. He was being pressed to go to America, and told us he had written to say that his advice was hardly worth bringing all that way, but that if they still wished for it he would go. His life in London seemed at a standstill. It was winter. The streets were gloomy and foggy, and even the adulation of two younger men, however sincere it appeared, could not dispel that faint tinge of melancholy and of self-depreciation which seemed to have crept into his thoughts. Only after we had been talking for some time and our minds had begun to warm did he appear to lose it. It was the same melancholy perhaps which led to that beautiful little poem which he sent to Seumas O'Sullivan shortly before his death, and then asked him to hold over as he would try and give him "something more cheerful" in its place.

> Art thou gone before me
> Unto that high air,
> Youth that was in my youth?
> And shall I meet thee there,
> Leaving this weight behind,
> Blurred mind and whitening hair?
>
> O do not wander far
> Before I too may go,
> I have need of thy sunshine
> As a lamp here below,
> Of thy youth as a staff to lean on
> Where the weary mind would go.

A few days later when I saw him again it had been definitely settled that he should go to America, and he seemed cheered at the prospect, and by the thought that he would be seeing his son there, and his daughter-in-law, whom he had never met. This last visit to America was paid at the request of the Government, that he might discuss the question of a rural civilisation with some of their experts in Washington. When asked to go he replied, as Plato had once done to the Syracusans, that he was an old man, but when the request was repeated a second time he accepted. One of those who met him on that occasion has described how he conferred day after day with those who sought his opinion, "advising out of the richness of his practical experience, and with great humility pointing out errors which he advised us to avoid". The same friend[1] describes how he gave up his evenings to talking informally with young people about poetry, life and philosophy, or whatever topic might crop up, his conversation full of wisdom and tolerance, maturity and faith in the possibilities of life and in the ability of the common man to rise to uncommon heights when need and opportunity offered. On the last day on which he was in Washington discussion, she tells us, had turned casually upon the intellectual contest then raging between property rights and personal rights and aspirations. He reached for a piece of paper and pencil and said he thought he could "make a poem" about that, scribbling on it the following lines, which he gave to her:

> How would they think on, with what shame,
>   All that fierce talk of thine and mine,
> If the true Master made His claim,
>   The world He fashioned so divine?
> What could they answer did He say
>   "When did I give My World away?"

He returned from America in the spring. He had been planning a visit to some of the native Indian tribes, a scheme suggested to him by one of his Washington friends, when illness overtook him, and he abandoned it to turn with the instinct of a sick man for home. In London he placed

[1] Mrs. Paul Wilson.

himself in the hands of the doctors until he should be well enough to go to Ireland. And it was in London that I saw him early in April. I had mislaid the note he had written me, and my mistake cost me much time and a journey to Covent Garden and back before I finally located him at Tavistock Square, quite near where my memory of the address had first started me searching. He had grown thinner and his clothes hung loosely about him but he was otherwise unchanged. There was the same abrupt handshake of welcome and almost the same zest when he began to talk. When I arrived Constance Sitwell was with him. After his death she was to write to me, "I remember how his face lit up when you came into the room that evening". He was better, telling us that it was the first day for many that he had felt like himself. "Look at Monk Gibbon. He smells of the sun and the soil and wild places", he said, deducing from my flushed face, the result of those peregrinations which I had almost abandoned in despair, and from the rough tweed suit which I was wearing, a health and spirits which I did not feel, for I had lost my father only a few weeks before. From the depths of his armchair he began to tell us about his visit to Washington, mentioning Lewis Chase, a mutual friend whom he had seen there, and regretting that he had missed the chance of seeing the primitive tribes which were all that was left of an ancient civilisation. I should remember more of his conversation if I had known then that I was speaking to him for the last time. But no such thought was in either of our minds. He spoke of the diet on which the doctor had placed him and how it would be difficult for him to go to his favourite haunts in Ireland, where both fare and cooking were so simple, as long as it had to be continued. But it would not continue for long; before summer was well started he would be back painting among his beloved mountains.

He was not to see them again with mortal eye. The voyage

was accomplished and the course set.[1] Years before he had written, "We may give up the outward personal struggle and ambition, and if we leave all to the Law all that is rightly ours will be paid. . . . We are indeed most miserable when we dream we have no power over circumstance, and I account it the highest wisdom to know this of the living universe that there is no destiny in it other than we make for ourselves." Looking back on his life it may have seemed to him not only in the multiple activities of brain and hand but in the domain of spirit, where the higher the achievement the more likely a man is to think humbly of himself, that he had fallen far short of the ideal which he had set himself. But that he had received other than the destiny he deserved would never have crossed his mind. He believed that others had achieved clearer vision and higher intuition. "There were some who had gone deeper into that being than I ever travelled. . . . The only justification for speech from me, rather than from others whose knowledge is more profound, is that the matching of words to thoughts is an art I have practised more." He may even have believed at times that he had scattered his energies, and that, though he could cry with Lugh in his own poem,

> Ask the high king has he in that dark house
> One who is master of so many arts.

there was little to show for this wide mastery; a few poems, a few lovely paintings in which beauty had found temporary resting-place, a few words of serene and patient wisdom to men whose passions were inflamed and vision distorted.

He had dedicated himself at once to beauty and to good-

[1] It was for A.E. that James Stephens' lovely verses 'The Mighty Mother' were written,

> . . . And with but the smallest sigh
> I shall get me whence I came,
> Shall not die to death but be
> Born into it, peacefully . . .

ness, to the service of art and to the service of men. He had never coveted material success. He told me once how at the age of twenty-five he was still earning what he considered the princely salary of thirty pounds a year. Later this was increased to thirty-five, and when, still later, it rose to be fifty pounds, it seemed to him that he was living in affluence and had abundance to lend to his friends.

It was Pindar who cryptically said that the business of a man in life is "to become what he is". This was the aim which A.E. had always set himself. To become what he was. No man that I know in the world of letters gave such an instant impression of being true to his purpose or of having so completely fulfilled himself. Moreover, the qualities for which he was loved were those one was always certain to find. As a friend said after one of their many meetings, "he talked wisdom and beauty as he always does".

And now the life so full of varied activity was drawing to its close. Some weeks before the end he went to Bournemouth to escape the great heat of July in London. There he was near John Eglinton, the friend of his youth, and there were Pamela Travers and others to surround him with kindness. Even then neither he nor those near him seem to have known that he was dying, though Eglinton in a letter to me, written a little later, seems to have suspected the truth. One of these friends, Myrtle Johnston, has described the house amongst the trees where he stayed and how he used to lie out in the garden overlooking the sea, shaded from the sun which "poured down fierce and steady with none of the wistful impermanence of a summer's day in Donegal nor with the mildness of Leinster sunshine". When she and her sisters came to see him he would talk to them about Ireland, the country from which they also came, calling up "visions of a beauty which had often made his brush slip unheeded from his hands". She speaks of his humility and how ten days before he died he hesitated to stay in bed for breakfast lest it should give trouble to those who were looking after him. Of his conversation she says, "he seemed to take for granted in all whom he met a spirituality equal to his own. He thought no-one fit to receive but of his best." She speaks too of his unfailing memory for verse, a faculty several of his friends have noted, and how Arnold's lines, "We mortal millions dwell apart", were often on his lips, but "never with any bitterness". Once they said to him, "What will be the next form of religion?"—"A religion of ethics."

Gogarty came over from Ireland before the end. Describing his death he speaks of his calm fortitude, his lovableness, "which made even his surgeon, whose skill must defend itself against sentimentality, turn away for a moment in tears".

> The change in his countenance was remarkable, and the way the mind threw off the veils of death to deepen the great blue light in his eyes as he rejoiced at seeing for a moment a friend's face, was something to impress the memory for ever. The hero in the man looked out and it was his friends who had to brace themselves against life with its loss. He said to a close companion as he lay dying, before he had altogether turned away: "I have realised all my ambitions. I have had an astounding interest in life. I have great friends. What more can a man want?"

Some years before, when her mother died, A.E. had written to Pamela Hinkson—"I think the dead are happier than the living. And I do not fear death for myself or others." And now, hearing of his own death, she was to recall these words and to say in her turn—"the world seems less safe without him; but, since he is dead, the dead to-day must indeed be happier than the living".

MONK GIBBON

SWANAGE, 1937

81

LITERATURE
AND
CRITICISM

LITERATURE
AND
CRITICISM

The Making of Poetry

THE BOOK in which I have found most wisdom tells me that the motive for action should be in the action itself and not in the event, that is, the making of song, the painting of picture; for the natural delight we have in the doing should be the sole reason for doing, not because we desire it or ourselves to be remembered. The making of poetry should be natural with us as the blossoming of the hedgerows, and we should be as little concerned about what we have made as we have been when the beauty of twilight has passed, because another beauty begins.

When I was young and had got over the first difficulties of the craft I wrote verses with this naturalness, having a pleasure in the making of them, and with no thought of the morrow or publication. Then a friend gathered my manuscripts and made a book out of them. I became self-conscious. I began to think that people would read what I had written, and lost some natural innocence of imagination which I never afterwards recovered. I think the poet ought to be shy about his public if not altogether unconscious of it.

There is a poem of Sappho's which it has always moved me to think of, though nothing remains of it, not even the names of the poets, lovers or warriors of whom it has spoken, nothing but a single line in which was recorded their belief that the world could never be forgetful of so great a beauty as their lives had known:

> I think men will remember us, even hereafter.

Why should we expect the beauty we make to be remembered? Every hedgerow has scattered prodigally in bud or leaf or flower a more miraculous beauty than man has ever made. If we could magnify primrose or lilac a million times we would only find new marvels of workmanship by the Magician of the Beautiful. The whitethorn of the spring that has passed, or the twilight which waved a peacock's tail of colour over the waters, the tumbling of foam, these and a million things like these we have seen; Nature produces them prodigally and they pass swiftly as they are born and are forgotten. But let us feel the beauty of any of these things, let us put it into words, and there arises in us that pathetic longing that what we have done may be remembered hereafter.

A Gold Standard for Literature

I AM TEMPTED to steal from economics some of its assumptions or principles and apply them to literature. I understand that the more you inflate a currency the more worthless does it become. The currency of literature is words, and the printing press enables writers to inflate that currency as readily as the printing press in Germany or Russia enabled the Governments there to manufacture marks and roubles, until at last a million mark or rouble note did not pay for

the cost of printing it. As a set-off against this evil, I understand that while inflation is going on the manufacturers
benefit, and there is some marketing advantage. Before
printing enabled the literary currency of words to be inflated
there was something approximating to a gold standard in
literature. The employment of scribes to multiply manuscripts was an expensive thing, and writers were forced to
concentrate their thought into fiery particles. How concentrated are the sacred books. A philosopher in the East could
boil his wisdom down into a series of aphorisms. One might
brood on aphorisms of Kapila, Patanjali or Lao-Tse for years
without getting to the bottom of them. Indeed, if one comprehended a single aphorism fully he could almost make
philosophies for himself. It is worth noting that William
Blake, the sole writer in modern times who not only wrote
but engraved, printed and coloured his poetry, is the only
writer whose power of concentrated utterance is on a level
with these ancient sages. There are aphorisms in his *Marriage
of Heaven and Hell* which are fiery and germinal, and there is
hardly any writer who has been more a cause of writing to
others who try to translate the gold of his literature into the
more popular silver and copper of intelligibility. Literature
has suffered so much from inflation that in my opinion it
can only be saved by a return to a gold standard. This deflation of literary currency will, of course, throw an immense
number of people out of employment. But we can only
secure the salvation of literature by martyrdoms. Literature
has less and less effect the more it is multiplied. Even a
century and a half ago writers like Rousseau, Voltaire or
Byron, none of whom could be called concentrated, had yet
an effect upon European thought which no writer since has
equalled. Books then were not so many or so cheaply acquired that words became powerless through over-multi-
plication. If Bernard Shaw had lived at the time of Voltaire
he would, in the sphere of the mind, have been the peer of

Frederick the Great or Napoleon in the external world of deeds and affairs. He would probably have awed Frederick more even than Voltaire did. It is impossible to imagine a literary man, no matter of what magnitude, exerting to-day the influence writers had a hundred and fifty years ago. The currency they trade with has been inflated. What is to be done? Return to a gold standard. Deflate the currency of literature; insist that every writer shall be his own printer and publisher. Only real genius, the men who must speak or die, will face the hard labour and survive. They will be forced to concentrate. We will not have these interminable novels, where the writer tells us how the room was furnished, what clothes everybody wore, what their personal appearance was like, how they spent their school days, their adolescence, and all their love affairs, wringing out the last drop of emotion. We ought hardly to endure such minutiae about titans like Napoleon, but to have mountains of words piled about imaginary, commonplace characters revolts me. What do we take out of books but some sentence in which there is a thought we can make our own? We can carry away with us the hushed melancholy of

A slumber did my spirit seal.

It is all embodied in eight lines of deathless poetry, but how much do we carry away from *The Excursion* that we can make our own? Can we imagine Browning, if he had, like Blake, to engrave, print and decorate his own poetry, producing *The Ring and the Book*?

Publication is too easy. I remember how a revival of stained glass came about. It was by a return to the methods of the mediaeval artists and craftsmen, who not only designed but carried out their own designs. They thought in terms of stained glass. Then came a bad period in which there was a division of functions. One made the cartoon, and another translated the artist's water-colour sketch into

88

glass. The ancient artists imagined in terms of their material, and their materials were precious to them. It must have been so with Blake. Words became precious things to him, and they glowed with gold and flame on his pages, as they well might, because his sentences were fiery particles of spirit. Of course hardly anybody could live by literature if this method was adopted. But is it right that anybody should live by literature? Is it not better that they should have some other employment so that their art might be entirely disinterested? One of the ancient sages concentrated a whole philosophy of disinterestedness into a single sentence: "Let the motive for action be in the action itself, and not in the event". That is, be artist, poet, musician, philosopher because you live to paint, sing or think, and to do so is your happiness. If you think of fame, large circulations, income, you must be deflected from disinterestedness. What you do is no longer an exquisite soliloquy between yourself and heaven. It is an effort to cajole others, to cast a glamour over them, and you are deflected from truth and beauty, and indeed from essential goodness. I have not the least hope that anything I say will bring about a deflation of literary currency. It will come about through necessity. The forests out of which paper is made are rapidly being cut down. In a hundred years paper will be so costly that it cannot be used except for precious thoughts. We will come back again to a gold standard in literature, and Patanjali, the sage, who wrote a treatise on concentration, will be the most honoured philosopher in the universities, and the literature of intensities will be the only literature which will be published. I would like to live in the future which I have conjured up. I could have boiled down this essay to a single sentence.

Yeats' Essays

I SPOKE OF THIS BOOK as the only important contribution anyone had yet made to an Irish philosophy of literature and the arts, and yet there is no definite philosophy, the unity of the thought arising from the peculiar temperament or imagination of the poet rather than from any logical system he has thought out, and into which all must fit or be outcast. It is much better as it is, for the intuitions of a poetical nature are more exciting and profound than any logical philosophy of literature could be. We find what seem to be contradictions, but these are the natural reactions we find in ourselves from all our moods. We do not betray our ideals when we react from them, if we react with full consciousness, giving good reasons for our new departure. We have always to strike a balance between our own opposites and the wisest thinker is he who is conscious that our nature is made up of opposing elements, all necessary, and who will not be afraid of speaking now from one pole of his being and now from another.

Yeats gives very good reasons why in his youth he desired to write popular poetry, and much better reasons for giving up the hope. He has found himself between the opposites so often that he has come in *Per Amica Silentia Lunae* to half expound a philosophy of these contraries, and it may be he will give us a complete exposition in the philosophical volume he is writing at present. I doubt whether the net of conscious mind will catch so many gay fish as were netted by momentary emotion, or that any house of thought built by a poet is large enough for a poet to live in. The poet accepts, consciously or unconsciously, Anima Mundi as his subconscious self, and if he philosophises too much he is in danger of substituting a bare theory for that rich depth. If there be any gods, says Plato, they certainly do not philosophise. In

90

the essays he has escaped limitation, and I doubt if he will ever stir us more by rationalising his impulses, and I would quote to him one of his own intuitions: "We make out of the quarrel with others rhetoric, but out of the quarrel with ourselves poetry". When we have explained ourselves to ourselves too clearly the quarrel is settled. I would rather the poet fished in that rich darkness for creatures of the mind which blaze when they are brought into full consciousness.

The Winding Stair

I HAVE BEEN TRYING to explain to myself the development in Yeats' later poetry, the new and strange beauty into which it has evolved, so that it excites us by a freshness we might find in the first volume of a new poet. So many poets labour to make a style for themselves, and then become the slaves of their style. They say nothing of which the style cannot be the vehicle, and so there is little development after. Almost all that Tennyson or Swinburne wrote which we care to remember was in their earlier volumes. Every now and then, but rarely in later years, something would be written by them which seemed like a brief revisitation of genius to the soul where it once was a familiar inhabitant. But in the case of Yeats we find the later poet is not only intellectually the lord of the earlier poet, but that as a stylist there is an amazing advance, yet without any diminution of emotion or imagination. It is one of the rarest things in literature to find a poet of whom it might be said that his wine was like that in the feast in the Scriptures, where the best was kept until the last. Here in this later poetry is the justification of the poet's intellectual adventures into philosophy, mysticism and symbolism, into magic and spiritualism and many ways of thought which most people regard as by-ways which lead nowhither. The prose record of these adventures made some lovers of his work think of him as a lost poet, and then he came back from these discarded regions of thought with poetry which was fresh and strange and beautiful.

It is his habit of continual intellectual adventure which has kept his poetry fresh. It is possible the Muse will forsake us unless we keep the intellect athletic, and she will reward us even if we forsake her and go mountain-climbing, if we return to her more athletic than when we left. Yes, I think after every book of poetry the poet should exercise himself in some hard intellectual labour before he begins to supplicate the Muse again. That dweller in the innermost will feel then we approach her with reverence, and will breathe on us the holy breath with a more intense flame than before.

We know now that it does not matter much into what by-way this artist of genius goes in his meditation. To us it may seem he goes into a desert, a jungle, into places that are barren of life to the spirit, but he comes back from his wandering with treasures none other had found.

The friends of the poet now know that wherever he goes he brings with him his Leonardesque power of evoking beauty, and he will return from a meditation as tangled as the bramble growth in some hollow on a hillside with a poem intricate and glittering with strange, cold and lovely lights, or with some song as simple and natural as a wild rose.

The poet has climbed into "the breathless starlit air", has tried to still the wandering intellect and to fix it upon that ancestral self, but he turns back from the thin and chill airs to work on things which are symbolical of life, and in a passion declares he would live life over again:

> Endure the toil of growing up:
> The ignominy of boyhood: the distress

Of boyhood changing into man:
The unfinished man and his pain
Brought face to face with his own clumsiness.

And there arises from that acceptance of life a sweetness
flowing into the heart:

We must laugh and we must sing.
We are blest by everything:
Everything we look upon is blest.

It may have been from his study of the Zen philosophy
that he came to this acceptance. The Zen philosopher discovered the possibility of a Nirvana in this world very
different from that mysterious cosmic Nirvana of the founder
of Buddhism. It might come upon the soul in a second, that
illumination which makes Earth and its creatures to appear
spiritual, as St. Peter after a vision found nothing to be
common or unclean. A Zen philosopher would have understood St. Peter, and he would have understood why the
poet, looking at the Japanese sword bound with some silken
embroidery, found, in these, symbols of conflict and love, of
all that made human history, and would not surrender all
that rich drama for the silence of the spirit. The acceptance,
the harmony between the self and the world it is born into,
brought that sweetness.

I fear the poet is not like the Zen philosophers who lived
in monasteries or hermitages, and could preserve in quiet-
ness the spiritual joy they had found. The poet is too restless;
he will come out of that mood which he cherishes only for
a day while he records it, and he will start on some other
adventure, perhaps again approach the gate to deep own-
being, or wander down some hitherto untravelled aisle of
the soul. It is that untiring energy of mind which has made
his later poetry as we read it seem new and strange and
beautiful, and the plain words seem many-coloured, as if

they had been dusted over with powdered jewels, not less glowing for all their absence of that vivid colour he used so lavishly in *The Wanderings of Oisin* or *The Shadowy Waters*. That was a colour put on more from without. In the new poetry plain things shine as by some inner light, as if they were lustrous by themselves and needed not any external light. Plain things shine when they have been bathed in dream. In dream we create our own light and impart it to the things we dream of.

A Journal of Yeats

YEATS HAS GATHERED some Fifty Thoughts from a diary kept by him in the year nineteen hundred and nine. His thoughts have much of the provocative quality of his father's letters. Whether we agree or do not agree, he starts us on a meditation of our own. In his early work the poet was but little conscious of estrangement from national movements. He ran with the crowd, thinking their thoughts were his own, though indeed they were not. And, if I remember aright some early essays, his ambition, so far as it was self-conscious, was to give more beautiful expression to moods which were common and popular among his countrymen. Life made him, as it makes most of us, self-conscious, and when he was setting down these thoughts he was, because of this self-consciousness, becoming aware of isolation. His poetry would not, I think, have isolated him in thought, but his intellect did estrange him.

Autobiography

W HAT I REGARD as the chief defect in Yeats' auto-
biographies will, I think, be considered by others as
their main virtue. The poet tells us but little about his internal life, but much about the people he has met, and as
he has met many famous people of his time, notabilities
like William Morris, W. E. Henley, Oscar Wilde, Arthur
Symons, Lady Gregory, Helena Blavatsky, John O'Leary,
Lionel Johnson, John M. Synge, John Davidson and Ernest
Dowson, his memories of these will be, for most readers,
the chief interest in the memoirs. I hold that there is only
one person that a man may know intimately, and that is
himself. If he be a man of genius, what he could tell us about
his own inner life would be of much more value than anything he could tell us of the external life of others, no
matter how notable these people may have been. I read the
Reveries Over Childhood and Youth, and into this river of
beautiful prose there hardly falls an image of the imagination
which was then wandering in *The Island of Statues*, or with
Oisin in Tir na n-óg. His mirror reflects almost everything his
eye has seen, but nothing of the imagination which was to
make so rare a beauty and which must then have been in its
rich springtime. The external world evolves its patterns
before his eye, but of the involution of the spirit into the
bodily nature bringing with it its own images and memories
of another nature, there is but little, and I read this biography as I would look at some many-coloured shell, from
which the creature inhabiting it, who might have told us
about its manner of being, had slipped away leaving us only
the miracle of form to wonder at. I am inclined to prophesy
a reaction from the objective treatment of life in literature,
and that the age which follows ours may value a writer only
for what he can report on the inmost mysteries of his life,

with the thought that from his candle we may set fire to our own. But of its kind, this mirroring of notable personalities in another, as notable as any he writes about, has unusual distinction. The prose in its cool, luminous flowing is a delight to follow. His portraits of his contemporaries are always interesting. If I do not recognise myself or my friends in the chapter he has devoted to us, I can understand how we may have appeared like this to another. But it is because I know myself and my friends so much better than the poet could have known us, and because I see the chasm between our inner life and the outer which he describes, that I am inclined to suppose, though I may be in error, that there is a wide gulf between the inward and the external life of others whom he portrays. I say this without reflecting in any way upon either the memories or the sincerity of the writer, which is made obvious in many passages relating to himself. But I return to my original conviction, that no true portrait can be made by any, save of themselves, though the doing of this would require extraordinary qualities in the writer, which not even a Rousseau had in the necessary fullness. Until we have such intimate revelations, all histories can be but little more than farthing dips, lighting the ages through which mankind has travelled.

Of Yeats' Style

HOW CAN ONE CONVEY any impression of that arrogant yet persuasive mentality, of that style where simplicity and bareness are suddenly varied by some image rich as a jewel, and we are as delighted by the contrast as if we saw some lovely gem-bedight queen walking along an undecorated corridor, noble only because of its proportion.

An Anthology

POETRY CAN NEVER BE MADE a business or occupation without losing that fine air of divinity which thrills us when we read the best poetry. There are many poets in this book who are, oh, so anxious to write well, and in a sense they do write well, but one could not bring the poetry born in a room and carry it out-of-doors, because it would seem too pallid a thing in the sun or not mysterious enough for the night.

I fear that much of this verse was written as deliberately as Walter Pater's prose. I do not expect prose to be composed out-of-doors. Prose is an indoor labour. But I mistrust poetry which does not seem to have come into the soul as naturally as a bird glittering on the wing might come before the eye. I think that just as things out-of-doors take on a colour they never have in the shaded room, so, when the poet is out-of-doors, some light from Anima Mundi illuminates the images.

A Poet

HE TURNS in his verses from his own speculations to dream of things which have that natural peace which seems so desirable to those who have lost it, and have not yet come to the peace which is won at length by the stern will and the indefatigable mind which have come through many tests to their own centre. But between the natural peace of unselfconscious things and Peace, there is long travelling for the soul and the endurance of all agony and experience.

97

Another Poet

THIS VERSE is impudent, like a dance in a French café. Its impudence pleases for a moment, and then one turns away wishing this child of the muse could find something lovelier to do with its agility.

Another ⌇

HE HAS chosen to write with a part of his nature rather than with his whole being. The poet is submerged in the clever intelligence. It is a pity that he should feed the clever at the expense of the imaginative, because when cleverness is pampered and exalted the poetic nature is starved, and after a time it becomes too feeble to create, and the clever self entirely possesses the house of the soul. The cleverness is a little arid, as all satire is which is without deep emotion or passion, and has only prejudice or dislike or contempt as inspiration. To be clever is to live in a very little house, packed with bright things, interesting literary knick-knacks, but without spiritual comfort.

Another ⌇

I CONFESS his verse is often obscure to me, because he reflects a stream of consciousness, with all the corks and dead rats bobbing up in it as well as the stars. The rats are more frequent than the stars in his stream, whereas I think the rats are rare and accidental, and the stars and sun are truly the normal, but this the moderns won't see. They are nearly all hunting rats. No, this is an exaggeration, but the psychological school are too insistent upon man's affinities with the animal creation.

Another ～ℓ~⌐

THE MUSE has many green, unripe apples to delay and deceive, as Atalanta had when she was chased, but this poet has not stayed to pick them up. He knows that he cannot, simply by taking thought, be inspired to make poetry out of poetic things, and he puts by the dreams that ask to be embodied with a gay gesture. He would like to satisfy them, hopes that inspiration will come, half promises it, but he knows in his heart that he is powerless unless the spirit choose him. He has a hope that he will find somewhere in the cellars of the heart vintages which have been laid down long ago, and which ripened while they lay almost forgotten. There are such beautiful resurrections in some of the lyrics, and they never suggest having being sought for, but as if they had sprung up from sleep to play with the poet, and he plays with them gladly while they are there, and lets them go as they will.

Another ～ℓ~⌐

HE WOULD, in my opinion, be better as a poet if he realised that the slightest personal experience of the spirit is worth *as poetry* more than all the greatest ideas of the world's greatest teachers, repeated with no matter how much reverence.

French and English Poets

WE GET THE IMPRESSION that life is more of an art and a pleasure to French than to English poets. They are less mastered by imagination and doctrine. They do not travel so far from the normal and they put a sweeter face on life.

They can be gay and beautiful together. There is hardly any poetry in English which is at once gay and beautiful. If the French poets do not, like Coleridge, Shelley and Keats, hurry us out of earth, they understand better than English poets how much beauty is in the normal life, in the things the eye sees and the heart feels, and they have a fine art.

A Woman Poet

ONE OF THE SAGES of India wrote about the soul: "Two birds sit on the same tree, one eats the sweet fruit, the other looks on without eating". It is rare in any poetry to find both birds singing together, one of the deed which is being done, while the other is aloof commenting as if from a distance, but it is still rarer in poetry written by women who seldom get apart from themselves, and who achieve poetry by a complete surrender to love, religion or nature. —— has this rare duality of feminine consciousness which enables one part of her being to surrender itself to its passion and another to be contemplative of it.

Modernist Poetry

MY TROUBLE with Modernist Poetry is not the trouble "the plain man" has with unusual metrical forms or condensation of language or even obscurity. It is that when the obscurities surrender to concentration of thought, the reward is rarely worth the effort. The important thing about a poet is finally this: "Out of how deep a life does he speak?"

Anthologies

I OPEN AN ANTHOLOGY with some apprehension always that my mind will be confused, and that after reading a few pages I will be unable to appreciate any poetry, however lovely. I never have such fears when I open the complete works of any poet. Anthologies too often are like museums and picture galleries, where works conceived in the most varied moods are set side by side. I find it difficult to change my mood passing from picture to picture. If I look at too many the effect is to stupefy. When the pictures are all by one artist, because they are harmonious with each other, we pass from one to another with heightening appreciation if the artist has genius. I think there are few lovers of literature who would not start to read through their Keats, their Shelley, their Browning, their Whitman, their Yeats with more certainty of sustained delight than they would start to read any anthology, though it contain only the most perfect poetry of the greatest singers. Anthologies, unless arranged with some psychological skill, affect us as contact with an inconsequent mind does, a mind which leaps from one topic to another, and which soon makes us irritable because of an instability our own nature cannot match.

Genius

ARTHUR GRIFFITH used to make plaintive appeals for Irish artists to paint historical pictures, but no Irish artist had the slightest interest in such things. He asked Irish poets to write patriotic ballads, but the poets had come to believe that poetry and politics were antagonistic. The idea that literature can be shaped from outside in response to the popular demand dies hard. When a genius is found he absolutely refuses to do any of the things the sentimentalist expects of him. He is just as likely to kick his country as to bless it. He follows a law of his own being which means that he can only express what is in him and not what is in the minds of other people.

The Memoirs of John Butler Yeats

WHEN THE POET'S FATHER began to write his memoirs he had come to an age when life casts overboard all its accumulations of experience which have not become precious to it. It was, perhaps, not conscious but unconscious selection, a process going on for many years, which enabled him when he began to write to tell us nothing which was not interesting in itself, and which was not made doubly so by the reverie which had distilled from circumstance its wisdom. In the portraits by the elder Yeats he seemed to divine what there was of lovable life in the men and women he painted. He was no flatterer, and whatever there was of strongly marked character was portrayed, but still what was best in the sitter looked out through the eyes, perhaps was evoked by the personality of the artist. I think he disliked the ugly and thought any artist who depicted it did so only to display technical mastery, and hence what was painted was purely mechanical. "Such men", he says, "are a weariness to a man with any tincture of a romantic imagination. I have seen drawings and read prose done with an appetite for the ugly that reminded me of the dogs that licked the sores of Lazarus." In his writing, as in his painting, the elder Yeats shows a delight in character, but he peers through that veil for what has beauty or charm, never for what is ugly. He asserts a dislike for controversy, but, as he is always controversial himself, we suspect what he really dislikes is vehement vulgarity or bad manners, and that he would have been

enchanted if he had found another fencer as swift and graceful in mental movement as himself. Minds like his in conversation with others of like quality rise above themselves,
and, as the poet makes out of three sounds not a fourth
sound but a star, so great talkers will make out of their
conversations a drama greater than the characters who take
part in it. Perhaps many of the wise things in this book are
memories of inspired things said in that brilliant conversation some of us remember so well; and which he himself
probably thought over with pleasure. All artists delight in
the perfect expression of their ideas, from the Architect of
the Universe, Who set sun and stars in their station and said
it was good, down to the least of His children who find the
inevitable word and are happy. In mere writing the memoirs
are distinguished. Not a sentence is heavy. That is because he
is in love with the idea he is going to express, and he moves
with lightness as a lover who goes to an adorable beauty who
is his only, and whose feet walk as if on air at the thought.

Stephens' "Deirdre"

THIS AUTHOR has done nothing more lovely and moving
than his story of the girlhood of Deirdre, her roaming in
the midnight woods, her meeting with the sons of Uisneach,
her calling of Naisi and their flitting through the dark forest,
their hearts so burdened with unborn destiny that not a
word comes to the lips. In passages where Eros is the shepherd of the heart, and leads it in an ecstatic wandering,
Stephens attains an extraordinary beauty in his prose. Everything external is melted in the emotion, all that the eye sees
or the ear hears becomes blended with the mood, so that we
feel we are moving in a nature which is not dead, but waits
panting to be one with us in the hours when the immortal
awakens in us. Even to Conachur, the King, and not all evil

demon, of the story, love makes all things beautiful. When the King falls in love, matter is changed to spirit for him, the divine is seen in all things, earth and sky are one music, women smile and all men are brothers. Whenever in this beautiful book the author's emotions are kindled what he writes amazes us with its vitality and imagination. Whenever he falls outside his own magic circle, and writes of an object-ive struggle or movement, he is less interesting, and we feel that others of inferior ability, who live less by the heart and imagination and more ¹y the eye and reason, could have done it as well. But there are but few chapters in this brilliant book where the author falls outside his own circle. We have often thought a book surpassing the *Arabian Nights* might be made by a writer of genius who would weld into a con-tinuous narrative the tales of the Gods, the Fianna and the Red Branch, so full of beauty, mystery and magnificence that, as the raw material for romance, there is hardly any-thing to equal them in the legendary literature of other countries. Perhaps James Stephens was born and endowed with that fantastic humour, tenderness and beauty of imagina-tion to write a better Hibernian Nights' Entertainment for the delight of youth and age alike.

A Platonic Criticism

WHEN ONE LIKES a poet it is easy to write about him, to become eloquent in his praise. We try to convey to others the enchantment he has cast upon ourselves. But how are we to be truly critical? We cannot apply to poetry any tests such as we can apply to the formulae of the chemist. They can be proved to be true or false in a laboratory. There is no accepted technique of criticism, no proof of beauty. We have little else but the expression of opinion. I have tried to formulate to myself some philosophical principles of criticism, but am uncertain about these. I ask myself about a poet whether his poetry is opaque or transparent; that is, does he rest on the surface of things, or does he see through things, and, lastly, I ask myself out of how deep a life does he speak. I formulated these principles of criticism after reading the *Banquet* of Plato, where Socrates suggests a hierarchy of beauty. First he says we are in love with a single person or form; then, as the soul becomes wiser, it realises that the beauty in one form is akin to the beauty in all other forms. We are released from this mean idea of beauty in one person or form only. Our search goes into the depths, and in this second stage of initiation into beauty we pass from the beauty of form into perception of the beauty of ideas, and at last are led to see beauty in its very essence. But he does not tell us by what criterion we are to esteem ideas. That is left to our intuition, and I could only think of this, that some ideas are opaque as some forms are, and stay us beside them, and that other ideas are transparent and we see through them as one looking through a glass at immense vistas. We are imprisoned—pleasurably, it may be—by the first order, and are liberated by the second order. I was started on this meditation by Richard Aldington's poems. This poetry, esteeming it as Socrates might, I class as largely opaque. It is imagist, resting on the surface or appearance of things, beauty of colour or form, and, indeed, the very titles of four of the volumes of verse from which this collection was made suggest the poet's preoccupation with images. Here is a poem which has for substance little else than a charming imagination for the eyes:

> We will come down to you,
> O very deep sea,
> And drift upon your pale green waves
> Like scattered petals.
> We will come down to you from the hills,
> From the scented lemon-groves,

From the hot sun.
We will come down,
O Thalassa,
And drift upon
Your pale green waves
Like petals.

That is a poetry made of what the eye rests upon, and
there is no attempt at transfiguration. The image is delicately
selected, but there is nothing more in it than the image
which has a charm. I think Socrates would say of many of
these poems that the poet had not passed beyond the first
conception of beauty as existing only in the forms of things.
I can understand this fanatic passion for things lovely to look
on, for in one of his poems he suggests childhood in an unlovely city. After a childhood like that we can forgive the
poet dreaming of white marble forms, blue waters, Sicilian
skies, old gardens, lutes and lyres, fauns and maenads, and
other images of ancient beauty. Almost always it is by pain
we are driven from a contented resting on the senses, and
the war seems to have broken up that mould of mind in
Richard Aldington from which came that early opaque
imagist poetry. But the ideas are still opaque. There is in
him rage and lamentation as he broods bitterly in the
trenches, but as yet he can see no meaning in the carnage,
perhaps nobody could. Now and then he is stirred to an
elemental meditation, but it reveals nothing. There is only
the tortured nerves, puddles of blood and flesh, rotting
bodies; phantom images of that lost beauty of Sicilian sea,
white forms, love, all remote and fading. But there is an
increased intensity even if nothing is transfigured, even if he
has not found some divine justice in the anguish he endures.
But he is launched on that inner sea, and will never be able
again to write contentedly of white marble beauties. Nature,
when we pass from one phase to another, closes the door
behind us, and we can never return to what we were, once

we have passed away from ourselves. I could find no verses suggesting that he had come to the region of the psyche where images and ideas are transparent or liberating. Nothing like

> Thy friends are exultations, agonies.

That was written by one who saw that for which all the long labours of the soul were undertaken, who could press the thorns into the soul, knowing that they would take root there, that they would break out into immortal flowers.

In the later poetry we find him wandering about in that new internal world into which his anguish has pushed him, not all unhappy, able to laugh, be cynical or serious, but never quite coming to that transparency where a light shines through idea or emotion, two worlds meet in us, and in every breathing there are martyrdoms or exaltations of sense or soul. Anyhow, he has begun to think. He even develops an ironical humour which has its appeal. He may find his way to the third circle of poetry, where ideas and emotions are transparent. But at present he is making himself at home in the second circle, salving his wounds with humour. He is the first victim to whom my Platonic formulae have been applied. I hope that genuine sense of humour the poet has developed will enable him to endure without rage my attempts to probe into his psyche with the lantern Diotima gave to Socrates.

Stephen MacKenna and the Genius for Translation

I HAVE ALWAYS THOUGHT the work of the translator more difficult than the work of the creator. It is easy to us to find words to express our intimate feelings. But how hard it is to put words on the thoughts of another. When a man is himself exalted the words which fly up to the brain seem to

be brought by some affinity, a law of spiritual gravitation
which acts as the power which attracts the filings to the
magnet. There is a swift collaboration between thought and
its symbols. We do not understand by what magic an idea
evokes swiftly out of so many thousand symbols those which
fit it with a body. We find ourselves speaking so swiftly that
the word seems to follow the thought as the shadow the
substance, there is hardly a second for conscious selection of
phrase. Indeed it may be said in most speech, and often in
the finest writing, there is no conscious selection of phrase
at all. The imagination of man is a despotic genie and words
are its trembling slaves who wait obediently on it to mirror
its lightest motions. But when a writer sets himself to
translate he has not this swift magic of the unconscious to
aid him. Everything he does he must do deliberately with
reference to the original. For him there can be no ecstasy of
swift creation such as enabled Shelley to write the *Prometheus Unbound* in a few weeks. There is one masterpiece of
translation, the old English version of the Bible, which
affects us by melody and magic of phrase as if it was a great
original work. But we may say that there are a thousand
original works of genius for every translation which would
be accepted as fine literature on its own account. Learning
alone will not enable a man to be a fine translator. No doubt
Jowett was as good a scholar as any of those who translated
the Psalms or the Book of Job, but is there a page of his
Plato which anyone would quote as beautiful or distinguished
prose? He was translating the greatest of Greek stylists and
the element of style has evaporated, and when that is gone
we wonder are we really reading Plato, for style conveys the
aristocracy of mind, and when there is no style what is
shining in the original loses its nobility. We apprehend the
original more by an act of faith, a flash of intuition on our
own part than by the sluggishly-moving sentence so burdened
by the anxiety of the translator to render the body of thought

that he was incapable of conveying the spirit, that impalpable shepherd who can make one sentence light as air and another solemn, and these act as an incantation, evoking in us the mood in which the thought was born. We have in Stephen MacKenna a translator of the highest quality, for while the learned applaud the accuracy of his rendering of the *Enneads* of Plotinus, we read enchanted by the distinction of the writing. We surmise what agonies of literary conscience went into the choice of words so that they might convey not merely intellectual meanings, but that we might ourselves fly into that spiritual aether and feel the ecstasy of the seer and tremble as he does with the beauty of his vision. Plotinus says:

> This is the spirit that Beauty must ever induce, wonderment and a delicious trouble, longing and love and a trembling that is all delight,

and to communicate this melting of the soul before the highest Beauty is the real labour of the translator. He must himself be melted and yet never forget that it is not his own delight he is giving us but the delight of another. How well he has succeeded.

There is not a word here which grates upon us. All is pure and cold and ecstatic as the vision the seer beholds. We are never let down to earth. The long sentences keep their up- ward flight like great, slow-moving birds which can soar upwards to the sun through the icy coldness of the lofty air and yet live and be full of exultation. How rare is this art which excludes every word whose associations are secular, or if such are brought in they appear purified by the choir of words to which they are joined and they shine along with the rest.

He has taken to heart Plotinus' own counsel to those who would create beauty:

Withdraw into yourself and look. And if you do not find yourself beautiful yet, act as does the creator of a statue that is to be made beautiful: he cuts away here, he smoothes there, he makes this line lighter, this other purer, until a lovely face has grown upon his work. So do you also: cut away all that is excessive, straighten all that is crooked, bring light to all that is overcast, labour to make all one glow of beauty, and never cease chiselling your statue until there shall shine out on you from it the God-like splendour . . .

Whoever will read these volumes shall find that exquisite labour everywhere. If he cannot rise to a full comprehension of Plotinus, nor know truly what he means by the Intellectual Principle or the Intellectual Realm, and their relation to the One, he will always find some subtlety which will delight him, some nobility of thought and invariable dignity of phrase. To see any being, to perceive any truth, we must, in some part of our nature, be in the same plane, and if we thrill at all reading this great philosopher it is because there is in us some incorruptible spiritual atom which can respond, and we know that we have not altogether fallen away from the divine image and that all of the heavenly man was not banished from Eden. We must perpetually ponder every sentence, for nothing is said lightly. When he speaks of the imperfect soul what he says is profound, but it needs meditation to discover its full truth:

A part is not self-sufficient, it must pursue something outside itself for its fulfilment, and so it becomes the enemy of what it needs.

How often do we find those who lack beauty or imagination pursuing vindictively those who have what would be the healing of the soul if they would but accept it!

I could quote endlessly sentences so profound that if one

brooded over them and comprehended them truly he would himself be a philosopher and be able to make systems. I hope Stephen MacKenna will forgive me if I quote here from a letter of his own written to me some years ago, talking of his feelings as translator: "I tremble sometimes; grandeurs, lovelinesses, humanities, raptures, great doors flung open suddenly—but we are hurried by with scarcely time to look: that is always to me the test of a spiritual value, that we scarcely dare to look at the thing, down the vistas, into the infinities." In such a mood great literature can be translated into great literature in another tongue and lose, I will swear, but little, but only the greatest thinking can excite such a passion. Here is one of the noblest minds of the ancient world. If any have escaped from that illusion that to-day is the day of wisdom because it is the last breathing of Time, they will find in these volumes profundities and beauties which no contemporary thinker can reveal to us. They are volumes for the slow and brooding mind, but once the soul has bathed in those depths it can never after sink to be altogether commonplace, it will always find some shining in itself and feel it has some relation to the divine order. Lastly, I wonder, thinking that this translation, a miracle of patience, has been made by an Irishman of our own day, labouring at this through all our disorders as if the light of the Spirit had absolved him from infection by the passions of the body.

Shakespeare and the Blind Alley

THERE ARE CERTAIN IMMORTALS whose influence it is literary sacrilege to deprecate. It is admitted that Homer nods at times, but by the way the admission is made it is almost regarded as one of his merits. There are passages in Shakespeare's plays which are not attributable to nodding but to the writer being too riotously alive, but the wor-

shippers silently attribute the worst rant to the more obscure dramatists with whom the genius collaborated. But if
anybody suggested that the genius himself had darkened
wisdom, that would be sacrilege. If I do suggest this let nobody accuse me of denying the marvel of the genius which I
affirm. There are certain figures in history which are pivotal,
and around them myriads have wheeled to new destinies.

Shakespeare was undoubtedly pivotal, more so perhaps
than any except the great spiritual figures. But did he lead
literature into a blind alley? Let us contrast Shakespeare
with his greatest predecessors, the Greek dramatists. Let us
take the *Œdipus* of Sophocles. As we watch the action we
suddenly become aware of an invisible presence, Nemesis,
a deity, who puts down the mighty from their seats and
exalts insignificance. Sovereignty, however august in that
realm to which the dramatist brings us, is as subject to that
invisible divinity as atom or molecule are subject to law.
Human insignificance is dignified by association with the
same deity, for it feels its being shepherded to its destiny by
august powers. The greatest of Greek dramas leave us with
this sense that the characters meet to reveal something
greater than themselves. We are almost always waking as a
Greek drama comes to its climax to a consciousness of some
enduring idea. When we waken from the dream we realise
how illusionary were the characters and how real the passion
or idea. Shakespeare was the first supreme artist in literature who seems to be absorbed in character for its own
sake. Nothing before or since has equalled the art by which
recognisable personalities are revealed in a few words.

But nothing is revealed in the Shakespearean drama except
character. What did the genius of Shakespeare do for literature? More and more since his apparition have dramatist and
novelist been artists of character for its own sake; and to be
absorbed in character for its own sake is to be in a blind
alley which leads nowhere. To the greater Greek dramatists

life swam in an aether of deity, and that again bathes all the circumstance of the *Divine Comedy* or of the Indian epic, the *Mahabharata*. We feel as we read that we are in the divine procession, and know ourselves more truly by this envelopment, native to the spirit, than by looking at a mirror which reflects only personal character. We know ourselves as we are known when we are drawn out of our personal reverie and placed in juxtaposition with elemental laws or divinities. When we are absorbed in character for its own sake we are absorbed in our own illusion, and have no perspective such as is necessary for judgment. Since Shakespeare became the shepherd of the artistic soul, dramatist and novelist have been more and more absorbed by this illusion; and we know in reality little more about ourselves when we have absorbed the literature of character than we did before. That is, we do not see ourselves in relation to spirit or to nature, where we are exalted or dwindle in a true perspective. This relation to spirit we feel when we read religion or poetry. This relation to nature we surmise studying philosophy or science. Balzac alone among the greater artists of character since Shakespeare had at times this supraconsciousness of spirit. With Shakespeare the imagination is so grandiose that we can imagine his greater characters as gods in exile, but rarely does he make the whole drama illustrate as the greater Greeks would have done the intuition revealed in single lines:

> There's a divinity that shapes our ends,
> Rough-hew them how we will.

> We are such stuff
> As dreams are made on . . .

We forget these intuitions in the dramatic clash of character, and come to conceive of them, not as fundamental to the drama, but simply as opinions uttered by characters. These intuitions are absent from the artists of character who

followed: Fielding, Scott, Dickens, Thackeray, George
Eliot, Hardy, and also from many famous Continental
novelists who, like the English, are in the blind alley.
Dostoevsky at times seems to be awakening. Tolstoi, in
trying to get another perspective, became only the moralist,
and was less of a seer as moralist than he was as the artist
absorbed in human life. Do we not feel weariness in reading
the most brilliant of modern novels, because, while every
nook, corner and cranny of human character is explored,
we know, or surmise nothing about the vast cavalcade of
humanity, its fountain, whither it is tending, or what laws
govern its being? I believe a reaction against this absorption
in character for its own sake is inevitable, and we shall once
more have a literature where humanity is depicted, acted on
by spiritual influences, or by its interblending with the life
of nature. Perhaps just as science, materialistic for a generation, has become etherealised before the mystery of the
atom, so psychology may discover at the last analysis that
there is a transcendental element in human life; and the
artists, always sensitive to spiritual atmospheres, may be
inspired to draw literature out of the blind alley where the
greatest of their tribe had led it, to conceive of life as part
of a divine procession in which the personal dwindles, but
the immortal may be exalted by a profound consciousness of
cosmic purpose.

Genius and Environment

I BELIEVE every great writer gets the environment which is
right for him, and what the creative poet wants is not
other creators about him, but men and women who, either
by sympathy or by antagonism, help to evoke his genius.
Some kindle by opposition, some by poverty, some by un-
happiness as others by comfort and love. Carlyle laid up in

brooding on his lonely farm in Scotland the wealth of passionate thought he spent so lavishly on literature, but who but God would have sent any soul to that nursery for spiritual food? I feel sure Keats' circumstance, antagonistic or sympathetic, was best for him, and he did in fact in that circumstance write more beautiful poetry in his twenty-four years than any other of the English poets in their youth.

Keats seems to me to have been on the whole fortunate in his friends. One wonders where he would have found better. He knew Wordsworth, but was Wordsworth a possible friend? Shelley was always generous, and he would have been a friend to Keats, as he was to many others, but genius is often dangerous to genius. When two men with creative imagination meet they draw each other from their secret base. They cannot draw so easily from their own fountain, they soon feel this, and hence it is rare to find creative poets desirous of close intimacy with one another. The work of the scientific man is built up largely on the investigation and research of others. But the poet must fall back on what is within him, and the incursion of another powerful nature, while it may fascinate for a while, will, the moment the poet feels the breaking up of his own natural mould of mind, arouse something like hostility.

Genius has a way of transfiguring those about it by its presence just as a woman in love with a man will reveal to him wit, tenderness and charm she can show to none other. The lover is the master who can evoke melodies others cannot evoke. I have no doubt that in Keats' society his friends were stimulated by his ardent imagination to be brilliant to him in a way they could never seem brilliant to us. At his best Keats is the greatest artist in words in English poetry after Shakespeare, and hardly behind him, and he seemed in the last years to be emerging from the fever of boyhood to an assured mastery.

I feel the inevitability of Keats' genius. It evolved from

within outward by a law of its own being as a flower does—
taking, indeed, from the sun, the wind, the rain, the earth,
but, all the time, transmuting what it takes inexorably to be
of its own nature, to be rose, and not another flower. So the
genius of Keats was evolving from within outwards. I doubt
if it would have been different in quality or character,
though the choice of subject might have been different, if
he had never met Hunt or others of his circle. He moved to
his own perfection as irresistibly as the acorn moves to be
oak, and not another tree.

Blake

IN WILLIAM BLAKE there was, perhaps, more of the element
of infinity than in any of his contemporaries, and for that
reason he is less easily exhausted. Byron and Scott, the great
ostensibles, were exhausted by their own generation. When
we are young we may read them with pleasure, but there is
no excitement of the spirit for us. Only Blake, the most
obscure of the great writers of his time, can still excite us
spiritually, for he speaks of truths to which the world has
yet to travel. His mind has not yet been completely charted.
Nor can it be charted until our psychology becomes more
profound. Blake himself wrote scornfully of the ignorance
which would limit all things by itself:

> Go, merciless man, enter into the infinite labyrinth of
>   another's brain
> Ere thou measure the circle that he shall run. Go, thou cold
>   recluse, into the fires
> Of another's high flaming bosom, and return uncondensed,
>   and write laws.
> If thou canst not do this, doubt thy theories.

The infinite labyrinth of the soul. Yes, if we could explore
that we could begin to be precise about Blake. Emerson says

of our consciousness that it is now on a level with the body, and anon with the First Cause. That is, we seem to run up and down a ladder set in clay, which at its highest touches divinity. Most of us are on the lower rungs, but Blake seems to ascend and descend with a swiftness which was bewildering to those who spoke to him, and which, I suspect, was sometimes bewildering to himself. Though Linnell says of Blake that he could always explain his paradoxes when he pleased, Southey says of him that he spoke of his visions "with the diffidence that is usual with such people". That diffidence I think arose because he himself could not always correlate his visionary consciousness with his normal mentality. When he could he was arrogant, and not diffident at all. His mind would become like a flame-thrower and he would scorch the doubter with fiery satire and bewilder him with subtle paradox. Was Blake mad? When he was on the upper rungs of his ladder, when he dealt with purely spiritual things, he was clear as any prophet. In the practical affairs of life he could be practical. When people speculate about Blake's sanity they are thinking of his adventures in that mid-world between spirit and matter, the world of dream, where all things exist in fantasy. Almost all have had adventures in this world in dream. But most people who have dreams forget them. But Blake entered the dream-world with his waking consciousness. All he saw he saw with extraordinary vividness. He could neither ignore nor forget. He tried to become an interpreter of his own visions, and it is because of his interpretations some people think he is insane. He said Isaiah dined with him. But did he mean anything more than that the prophetic in his nature was stirred and that he named the prophet in himself by the prophet of Israel? He could, Linnell says, always explain his paradoxes. But if he did not choose to explain, those who listened might easily come to think of Blake as an inspired lunatic. Even when we do not agree with Blake's interpretations, we need not think him insane. He lived at a time when psychology was even less of a science than it is to-day. He had to make some guess at meanings, and though he was a great genius he had not, I think, a very wide general culture, and his interpretations were limited by his external knowledge. A peasant girl to-day seeing the vision of a beautiful woman might think it was a vision of the Blessed Virgin. Two thousand years ago a girl, seeing such a vision, might have assumed it was Dana. The interpretation would depend on the thought in the waking mind, and Blake was like this in giving famous names to the apparitions he saw. He may have been wrong, but there was nothing of insanity in his interpretations, only an incomplete philosophy of the world of fantasy into which he passed so easily.

Blake's Prophetic Books

To us WILLIAM BLAKE appears the most potent and original genius of his time, the one whose ideas are still exciting, whose influence is still unspent, almost at its beginning indeed, for in spite of many commentators his image still remains dark to us with excess of light. For all that darkness, we get more from Blake than we get from the more intelligible poets, because we come to him with the mind tense, and the difficulty in interpretation forces us to evoke the seer in ourselves. The lyrical poetry has had many lovers. Will those who read with delight the *Songs of Innocence* and the *Songs of Experience*, where every song has its own light, enter into the darkness of the Prophetic Books, where they must kindle their own light if the palace chambers of Blake's marvellous fantasy are to seem brilliant, as they undoubtedly were to the seer? In this world we can see by another light than any we kindle. In the mystical world none can see who does not kindle a light of his own, and it may be doubted whether any mystic made comprehension of his vision more difficult than Blake.

Blake made discoveries about the spirit in a country whose people were very content with this world. Like Adam he was the first inhabitant of his world, and like Adam he had to give names to the creatures which he found there, and sometimes he put on them names taken from this world because the person or country or continent whose name he used stood in his own soul for some quality or character which made them fitting symbols of their more grandiose counterparts in mystical nature. At other times, where this world helped him not at all, he used mythic names of his own invention. All these creatures are but parts of our own nature dramatically sundered from the primordial unity of the spirit. In dream we divide ourselves into this and that and thou and I. In the dream of life the primordial unity of the spirit is so divided and its genius becomes broken up and manifold.

We adventure into the more obscure books hoping for the same psychic exhilaration, but while we find marvellous oases we become more doubtful about the inspiration of much that we read. He has created a system and become enslaved by it. He writes out of his own convention, using the secret shorthand he invented to record his psychology. It may have a subtle thread of meaning in it all but it is not inspiration. Indeed it often seems to merit the castigation he himself gave to work which he described as "confident insolence sprouting from systematic reasoning". I think his ambition was greater than his genius in the longer prophetic books. That genius could at white heat transcend any genius of his time and get glimpses of the eternal world, but could not remain for long in the high air, and when he attempted spiritual epics there are long symbolic bridges built by the reason, not by the imagination, between illumination and illumination. When he is buoyed up by his genius he is

dazzling. When he is not buoyed up he confuses doctrine
with illumination and preaches in his obscure jargon and
misleads the devotees holding to his skirts, who do not see
that his lamp is blown out and the seer has become the
rationalist he abhorred. They would know this, only that his
rationalism is wrapt up in mystical rhetoric. The bird is not
flying. It is only walking and the flapping of the wings do not
lift it from earth. But when it does fly he reminds us of that
enchanted bird seen by Coleridge:

> He sunk, he rose, he twinkled, he trolled
> Within that shaft of sunny mist:
> His eyes of fire, his beak of gold,
> All else of amethyst!

It flew beyond faery, which was all Coleridge's genius enabled him to see, into a spiritual universe, and he comes back
almost dark and blind with glory crying out what wonders
his "enlarged and numerous senses" have seen, as at the close of
the Epic of *Jerusalem*, where the whole universe is redeemed
from the Fall, and "living creatures, starry and flaming with
every Colour, Lion, Tiger, Horse, Elephant, Eagle, Dove,
Fly, Worm and the all-wondrous Serpent clothed in gems
and rich array humanise" in the final forgiveness of sins.
Even the Tree, the Metal, Earth and Stones return to that
ancestral beauty they had first in the mind of Jehovah, from
their "going forth and returning wearied into the Planetary
lives of Years, Months, Days and Hours, reposing and then
awakening into His Bosom in the Life of Immortality". This
is his vision of the New Heaven which is the earth transmuted and made marvellous so that nothing conceived or
created by the Father is lost, but is transfigured in His
Eternity and enters into some mystical communion with us,
even the worm becomes radiant and the mole creeps out
into that sunlight, fierce things becoming gentle and small
becoming great. Not any poet, not Dante, imagined a Para-

dise which lingers longer in our imagination than that brotherhood of all living things with which Blake ended his greatest song.

Blake's Designs

I DO NOT WANT to read any more interpretations of Blake's prophetic books, but I would like to read a study psychological rather than aesthetic on the designs to these works. The designs have been praised, sometimes over-praised, as works of art, though I admit that it would be difficult to over-praise the very finest of Blake's inventions like that of the Morning Stars singing together. But the designs are given to us as visions. What exactly does that imply? Are they visions in any sense different from that in which Michael Angelo's "Awakening Adam", with finger outstretched to meet the finger of the Almighty, is a vision? It is obvious that the picture in the Sistine Chapel is not a product of reason, of models posed after experiment by the artist. The images were born in the psyche of the painter. Were Blake's visions in any way different? That is, do they represent real beings, entities in the Archaeus visible to the seer, or are they only peculiar to Blake's consciousness? Every now and then there are figures which almost convince us of their authenticity, while a still larger number seem to be purely symbolic, for we cannot imagine that anywhere in the universe there were figures bending down with compasses to measure out space, or ancients carrying stars or stooping over planets. These have no more external authenticity than Watts' picture of "Hope" on the world playing on the lyre on which there is but one string unbroken. But while we deny authenticity to the symbolic pictures, that is, we do not believe, as it is said Blake did, that they represent real entities, there is still a mystery about them, for they are obviously things seen, not reasoned out, as so much that purports to be imaginative art is. I feel convinced that Blake with inward eye saw in some psychic aether the images he depicted.

What is the explanation? Is there a transcendental ego which is the creator of these images and of symbolic dream? When we dream the images of dream appear entities to us. When we waken we believe they were self-created. But by what self? The dreaming self is unconscious of creation. There should be some psychological study of these visionary pictures of Blake. No one explanation will cover all. I myself have had experience of clairvoyance in dream. That is, I have seen people and places at a distance, and have afterwards verified the truth of the vision. But in dream also I see persons who, I feel sure, are self-created, created by some power of the psyche transcendental to both the waking and dreaming consciousness. Possibly Blake's figures are of two kinds; occasionally there may be pictures of entities which have some external psychic reality, and at other times the internal artificer of symbolic forms was active. I am forced by my reason to deny to most of them any external reality, just as I must deny any external reality to Watts' "Hope" or his "Love and Life", but these were doubtless seen clearly in the imagination.

Magic is rarer in art than in literature. In literature Keats, Coleridge, Francis Thompson, our own Yeats make a magical use of words. But in painting how rare it is. We think of some, Turner and Monticelli. But it is Blake more than any other who suggests magic in his art, to whom many will turn again and again to get an excitement of spirit which far greater craftsmen are unable to communicate.

The Hierarchy of Ideas

WHEN WE CLOSE the eyes and are alone in a darkness with imagination, feeling and thought, the mind which is so certain a guide of the body becomes but a blind shepherd of its own internal wanderings. How surely do we know what is loveliest in Nature! How doubtful are we when we pronounce judgment upon ideas! Lovers of literature too, speaking of what they approve as best, are for the most part in agreement when the writer appeals to the inner senses, but they become dubious or controversial when the writer evokes the intellectual rather than the image-making faculty. Whoever disputed this beauty:

> Gilding pale streams with heavenly alchemy.

Or this, written of the world under water:

> One faint, eternal eventide of gems.

Or this, spoken of the Evening Star:

> Speak silence with thy glimmering eyes
> And wash the dusk with silver.

Or this:
> The moan of doves in immemorial elms.

Or the praise Yeats' peacock bestows on its divine Original:

> He is a monstrous peacock and He waveth all the night
> His languid tail above us lit with myriad spots of light.

This kind of beauty is never questioned, because the magic of the poet recalls the magic of nature, and half the delight we have in reading is that he unlocks for us our own treasure-house of beautiful memories of which we have lost the key. But how shall we appraise ideas which all come to us clothed with equal verbal felicity, and can we place them in hier-

archies, setting the higher above the lower? Socrates in the
Banquet tantalises us when he indicates such a hierarchy of
beauty, the soul passing from the perception of it in form
until it perceives the higher beauty of thoughts and ideas.
But he does not tell us by what means we are to esteem ideas
so that we may say this is of a higher order than that. I have
come myself to make one distinction, which is between ideas
which are opaque, on whose loveliness we rest and are not
carried beyond it, and ideas which are transparent and which
open for us vistas and start us on imaginative travels of our
own. I choose to illustrate my meaning passages where the
verbal felicity is of the highest order, whether the idea chains
us to itself or liberates us. Are we not tranced in a motionless
delight at this from the *Ode on a Grecian Urn*:

> Thou still unravished bride of quietness.

And when we read:

> Brightness falls from the air;
> Queens have died young and fair;
> Dust hath closed Helen's eye;

are we not stayed by this melancholy beauty? But is not the
imagination set free by this:

> And beauty born of murmuring sound
> Shall pass into her face.

Or by this:

> A pity beyond all telling
> Is hid in the heart of love.

Or this:

> The angels keep their ancient places.
> Turn but a stone, and start a wing.

Or by this marvellous line, which comes to us like the angel
who opened Peter's prison:

> Thy friends are exultations, agonies.

Or by this line, which might be written over the gate of the second circle of the poetic Paradise to make known that every thing, visible or audible, has its spirit bride:

Heard melodies are sweet, but those unheard are sweeter.

In the first order there is a lovely finality. In the second the thing seen or heard is the symbol of another unimagined beauty, and because we are so excited to journey for ourselves, because we cry out in our hearts:

Bring me my bow of burning gold,

we feel that ideas which have this translucency are of a higher order than the ideas which compel us to stay by them because they suggest nothing lovelier than themselves. The highest Muse sits by the parting or the meeting of the ways, where she can see together past and future, outer and inner, flesh and spirit, Death and Love, Heaven and Hell, and her highest utterances have in them always a marriage of diversities, a marriage which is fruitful. The unwedded thoughts or images have not this power of begetting their children in our hearts. We look on them as lovely statues which we desert when a living beauty comes to companion us. The symbolist movement was succeeded by the imagist in modern literature, and I cannot but think it was a descent in the hierarchy of intellectual values. There are many other canons we might formulate. We might ask out of how deep a life does the man speak, but that is the question of a philosopher rather than of the artist. The artist asks of a work of art whether it gives us itself only or whether it multiplies images of beauty in us to whom it is given; or, to put it in another way, he has genius who can make us see the beauty he sees, but he is a master who can give us his own power of seeing.

The Architect of Dream

GERALD BULLETT discusses my *Candle of Vision*. He is dubious about my own intuitions and speculations. I have considered his doubts, and I am not made any wiser. He quotes a passage from my book describing some visionary picture. This, he says, proves nothing except that I possess in a high degree the power of visualisation. But what is the power of visualisation? What is it that projects before the inner eye in day-dreaming or night-dreaming images which are so precise? Are we not to speculate? Must we be content with a word like "visualisation", which explains nothing at all? He goes on to quote from Coleridge, who, before dreaming his Kubla Khan, had been reading in Purchas' *Pilgrimage* about that monarch, and he asks: "Are we compelled to believe that the palace and the garden of Kubla Khan and Alph, the Sacred River, having been seen in a clear vision, must at one time have existed geographically?" I can agree that this creation of images is no more mysterious in sleep or trance than in waking life. But there is a mystery which it is worth while trying to explore. Freud may be right when he interprets a dream, but he throws no light any more than Gerald Bullett does upon the architect of dream, and all my probings and intuitions and speculations were to show the mystery involved in the architecture of a dream, which may be built up in a second, and yet be coherent, be prodigal of character, incident, scenery, in which we see things from an angle of vision we have never seen them when waking. It may be that our dreams are memories refashioned; but by what process are they refashioned? Give an artist a hundred thousand life-size photographs of human beings, and tell him by cutting, snipping and pasting together to make a single new figure out of these. It would be a labour of infinite difficulty, a patchwork at the best; the joinings would be visible, the chiaroscuro would be incorrect. But the figures created in an instant in dream are not like this. They have the swift movement of life. Light, shade, colour, anatomy, are correct, and the recombining, if it be recombining, which we could not achieve in months of waking effort over photographs, is miraculously done in a second by the architect of dream. Let us assume that Coleridge saw in dreaming as pictorial images the deep romantic chasm, the sunny dome, the caves of ice, the whirling enchanter. How was that succession of images created? Were memories recombined? How are they recombined? With our waking intelligence the recombination of pictures into new pictures is a practical impossibility, or, at the most, a slow labour choosing from this and that picture a tone, a fragment of form, a light or shade to fit in with some other fragments. Are we forbidden to speculate about what takes place when what happens is amazing, almost miraculous to the waking consciousness asked to do the same thing?

Now must we not consider about dreams the measure of time, so different from the waking state, and the incredible swiftness of creation? Is there not some intellectual activity in the swift assembling of many images in a second? I divine, as many others have done, that there is in us an unwinking vigilance, a consciousness which transcends waking or dreaming, which has a faculty of swift creation which we cannot rival in the waking state. I will go on speculating over this genius which exists in everybody in dreams. The last pages of Gerald Bullett's book suggest that to him both waking and dreaming are miraculous states; that if he must declare his philosophy he would say our dreams are but fragments of the imagination of an Eternal Dreamer, and if he can speculate in that mystical fashion, why does he quarrel with me?

Personal Immortality

THERE IS HARDLY any discussion we can imagine in which humanity should take more interest than that which arises over the problem of personal immortality. But while we all when sick put ourselves into the hands of a doctor in the hope of prolonging life by a few years, while we obey every instruction, how few of us take a scientific interest in the evidence for the survival of a soul after death! The literature dealing with this problem is very disappointing. Our libraries are filled with works by men of science, but how few approach this subject with the intellectual intensity and thoroughness which they will devote to a problem of engineering. I have myself only come across two books dealing with the possibility of survival after death which I could read with the feeling that the writers were intellectually competent to state a case or form an opinion. One of these I read thirty years ago. It was called *The Unseen Universe*, and the author, Balfour Stewart, a scientific man of some eminence in the middle of last century, asked by his religious friends if his science suggested any intelligible method of approach to the subject of survival after death, considered the existence of aether, a subtle element, out of which visible nature was born and unto which it returned, and the percussion on that subtle element of thought and emotion. He considered the possibility of the aether retaining images of our psychic activities, in fact the preservation of memory, for without memory of the past there could, of course, be no personal immortality in any sense which could have meaning for us.

The other was Frederic Myers' monumental book, *Human Personality*, which is, I think, the best of all the works I know dealing with human personality and the possibility of survival after death. Neither of these books is easy reading.

The majority are, I think, content with belief and rarely look for proof.

I do not think H—— has written anything comparable to the books I have mentioned. He is skirting all the time on the outside of the problem rather in the fashion of the Victorian rationalists. He wastes an immense amount of space discussing the ideas of savages and primitive people which, of course, have interest as history but are not worth considering if we are endeavouring to discover truth to-day. We would attach no importance to the opinion of a savage on chemistry or bacteriology, and their views upon immortality may be dismissed in a scientific discussion. Whether these beliefs arose out of dream or hallucination does not help us, without our infinitely more complex intellectual and scientific apparatus, to get at truth now.

I get the impression that H—— is, perhaps without knowing it, all the time more concerned with making a case against religious belief of the more stupid kind than in discovering a new avenue to truth, and the savage is brought in with the intent to show that the religions of to-day are living intellectually and emotionally on the beliefs of ancestors and have little more substance. All that shooting of arrows against the foolish is unworthy when we are endeavouring to discuss a subject of prime importance. It can be approached through psychology as Myers approached it, making careful study of the supernormal human faculties, of thought transference, clairvoyance, apparitions, trance, dream, etc., and drawing deductions from carefully observed phenomena. Or it can be approached experimentally as the spiritualists do who endeavour to get into communication with the souls of the dead.

There is a third way which theoretically might lead to truth, the way of the mystics who by intense concentration and meditation raise themselves above the visible world and enter another world, perhaps clothed with that psychic body

St. Paul spoke of, and who, by parting the soul from the physical form during life, get personal proof that soul can exist apart from body. These are theoretically three ways of approach, but H—— is, in my opinion, superficial and not at all subtle when he discusses the method of Myers and the Psychical Research Society.

He must be classed with those who have some unconscious bias, and his objections grow in his mind with much of the fertility he attributes to his growth of a good story. His bad story is built, to my mind, on exactly the same psychic foundation. He takes pleasure and wastes time in exposing fools when he should be concentrating purely on the thoughts of wise men. We all know there are lunatics in the world, but why give us quotations from lunatics or obsessed people such as this description of a baby in hell?

> Hear how it screams, see how it twists itself about. It beats its head against the roof of the oven. It stamps its little feet upon the floor. On its face is an expression of the most appalling despair.

This is quoted in a chapter on current arguments. It is the raving of a lunatic. What bearing have his ravings upon the intellectual consideration of a world after death? It is this tendency on the part of H—— to throw stones which cannot miss, at the fools he sees, which makes his book have little or no value as a serious study of a great problem. What would we think of Helmholtz, Maxwell, Einstein, if their scientific writings were filled with shrieks of laughter over the ignorance of bygone generations or the folly of inferior minds to-day? The great men of science concentrate on their subject. H—— is so occupied by narrating the errors and fancies of others that he really has nothing at all weighty to say on the subject of immortality. It is a very disappointing book on a subject of the highest importance.

Dunne's Experiment with Time

IT IS RARELY that profound ideas present themselves to the common people in a form which attracts them, so that they can begin to apply them to life, to experiment with them for themselves and make a really exciting game out of their experiments. The founders of world religions have always had the genius to interest not merely the intellectuals but the common people with great ideas. The philosophers never had this gift. The profundities of Plato, Plotinus, Spinoza, Berkeley, Kant or Hegel are appreciated only by the aristocratic intelligence. You will find the half-educated thinking intensely about religion. But did you ever enter a room and find our young barbarians talking excitedly about the ideas of any of these philosophers, feeling that they had possible personal applications to themselves, starting them in adventure or experiment with much the same zest that they might start to work out a cross-word puzzle? No, nobody could say that these great men affect our young barbarians in any lively way. The divine philosophers have speculated upon Time, upon an Everliving in which past, present and future co-exist, but these speculations were as intangible to common mentality as that dark aether full of stars which glows above them night after night. It is quite possible that a man of our own time, who is neither a great writer nor a great philosopher but who has only a very acute intelligence, may have found a way of exciting the common people to make explorations in that Everliving. Dunne's book may possibly be the pivot around which great numbers of people may turn to the practical consideration of that transcendental conception of an Everliving in which past and future glow in an eternal present. Any who dream can, if they read *An Experiment with Time*, become fishermen in that Great Deep. Most of us forget our dreams five seconds after we waken. Once in a year or so a dream impresses itself on us so that we remember it vividly. Mr. Dunne was struck by the fact that now and then he dreamed of things which happened a few days later, or in some cases months, or even years later. His dreams were rarely accurate enough to have a complete identity with the event they foreshadowed, but they were close enough in detail to make him ponder over them.

His book and a little personal experience should start people on speculations of their own. If we move through an Everliving in which past and future co-exist, if there is a seer within us who has vision of a being so vast, we must assume an eternal relation of the seer within us to that Ever-living. Even if the waking or dreaming consciousness is normally so clogged that its share in the vision backwards or forwards is slight and confused, any prevision it has must depend on that eternal relation of the seer within us, or shall we call it the spirit, to the marvellous nature in which it lives and moves and has its being. It may be found possible after a time to bring the waking consciousness, the traveller in time, into more intimate relation with that interior consciousness which has relations with a timeless universe. All kinds of fantastic possibilities spring up in the imagination. If the inner seer contemplates so wide an empire extending into the three times, does it ever use its knowledge to influence the waking self? Has the future an influence upon us? If I waken with an inspiration for action, has that been because the inner seer in forgotten dream has seen some hero yet unborn? We might ask whether Alexander was in some way inspired by Napoleon or whether Sophocles had some partial vision of the genius of Shakespeare, whether wars in the womb of time may not influence the thoughts of statesmen. It is all fantastical. Must humanity, which has so long travelled outward, sometime begin to travel inward? Will it discover majestic things in that dark sphere, the things the great seers and poets have reported to us? Will there come a time when the average man will be as excited about his adventures inward into his own being as he has been in the past absorbed in the adventures of the external self? It will be an extraordinary change in mass psychology if he comes to believe he has access to three times.

The Professor and the Myth

PROFESSOR RICHET has repute as physiologist and investigator of psychic phenomena. He will not add to his repute by rambling, rather hysterical writing about the idiocies and follies of mankind. Nothing is easier than to make a selection of the follies of humanity, and to denounce mankind as being really less intelligent than the animal creatures, because they do not do the things we do. We suspect the Professor's knowledge of history and literature is not equal to his knowledge of physiology, and, indeed, his arguments are so devoid of subtlety that one wonders could he really be a first-class thinker on his own specialities. When he cries out against spiritual myths he obviously takes the literal materialistic meaning of everything he reads. Minerva sprang from the head of Zeus. How ridiculous! Brahma came out of an egg! Jupiter turned into a shower of gold to allure Danaë! Millions of angels revolted against Heaven! People believe in Angels, Thrones, Principalities and Powers in a Heaven world! What madness! The animals have more sense! Our good professor has not learned to understand myth. He seems incapable of the interpretation of symbol. His culture has been neglected.

The Antecedents of History

I HAVE A QUARREL with historians, for they seem to assume that the birth of great imaginations is not subject-matter for history as much as great wars, or treaties or political or economic systems! Is history only to deal with effects, and not with causes? Great wars are the result of conflicting imaginations, which are anterior to wars as causes precede effects. Treaties are the equilibrium established after the imaginative storm has worn itself out. Economic and political systems represent more or less fixed or solid states of soul in a civilisation; but once they had their fiery and volatile states in the imagination of humanity. The true history of Ireland would attach as much importance to the creation of bodiless moods as to material events, and be as concerned with literature as with laws, conflicts, warriors or statesmen. What is a nation but an imagination common to millions of people? Is there anything else to it? I doubt it. Race does not make nationality, for nearly all the greatest nations are composite. Natural boundaries are not a justification for independent states. There are mountains and rivers inside states which might equally split them up as the rivers or mountains on their borders. Religions are no mark of nationality, for they are international.

It will be found that the basis of nationality eludes us, unless there is agreement that the bond is psychic, that a nation is nothing but a collective imagination held with intensity, an identity of culture or consciousness among millions, which makes them act as a single entity in relation to other human groups. How, then, can historians ignore the great imaginations which have brought about this unity? What does it matter whether Cuchulain, Deirdre or Maeve ever lived or acted on earth, as legend relates of them? They are immortals and find bodies from generation to generation.

What was in Padraic Pearse's soul when he fought in Easter Week but an imagination, and the chief imagination which inspired him was that of the hero who stood against a host. Though Cuchulain be as much mind-created as Hamlet, or Deirdre as Rosalind, yet to those who have been inspired by the first or moved to pity by the second they are real as flesh and blood. The national being is made up of countless memories of beings, some of whom, like Red Hugh or Wolfe Tone, have passed from earth to become part of its immortal memory, while others, like Cuchulain, Oscar, Oisin, Deirdre, have descended from the heaven-world of the imagination into the national being. But, whether risen from earth or heaven-descended, in the national being they are all stars; and, as the national being is the cause of history, whatever is most powerful there ought to be of the deepest concern to the historian. It is possible to argue that as an historical event Shakespeare's imagination of Henry V, the first imperial mood in English literature and the begetter in millions of men's minds of like moods, was as important an historical event as the execution of Mary of Scotland. We might make a case that Burns' poetry made the Scotch the dissolute people they are, and that Moore's songs gave to too many Irish people an Irish soul as artificial as a periwig. The poetry of Burns tended to create a drunken but sincere people. The poetry of Moore tended to create a tipsy and insincere people. Yeats, no doubt, will incline the next generation to gravity and beauty, while James Stephens, who is so full of humour and understanding, will save them from being prigs. They will act through many men and women, and the birth of their imaginations will be as important in the evolution of Irish character and nationality as the fight in Easter week. Both will enter into national imagination; and in the long run the things which come out of the spirit are as powerful as the deeds done upon earth. Standish O'Grady, among our historians, realised this with most intensity. Carlyle, whatever one may think of him, knew that it is the soul makes history, and his *French Revolution* contains as vivid realisation of ideas as of external events.

In that delightful fantasy, *In Tir na n-óg*, which James Stephens found or invented, his hero, Nera, sees the overthrow of Cruachan a year before it happens. When we read great contemporary writers we are like Nera seeing into the future yet knowing it not. If we had true intelligence we could prophesy. We are afraid to speculate what came out of *The Playboy of the Western World*, or how many playboys may yet come out of that lawless imagination! What will come out of *Juno and the Paycock*? Here is history in the making rather than history dramatised. What may not come after the first deep sounding of the horn of humanity in a country? Our literature hitherto has been noble, beautiful, mystical, passionate, gay, witty or fantastical. Any adjective could be applied to it except that it was human. Here we found pity for humanity, pity, the deepest mood its spirit knows. True, the note was not altogether new. Stephens at times has ceased to be the changeling and has been passionately pitiful, and Colum's love for his kind shines in all he does. But O'Casey is quivering all through with pity for life. His most tragic effects are created by his humour. All the while we laugh we feel we ought to be sorrowing that man the immortal should have degenerated into these grotesques, that he should live in such remoteness from beauty. Is there an answering deep or height in Irish nature to respond to this *De Profundis*? Will it start the fury that will erase the slums, the petty Bastilles in which life decays? Something is bound to come out of it, for when humanity looks on its own image and finds it terrible it changes its own heart or else it breaks the mirror.

Reaction in Literature

WE ALL KNOW since Newton how exquisitely Nature keeps the balance of its powers, but I do not know whether it has been yet accepted as a law that life maintains its balances as exquisitely around some mysterious norm. We can see this in little things. I look at the sun and that intolerable brightness is balanced by black spots which swim before the eyes until the norm is regained. I look at a red circle and when my eye wanders from that a green circle appears for a little and then vanishes. Action and reaction seem to be equal and opposite in life as in Nature, and I am tempted, partly by the spirit of scientific inquiry and partly by sheer impishness, to inquire into how that law of reaction operates in literature. Twenty-five years ago Anglo-Irish literature was romantic, idealist or mystic. But what a change in the writers who came after these!

From the most idealistic literature in Europe we have reacted so that with Joyce, O'Flaherty and O'Casey, the notabilities of the moment, we have explored the slums of our cities, the slums of the soul. Is there a law in these oscillations like that which brings centrifugal to balance centripetal? Are these writers the black spots which balance the bright stars? If a writer of powerful character appears, is it inevitable that his opposite must be born? Or if Nature cannot find any single person powerful enough to form the balance must it inspire a school of smaller men and cast them into the scale? It is the spirit of scientific inquiry which prompts the question. It is, perhaps, the imp in me which makes me speculate whether James Joyce was not made inevitable by W. B. Yeats, is not in a sense the poet's creation, his child, born to him, not out of his loins, but supplied to him by Nature, being called forth by a kind of necessity to balance in our national life an intense imagination of beauty, by an equally intense preoccupation with its dark and bitter opposites. It amuses me to consider this parentage. Father and son have this in common, that they are stylists even to elaboration. There was also a little poetry in the youth of James Joyce, and if Nature, or the national being, had not to preserve the balance of things, if there was not a force pulling the pendulum of literature from the height of dream it had swung to in Yeats, Joyce might never have written *Ulysses*. He might have gone on writing *Chamber Music* and further innocencies of that kind.

What damp and depressing literature have not the fiery and volatile elders made inevitable! Perhaps it was as well that George Bernard Shaw was removed from Ireland before he began to write. If he had remained here, if we had to bear the full force of the reaction which that transcendental puritan virtue of his would have involved, what a literature we might have had, a literature as loose as the Restoration literature in England! And now I must dismiss the imp who has been prompting these speculations, but who refused to depart until he was allowed to make them, lest I be suspected of holding the heresy that every good deed leads to a bad deed. I think it true that every intellectual effort has a two-fold effect. It tends to multiply images and shadows of itself, and also to stir into activity an opposite or balance. The moral character of that balance is not predestined, but depends on the individual who may be caught by the balancing forces. I would say that an idealist movement must create by reaction a realistic literature, but that does not imply a literature without moral character, though there are people here who seem to think that the person who refers to a sin in literature is as guilty as the persons who commit the sin. The moment we read a book either of two things takes place. We find the book is akin to us and we accept it, or if it is not ours we react from it and tend to give birth in ourselves to the opposite idea. This law of action and reaction is observable not merely in our own literature but everywhere. The pseudo-classical literature of the eighteenth century was followed by the romantic, and the romantic gave birth by reaction to the realist. Hugo and Dumas necessitate Zola and Flaubert. After the realists have made life weary come the symbolists. The general truth of the law I have stated will not be denied. The only point in doubt is whether individual writers are the inevitable consequence of others who preceded them; whether the imp in me was justified in proclaiming so precisely a law of literary heredity attributing particular children to particular parents. I am not sure that these illegitimate children, after the first shocking effect of their attribution has worn away, would not be regarded with more pride than those others whom I might call the legitimate children, that is, the imitators of genius. Was there ever a leader who did not wish to turn the hosepipe on his followers?

Joyce ~~~~

HE IS CREATING a psychological following who are trying each to evolve a language of his own, as he is doing. I wonder do master and pupils ever meet? Do they ever speak to each other in the language they use when speaking to the public? How enchanting it would be to listen to such a conversation!

I feel a little sadly about Joyce, who has an astonishing talent, which, in spite of my chastening recollection of unintelligibles of the past who became merely obvious to a generation who succeeded them, I feel he is burying in a jungle of words; and the burying is none the less effective because all the weeds in that jungle of words, which spread so prolifically over the grave, have been carefully selected. One suspects with Joyce some truly profound idea, some dark heroism of the imagination burrowing into the roots of consciousness, the protoplasmic material for literature, where there are strange blurrings and blendings of words, moods, passions, thoughts in a mysterious mush. Normally these are transfigured into the intelligible by their manifestations in speech or literature. But Joyce does not desire in his later work to allow that transfiguration to take place or allow the murky chaos to lose its formlessness. He desires to give us that murky chaos itself. Well, I believe the evolution of the spirit will bring it to a clairvoyance where nothing in the universe will be obscure to it. And it may be in that faith that Joyce begins to dig the subconscious out into consciousness. I wish he had tried to penetrate into the palace chambers rather than into the crypts and cellars and sewers of the soul, and written after *Ulysses* the effort of his hero to rise out of that Inferno through a Purgatorio to a Paradiso.

Reticences

WE HAVE ALL RETICENCES about our own nature, and it is difficult to say whether it is wiser to keep our worst and give our best than to thrust the whole personality, palace and slum together, at the reader in the fashion in which Rousseau gave himself to his generation, or James Joyce gives himself to ours. The poets who give us only their best get us to start with them in the journey to Paradise, and to do that is a great thing, but because they will not let us know what is in the dark there are often betrayals and ambuscades of the pilgrims who start on that journey. How many a boy and girl who were brought up on the literature of pure beauty selected for them by critical guardians have been horrified to find obscene beasts prowling about the corridors of the palace that was built, and they were never told they were there.

MEN
AND
WOMEN

MEN
AND
WOMEN

Standish O'Grady

IT MUST BE about forty years since I first met O'Grady. He received with a most delightful courtesy the stammering young poet who had read the Bardic History and had become enthusiastic about it. He had passed through his own enthusiasm after he had written his greatest work, and had, I think, begun to meditate more on the future than the past. After staring intently at any colour we begin to see an apparition of its opposite. He only occasionally spoke with enthusiasm of the myths he had revealed with so poetic an imagination. But I think he knew that the work which lay behind him had elements of genius in it, and he would never do better no matter to what cause he devoted himself. His mind had a shining simplicity. His depths were the depths of consciousness on which heroism bases itself, not the depths of the philosopher, but I always felt the life out of which he spoke was as deep as, if not deeper than, that of the profound speculators of his time. There were contradictions between the outer and the inner O'Grady. The outer O'Grady was unionist and imperialist. The inner O'Grady was passionately national. The outer mind was simple and unmystical. The inner being rested on some fundamental spiritual reality, and clung to it without ever being able to rationalise his faith. He thought I was too given to arcane meditations, and told me I was too subterranean in my thinking to suit him. Yet, in spite of his external doubts about such ideas, I feel in the subconscious he was close to me. For myself, I felt that there was none of my contemporaries with whom fundamentally I was more in harmony. My mind or my speech was too rapid to please his own mind, which was graver and gathered itself more slowly to convictions. He grew to mistrust himself when I was with him, and he came to keep me at a distance, writing affectionate letters in preference to speech. My mysticism existed in his imagination in my early days, for he told me he had me in mind when writing those sentences in *The Flight of the Eagle* about "some youth wandering unconsoled, o'erladen with the burden of his thoughts, rapt with visions, tormented by the gods". I think he was rather more in sympathy with mystical thought than he could bring himself to express. O'Grady said of the ancient legends of Ireland that they were less history than prophecy, and I who knew how deep was Pearse's love for the Cuchulain whom O'Grady discovered or invented, remembered after Easter Week that he had been solitary against a great host in imagination with Cuchulain, long before circumstance permitted him to stand for his nation with so few companions against so great a power.

Rarely has so fine a voice as his had so limited a circle of listeners. He affected Ireland rather through others than directly. I think it possible that if one could track back the forces operating in Ireland during the last forty years to their fountains it would be found that some of the greatest owed their inspiration to O'Grady, to some sentence or some image which exalted or ennobled the imagination or nerved the will. His physical presence was dignified: his face grave and beautiful, with so sweet a smile that it could melt any anger. He had a quite delightful humour. There is in the gallery at Harcourt Street a portrait of him, one of John B. Yeats' very finest pictures. It shows O'Grady in one of those melancholy moods when his country had become to him "the Lost Land", when all its heroisms and nobilities seemed extinct, and its fires of morning had sunk in his vision of it into gleamless sleep. That was painted before there came a national resurrection, and I do not know whether O'Grady would have recognised our Irish revolution as a resurrection, for his last years were spent outside Ireland, and he wrote me nothing about Easter Week, or what came after. He did not know what his own work meant to Padraic Pearse or how he had helped to kindle that spirit, and he may for all I know have shrunk from an upheaval to which it is possible in the sight of Heaven he contributed the first spark of ignition. There were fiery particles in his soul, which he scattered about, not knowing what other fires might be ignited besides that he wished to kindle.

Susan Mitchell

IT IS BUT A LITTLE part of life can be reflected in literature. The moment we try to embody in words an emotion or a character we feel how much is lost in the brief journey from being to speech. At every second of the journey something is dissolving or deserting us, delicacies, essences, breaths, which fly back to the heart. They cannot be embodied. They will not enter the narrow house of words. I thought of this when I took up the little volumes which are all that a rich and lovable character has left behind, and tried to find a sentence or verse from which, as from a seed a flower may be grown, the character might be imagined.

I think Susan Mitchell had the genius for life, and she never neglected that exquisite gift in order that she might make herself better as a writer than as a woman, though I am certain that if she had turned her genius for life into letters there were few women of her time who could have written more brilliantly. Her love for life, for her friends, was primary; and what she wrote was but the overflow of an abundant vitality at some moment when it seemed there was no kindness to another to be done and the hour was her own to play with.

The life of letters is a hard one, and to win high distinction the heart must always be pondering on its art, must often seem cold in its absorption. Susan Mitchell did not choose so to desert life for letters, and her finest wisdom never got into her books. There were few human problems, however abstruse, one could talk to her about which she could not comprehend and illuminate by some flash of intuition. Her range of reading was wide, from the sacred books of the world, which she pondered over, to the last play or novel. This range of interest made her one of the best of companions. I have known her to enchant scholars and professors as well as her literary friends by her wit and understanding. But there was no snobbery in her friendships. She gave the best which was in her to give to the least notable acquaintance. How shall I choose verses which might indicate the plenitude of her delight for the earth she lived on, in the friendships she had, in the life which never seemed to weary her.

What was the secret of this unfailing delight in living? Why are some souls grey and others so sweetly coloured? I divine some law governing the motions by which the soul absorbs and transmits the interior light. In those who restrain it within themselves, in them it is restrained. Through the free giver it freely flows. I think Susan Mitchell surprised long ago this lovely secret and the use of it became with her as instinctive and unconscious as breathing. There are many whose sole passion is for the world because they know of none other, but to Susan Mitchell this world was always casting up images of its Original.

Those to whom life has these divine transparencies are happiest of all of us. These have perpetual compensations for what is perpetually passing away. Every moment heaps up some new beauty which is still the Ancient Beauty. There are many people who have thought this without realising it. I think Susan Mitchell realised it hardly thinking about it at all. I am one of those who are always pondering over the mysteries, always imagining a delight in knowledge which but rarely comes to me.

I found in her one of those rare natures whose spirituality turns them to the world, taking it with outstretched hands and laughter as if they knew what precious ores were in its dross and they had the instant alchemy by which the ore was revealed. She was of middle age when I met her and she became my daily associate in work until she died, but even when she was white-haired she was, I imagine, no older within than when she was the beautiful girl earlier friends than I remember so fondly. It might almost be said of her what Swedenborg said of the angels, that she was perpetually advancing to the springtime of her youth. Youth always attracted her and she loved to have young people about her. She could write with tenderness of the play of youth after she had long passed from girlhood.

In her lyrics may be seen her delight in lovable and desirable life, in what was sweet and natural. Many crowded about her to hear the witty speech, and she could use perfectly the speech of a Beatrice or a Rosalind, her eyes brimming over with fun, and it was as the wittiest woman in Dublin that most knew her, but because that apparition was so well known I am trying to suggest the spiritual nature which was the reality behind that brilliance, the affectionate heart which remembered everything that was lovable and forgave or forgot all that was contrary.

Though in her later life I was probably more intimate with her thought than any except her sister Jenny, for whom she had a deep affection, I could not know how deep the sadness I divined lived, a concealed spirit, along with that obvious gaiety; yet I am certain one must have been the measure of the other, but that she hid the sad spirit and let the gay spirit have full play. I divine this wistful spirit, for I believe nobody can be altogether gay without revealed or hidden gravities; but that kind soul but rarely spoke about its sorrows, though of its gravities she would often have speech. I think she was never so absorbed as when she discussed some problem of the Soul, Heaven-world or Immortality. Yet after doing so with tremulous eagerness and sincerity, a moment after she would fling off the gravity and delight in some absurdity of life which caught her quick eye. I think she ran away from these serious discussions as a child might who had got a surety of some precious thing and who then ran off in sheer happiness of heart to play any prank, keeping all the while the secret thing she had found as an inspiration for her frolic. How wild that fun could be all her friends knew, how good the fun was and how little malicious, or if there was a touch of malice it was so wrapt up in humour that even the victim must laugh and be the better of it, for there was no bitter flavour in it.

I do not think of any I have known who have left more endearing memories of themselves among their friends than this kindest of women.

John Butler Yeats

W E ADMIRE SOME because of their accomplishment, others because of what they are. I admire John Butler Yeats as an artist as much as any, but I feel that Nature's best gift to him was a humanity which delights in the humanity of others. Few artists I think found it more easy to be interested in the people they met or painted. All his portraits, whether of men or women, seem touched with affection. Rarely has he portrayed any, young or old, where something like a soul does not look at us through the eyes. I have liked people after seeing his portraits of them, and I am sure I would not have liked them so much if I had not first looked at them with his vision. In his delightful letters, of which extracts have been already published, and in his essays he lets us unconsciously into the secret of his meditation about his sitters. He is always discriminating between themselves and their ideas, searching for some lovable natural life. He complains in one of his essays that the American women whom he admires cannot be easily natural. They want so much to be the ideal daughter or the ideal wife or the ideal friend that poor ordinary human nature is not good enough for them. When Lao-Tse says in his ideal state people would be contented in themselves, think their poor clothes beautiful and their plain food sweet, I think of Yeats and his fear that the reformer will improve the Irish peasant off the face of the earth. He delights in him as he is. Why should anybody want to alter what is already natural, wild and eloquent? To be primitive is to be unspoiled. He seems to be seeking everywhere in art and letters for the contours and emotions which are the natural mould of face or mind. Orpen can astonish us with technical accomplishment and John with masterly drawing, but if we look at the face of a woman painted by Yeats we will be attracted, not by the transient

149

interest of novelty in treatment, but because of some ancient and sweet tradition of womanhood in the face, the eyes, the lips. We find the eyes so kind that it is so we imagine mothers or wives from the beginning of time have looked upon their children or have bewitched men to build about them the shelter of home and civilisation.

In his art he has this intimacy with the heart's desire, which is not external beauty, as those who have degenerated art into the portrayal of prettiness suppose, but beauty of spirit. Those who knew him will remember that enchanting flow of conversation which lightened the burden of sitting; and Nature was wise in uniting the gift of conversation with the gift of portrait painting, because the artist was so happy in his art and so reluctant to finish his work; without that grace of speech few sitters could have endured to the end with an artist always following up some new light of the soul, obliterating what already seemed beautiful to substitute some other expression which seemed more natural or characteristic. To those who knew him his essays will recall that conversation with which we did not always agree but which always excited us and started us thinking on our own account. The reader finds there thoughts which are profound said so simply that their wisdom might be overlooked, and also much delightful folly uttered with such vivacity and gaiety that it seems to have the glow of truth.

How witty he is those who read the essays will discover. "When a belief rests on nothing you cannot knock away its foundations", he says, perhaps half slyly thinking how secure were some of his own best sayings from attack. I refuse to argue over or criticise the philosophy of the man who wrote that, for I do not know how to get at him. I am content to enjoy.

Perhaps these fantasies and freaks of judgment are as good as if they were true. One of the most delightful inventions of Nature is the kitten chasing its own tail, and this and many other inventions of Nature seem to indicate that a beautiful folly is one of the many aspects of wisdom. What is it but mere delight in life for its own sake, in invention for its own sake, or, as he puts it elsewhere, a disinterested love of mischief for its own dear sake? How dear that is to us Irish who have often had nothing but love of mischief to console us, when all the substantial virtues and prizes of life had been amassed by our neighbours.

Katharine Tynan

KATHARINE TYNAN was the earliest singer in that awakening of our imagination which has been spoken of as the Irish Renaissance. She was a born singer, almost everything she has written seeming effortless. I think she had as much natural sunlight in her as the movement ever attained. The Irish imagination is little interested in normal humanity and its affections. It deserts centres for circumferences. It goes adventuring in Over-world, in faery, in fantasy, in Under-world, in the crypts and sewers of the soul. All these Irish men of letters, Yeats, Synge, O'Grady, Stephens, Dunsany, Joyce, O'Casey, O'Flaherty and most of their contemporaries, have this tendency to turn from the hearth and to roam in uncharted regions of the psyche. Katharine Tynan had her own spirituality, but she has kept closer to the normal than any except Padraic Colum. She had something which is rather rarer among poets than most people imagine, a natural gift for song. In me there is a great distance between body and soul. It was with so much difficulty or anguish that soul could melt body, and body be made transparent for poetry to come through, that when young I was in despair, believing I was not naturally fitted to use this precious art. I found it so difficult to make a shapely verse that I wondered at Katharine Tynan, to whom the craft seemed to come so easily, who had such a gift for melody. The first perfect saying of verse I ever heard was when she read me the just-written *Children of Lir*, and I listened to a voice which gave its perfect resonance and rhythm and emotional quality to every line. I may be mistaken, but I think it was easier for her to work in the craft of poetry than it has been with any of the poets I have known. But because it was easy and because she has written many books of verse, it would do her wrong to think that what was written with a natural ease was not memorable. There was a mould in the psyche into which thought and emotion were poured, and the lyric record was almost always shapely. No one can be always on peaks of intensity. We, all of us, vacillate between our surfaces and our depths, from verse which makes itself lustrous and decorative with external colour or symbol to verse which embodies profundity of feeling. What is common to her lyrics, out of whatever mood she writes, is a shapeliness in their architecture. This can be seen to perfection in *Sheep and Lambs*, in *Larks*, and in *Lux in Tenebris*. I think of this shapeliness of a song with the same pleasure I have when I look on a picture where everything in it, colour, form, tone, are harmonised and fit delicately into its four walls. That artistic shapeliness is in danger of becoming a lost art to a generation which grew tired of the traditional courtly dress of poetry and listened to so much free verse that it almost forgot what melody was. It may appear old-fashioned, this adherence to metrical tradition, but I confess I like those who bring their gold, frankincense and myrrh, and put fine raiment on the children of their spirit.

Katharine Tynan said of herself that she was "born under a kind star". It was true. She was happy in religion, friendship, children, instantly kindling at any beauty in gardens, flowers, in sky and clouds. A friend passes and he is sped on his journey not with despair but hope, almost with imaginative gaiety.

Traveller from the realms of gold,
　Sydney's brother, Raleigh's twin,
From this cynic world and old,
　Some strange jest had placed him in,
Eldorado and the morn
Unto these he shall return.

It is a great gift this, which on a sudden changes our gloom
to a glory. She imagines celestial adventures for those boys
who met death in the Great War; and who can say, after
the purifying fires, what transfiguration may take place; that
there may not be some exquisite mingling of earth-born
desires made heavenly by the Holy Breath in some land of
Heart's Delight? The fairy-tales of the heart may come to be
true for us in the Pleroma.

I like her poetry best when she draws some shy beauty out
of its recesses as in this little lyric, which she named *Drought*,
but overlooked when collecting her poetry. I rescue it
because I love its dim colour and the brooding gentleness
with which she fondles the thirsty leaves.

The sky is greyer than doves,
Hardly a zephyr moves,
Little voices complain;
The leaves rustle before the rain.

No thrush is singing now,
All is still in the heart of a bough:
Only the trembling cry
Of young leaves murmuring thirstily.

Only the moan and stir
Of little hands in the bough I hear,
Beckoning the rain to come
Out of the evening, out of the gloom.

It was the same brooding love which enabled her to interpret *Summer Airs*, to pass beyond odour of heather or ocean,

beyond memories of lakes and islands, to discover that some wind out of Paradise is mixed with the air we breathe.

> What soft invisible loving clings
>   About my neck and lifts my hair?
> The Eternal Love in these wild wings
>   Meets me and clasps me everywhere.

It is love only which has this clairvoyance, which discovers there is no hollow of air, no desolation of desert or stone which has not upon it somewhere the divine signature, which knows that nothing was born out of the Divine Mind which is not milk for its children.

Every creature seeks for the things which satisfy its own nature. Others may take much more pleasure in poems whose art I admire but which are born out of emotions I have not shared, using a symbolism with which my childhood was not familiar, so that I cannot make it a stepping-stone to the reality it stands for. But to the majority of my countrymen the symbols she uses are keys to a sanctuary they often enter. I am like those others I spoke of who go on lonely adventures. I was not fortunate enough to be born under a happy star.

Philip Francis Little

WHEN I HEARD that Philip Francis Little was dead, my memory ran back forty years or more to the days when I first knew him. We both then were a little wild. I was sufficiently remote from terrestrial affinities for Philip to think of me as a brother mystic, for he said to me a little later: "There is an overturned truck on the East Pier of Kingstown. We two shall live there, and we shall teach the people, and we shall be known by the name of 'The Wonderers'. The people may jeer at us, but they will get tired of jeering at us sooner than we shall get tired of doing good to them." I was perhaps a solemn youth, but I had a faint sense of humour, which overcame my sense of his moral heroism, and the thought of myself living in that overturned truck fanned the faint fire to a glow which I hastily tried to shroud. But Philip saw the flicker of a smile and he pointed a condemning finger at me. "You smile", he said. "You never saw me smile". Therein he did himself an injustice, for he had a rich sense of humour, and I think this sense of humour, private to himself, inspired much freakish conduct in later years, as when he entered an assembly of the very godly and denounced them for the immorality of their costumes. I remember many years ago when I visited him at his lodgings he thought it necessary to explain his solitary existence: "I am very fond of my people," he said, "but they cannot get on with me. Because, whenever I think anything, something says to me, 'You think so! Why didn't you say so? You are a coward! You are a damned coward!' and I say 'I am damned if I am', and out it comes. And just because of this my people are paying me a hundred and fifty a year to live away from them." Then the humour broke out and he added slyly: "I think it should be two hundred. Don't you?" Perhaps the comfort of living at some remove from so devastating a conscience was better appreciated later, for he had become satisfied and was always affectionate in his references to his people. I often gave occasion for the use of this frankness enjoined on him by his interior tyrant. I am glad to think I received his admonitions more in admiration than discomfort, though once, in a public place with crowds of passers-by, some incautious remark of mine led him to lift his arms above his head and to denounce me as Jonah might have denounced the dwellers in Nineveh: "There shall be a great fire hereafter and great rejoicing outside your burning". The insistence of conscience that he must not be a damned coward was, I think, the reason why he came to be often in trouble. I think myself his moral courage was proved and undoubted, and he might very well have ignored the jibes of conscience, for his yielding to these seemed unreasonable to me and others, though it is only when the Scroll of Life is unrolled that the picture of a personality recorded there shall be seen in relation to an absolute rightness, and I would never prejudge that judging because I found him a little trying at times. That there was a fire of genius in him I have always believed. I listened long ago entranced to that eloquent voice every now and then lit by an ample imagination or inspired to the improvisation of poetry. He was master at times of a subtlety which used to upset me in argument, so that I grew cautious of agreement with statements which seemed innocent. I found that he could foresee the logical outcome of my rash agreement, and half an hour afterwards I would be bound, intellectually, hand and foot as a consequence. In later years there was less natural poetry in his speech, and he was preoccupied with moral and religious questions.

The only occasion I remember on which I enjoyed what, I think, was a victory over him in argument, was when I criticised the conventional phrases he used. I said to him: "Philip, when you write poems for your fellow creatures you use all your power to create original imaginations, and all your art to find the new, beautiful and fitting words. But when you speak to God you pray to Him in an outworn language, and I do not think God will be pleased that you show a less tender art in your prayer to Him than you do when you are supplicating the interest of mere mortality." He started to say something in reply, but stopped as if that conscience which was so stern a monitor to him had constrained his speech.

His poetry was a wilderness in which one might come across in deserts of sonorous syllables oases of a noble dignity, and now and then sentences which might follow after "Marlowe's mighty line" in memory. Even in serious verse his sense of humour would lead him to invent flowers or other creatures, and he would watch the listener as he chanted the verse to see whether the invention passed without question. He deceived me with some lines which were certainly well imagined:

> The grey
> And cindery smock-weed, and the flickering, blue
> Sea-poppy.

He tried to pass them off upon Dr. Sigerson, but that alert elder would have none of them. "There is no such flower", he interrupted the reading, to Philip's discomfiture. In his isolation he seemed to have grandiose visions of earth and sky, and some remote beauty in these would be captured in verse which had delicacy as well as dignity. He built up his shadowy pictures with a solid masonry of words. He had the artist's eye and he omits no image necessary for the conjuring up of his world in our imagination. I think that visionary faculty might have made a fine artist of him if he had continued his early study as an art student. His room had many pictures, though here the technique was never on the same plane as his vision, but almost always there was intensity in his drawing to make us forget the elaboration of forms of whose true architecture he was ignorant. He was a romantic by nature, a romanticism I think kindled originally by certain lines of Milton which started him off on a journey of his own.

He will go on for pages elaborating a tremendous imagery, as of some larger world than this we live in, and as I heard much of it when I was young, and my own imagination readily created pictures at the evocation of Philip's voice, I have never been able since to think of this verse as coldly and critically as I would of poetry which came to me in later years. I still think he often showed a fine imagination and a fine quality of sound when he gave utterance to it. I am told he has left much manuscript, a book of parables and other matter. I hope if it is poetry it will be sifted to see whether the imagination of his later years was as rich as in the best of the early poetry. I think it probable that much of it is religious musing, for he drew me into his rooms a couple of years ago to listen to a long passage which he read me. I thought it eloquent, but conventional in phrase.

He was born, perhaps, out of his due era. Seven hundred years ago he might have been a great preacher or saint, or in the Elizabethan period his imagination might have run riot magnificently at a time when mighty mouthfuls of words were listened to with equal mind by mighty men and adventurers. He seemed like one who ought to have been driving the huge mastodons of thought, and had come, in a world dwindled in size, to hold forth to conventional little folk, who shrunk from him and to whom indeed it was hardly worth while preaching at all.

A Bibliophile[1]

UNLIKE MOST POETS, the poet I was talking to was a book-lover. He held rare and first editions in a reverence which was at first unintelligible to me, who prefer the edition most convenient to read. But as I listened I began to be stirred to wonder and speculation. Books became animate things with mysterious laws governing their being, their relations to each other and to the book-lover. I had gone about the quays with this poet watching him, and I remembered how surely the rare book, the first editions, brought themselves under his notice. He did not seem to peer about or to look at titles. He dropped long delicate fingers, casually as it seemed, into a welter of books on a cart, and drew out what was rarest. It was attracted to him by some law of

[1] The poet Seumas O'Sullivan.

affinity like that which attracts iron filings to a magnet. It must be so, for when I dropped my fingers into a cart in deliberate imitation of him I brought out nothing more valuable than a book of sermons or an out-of-date directory. Books did not recognise in me any lover of their rarity. The expert fisherman on our rivers does not know more surely that the fly cast will cause the fish to bite than the poet knew the unfailing attraction of the magnetism of his fingers. It was most amazing. There would rise out of that pool of books a first edition of Shelley or Wordsworth, or a rare pamphlet. Or if he drew out a book of sermons he knew by some instinct that it contained matter of literary interest. Mere unadulterated piety would never attach itself to those fingers. He would bring the volume home and set himself to discover what was the affinity between himself and the book, and he would find it. In one volume of sermons he found where Vaughan had stolen

bright shoots of everlastingness,

and in another the sermon from which Wordsworth had rescued without acknowledgment

thoughts that do often lie too deep for tears.

Dr. Osborn Bergin tells me that once as he came near a book cart he had an intuition that he would find there a Sanskrit text, and he found it. All this is to me very exciting. Has the book, once it is printed and bound, a consciousness of its own? Or is it endowed gradually with consciousness by those who have pondered over it? Does this consciousness grow intense with years of use as one generation after another read it with love? Does it come at last to a state where it is sensitive to the aura of the true book-lover? When the fingers come near, does the book intensify its consciousness and attract the fingers to its precious pages? We may never know these mysteries until the universe goes back into God and all mysteries are revealed. But even more astonishing things than this happen when the poet is on the prowl. He found in one shop a first edition of Shelley, but with the title-page and some ten pages missing. Within a week he had discovered the title-page by itself, and the missing pages elsewhere, so that they could be bound together. The first edition here appears almost to have the magic attributes Milton bestows on spirits which, when their substance is severed, by some mystic power bring about a uniting of the severed parts. Was it so? Or was it clairvoyance? We know from Dunne's *Experiment with Time*, and from many other psychical researchers, that there may be clairvoyance in dreams. Did the poet go to sleep thinking unhappily of his tattered copy of Shelley? Did the soul set out on a prowl, using its mysterious insight to discover where was the lost title-page, where the missing pages? Did it, before wakening, impress the subconscious mind of the poet with a desire to go along the quays once more? Was it the dreaming soul led the waking self to the spot where the title-page was lying, or to peer between other books to find the missing pages? Here are two explanations. Either the book is animate and draws the book-lover to itself that it may find a refuge for its old years, a shelf where it is honoured, or else we must fall back on the explanation of dream. Perhaps dream may explain it better, though I do not put altogether aside the idea that a book may have a life of its own, as Kipling found a ship had a life of its own. Once the poet dreamed of a house where there were specimens of fifteenth-century printing. It was an eighteenth-century house, and there were broad stone stairs in it. Afterwards he discovered the house with its fifteenth-century books and its stone stairs.

I grew more and more excited listening to the poet as he sat in his garden. He talked in a melancholy way about a fall from grace. Poverty once compelled him to sell some of these precious volumes, and after that he felt that virtue had

departed from him. Books no longer came to his fingers with
the trustful confidence of children to a kind guardian. They
felt the element of base alloy which had corrupted temporarily the pure gold of his nature. They allowed the fingers
to pass by without rising to the bait. He had to search hard
at that period to get rare books. In fact, he felt himself
declining to be the mere industrious hunter of second-hand
bookshops pitting his knowledge against the ignorance of the
bookseller. Of course he discovered books, but it was not
by any transcendental process like that which enabled him in
those days of innocence before his fall almost unconsciously
to pick up masterpieces. He was conscious of the fall and was
unhappy. He would never have fallen but because of necessity. Then he came back heroically to himself once more
to be the disinterested book-lover. His books lie now on
shelves confident that they have found a safe hermitage. Rare
volumes, as of yore, attach themselves affectionately to his
fingers. It is all very romantic, very mysterious. As I sat in
the poet's garden new laws of the universe hitherto unsus-
pected were apparent to me. I felt like stout Cortez when
with eagle eyes he gazed with wild surmise on the Pacific,
silent upon a peak in Darien. The garden chair I sat on was
a peak from which I contemplated hitherto unexplored
mysteries.

I wanted to tell my discoveries to a Fellow of Trinity
College, a biologist, who was there, so that he might with
his trained faculties investigate the life of books and bring
them into his scheme of things, into some fitting place in the
long chain stretching from protoplasm and unicellular organisms up to humanity. But as I looked at his eyes I felt he
would be sceptic unless to convince him I had instruments
delicate as those Sir Jagadis Bose invented to assist him in
his explorations into the life of metals and plants. I am
certain that if that instrument of Sir Jagadis Bose, which
magnifies vibrations two million times, had been applied to

a first edition of Wordsworth with my fingers resting on it, and afterwards when it was touched by the fingers of Seumas O'Sullivan, there would be evidence enough to startle the most sceptical biologist. He would have found at the second experiment the spark on the screen had begun to dance, the book would have communicated its ecstasy to the scientific observer, and the real laws governing the animation of books would have been placed on a scientific basis. I am certain that if the delicate mechanism was attached to the *Book of the Dun Cow* when Osborn Bergin's hand was on it, it would be found that the spark on the screen was frolicsome and conscious of the presence of the true scholar. With my hand on the book the spark would fall asleep. If the instrument could express itself in sound it would snore. I know the truth will be found out some day. So I am staking a claim as first hinter or expositor of the law. These words may pass as unnoticed as did Mendel's great contribution to science for many years. But some time, perhaps fifty years from this, in an age when Sir Jagadis Bose's instruments shall have been perfected to reveal the minutest vibrations in things hitherto considered inanimate, the joyfulness of books when approached by the perfect bibliophile will have been apprehended. Then this paper will be rescued from the obscurity in which it lay so long; a new branch of science like Mendelism will have been created dealing with the life in books. It may even be called Aetheism.

Eva Gore-Booth

WHEN I LOOK BACK along the aisles of memory I can conjure up the image of Eva Gore-Booth as I saw her a quarter of a century ago, like a star half hidden in mist, a fragile yet gallant figure breaking out in sudden transcendentalisms from cloudy, luminous silences, a little

breathless, always in pursuit of the spirit, just as her sister
Constance was a little breathless in pursuit of her national
ideals. Neither, I think, had much of that wise passiveness in
which ideas cease to be glittering things beyond us, but
silently sink into and become part of our being. She seemed
to me, while never wearying in that pursuit, to be too hasty,
and not to allow herself leisure for a true contemplation.

In her verse there is more continuous preoccupation with
spiritual ideas than manifestation of a profound spirituality.
An ancient scripture says of the spirit: "It is not understood
by those who understand it. It is understood by those who
do not understand it." This may seem paradoxical, but by
intuition we comprehend the truth in it, the difference
between being a thing and thinking about a thing. Here we
have continual exposition of spiritual and transcendental
beliefs, but there is more exposition than poetry. Not that
there is not evidence of a talent. Every now and then we
come across verses where feeling and vision are blended
together, and the words are melted by emotion and make
lovely rhythms:

> Here the white stars brood high above the austere pines,
>   And the long pine-stems seem to gather up the shadowy
>   stream
> Of the earth's beauty, all her flowing curves and rapturous
>   lines,
>   Folded together and lifted up in a long ecstatic dream.

To her the soul must always be on its travels. It is rare
to find a phrase which suggests that she had brooded long
enough over any one place or any one idea to make it her
own, to become one with it. She is the poetic Peri always
outside her Paradise. But she never turns away from it. Her
wings are always fluttering at some divine gate. I doubt if
she ever looked away from it long enough to feel the lure of
another pursuit. She was like that mystical mariner she
wrote about in her first book of verse. I quote from memory:

Thus did the swift boat past the islands glide,
The pleasant Islands of Delight and Youth,
Where dwell the sirens; as it sped along
He did not even hear their fatal song,
For Orpheus was standing by his side
Making sweet music of an unknown truth.

She had all her life that preoccupation. She did not hear
the fatal song, and I am inclined to believe that if she had
listened, and had turned away after, she would have had
strength to have gone further and deeper on her spiritual
travels—for power is born in the soul from its struggle with
itself. Never in a single line is there a hint that its purity
was muddied by desire, that it was entangled by any passion
except that master passion for the spirit. Other poets have
at times fallen into

some slough of sense or soul
Forged by the imperious lonely thinking power,

and have made great and moving poetry out of their struggle.
She seems never to have suffered any human temptations
from world, flesh or devil, from the wrestling with which
so much of the greatest poetry is born. As it is, she too
often wrote about beauty and the spirit, as if when she had
named the divine powers she had invoked them and made
them visible. She was too impatient to labour over her art.
She wrote too much and too hastily, and her haste is her
undoing as an artist. She was almost irritated if one spoke to
her about the technique of verse. She did not realise that in
poetry the body is part of the soul. In the same lyric she will
sometimes wander from iambic to trochee, and from trochee
to anapaest, so that there is no continuity of mood expressed
in sound. We are rushed in one line and delayed in another,
and there is no change in the thought to account for the
alteration. It is mere haste in writing due to that breathless-
ness I have spoken of. She was probably afraid the mood would

fly if it was not at once put into words. She did not seem to know that poetry is first imagined in the dream consciousness, and the perfect poem is there if the waking consciousness will try patiently enough to bring it from soul-world to earth-world. Just as we have a moral conscience which tells us when we err from the good, so there is in us an aesthetic conscience, and the artist listens to its whisper and will let nothing pass until the aesthetic conscience is silent and he knows that inner and outer are in as close a harmony as may be. A little less of the moral conscience and a little more of the aesthetic conscience would have made Eva Gore-Booth a finer poet. She would not have sung so often about Beauty, but would have made much more beautiful songs. Yet, in spite of this imperfect craft, we feel respect for the poet because the nature is so steadfastly set on noble things, and here there was no insincerity. It is proof of this that she was not content to be the spiritual dreamer but must try to change her world. We get some revelation of the woman, ardent for reform, whose good heart compelled her to social service, to build up women's trade unions, to work for the poor. But all the while she speaks before the crowd she speaks as one whose heart is indeed moved by her message, but whose spirit is otherwhere. The world she looks at seems a dream. The reality is some spiritual world of which the symbol in memory is the mystical hills which rose above the home of her girlhood.

Though her life was spent mainly outside Ireland since her girlhood, her affections for the country never seemed to weaken, and when she writes about Ireland her verse becomes less abstract and more intimate, as in her best-known lyric:

The great waves of the Atlantic sweep storming on their way,
  Shining green and silver with the hidden herring shoal;
But the little waves of Breffny have drenched my heart in, spray
  And the little waves of Breffny go stumbling through my soul.

It is too rarely she writes a line like that about the waters shining with the hidden herring shoal, a line which shows more than superficial observation. Sometimes she could be quite simple and give us revelation of herself rather than of her ideas. She loved the beauties of earth, but her allegiance was not to it. She was too content to generalise about the lonely winds of twilight and haunted hills and the silence of the stars, for her heart was always hungry for its "unknown truth". This preoccupation with other-worldly thought, which made her so careless an artist, made of her a very notable personality. It is a victory for the soul to sustain itself firmly through life, so that it always appeared clear and flashing as a crystal. She seems to have known only occasional weariness, transitory discouragements or melancholy, but she soon recovered her mystical steadfastness which never weakened to the last.

She had ideas and intuitions to overflowing, as many as any poet of her time, but she had not patience to carve out these jewels to that exquisite perfection which the artist gives. A diamond seemed a diamond to her, polished or unpolished, cut or uncut, and the cutting or polishing was often of the hastiest, but she had a most radiant, iridescent personality, and one clings to the memory of that flashing spirit while rarely remembering its utterances.

Tagore

IT IS TAGORE who more than any other maintains in our Iron Age the dignity of poetry and makes us understand why in the ancient world the poet held so great a sovereignty over the spirit of man.

How wise he is reflecting on the intense nationalism of his own country, and how this jealous passion limits the heart. "The complete man must never be sacrificed to the patriotic man." How often in Ireland have we not been asked to sacrifice our complete humanity, beauty, love, justice, as an offering to patriotism? All have been sacrificed to an emotion which can never leave earth and journey with us to Paradise. It is a bad patriotism which demands from us the sacrifice of things which are higher than itself.

Rhetoric has a dulling effect on the spirit, and I know for myself all the radical element in my nature would fade if my spirit had for diet those revolutionary verses, which I think come because the writers have read too many leading articles and political speeches which have made them angry. But to be angry is not the way to evoke the soul.

The poet always has his heart fixed on life in its fullness, on the complete man, and will not starve life for the sake of the patriotic man, and he is a truer patriot than those who have nothing else but patriotism. Our spiritual, intellectual and economic life, all that is necessary to our humanity and its fullness, has been ravaged by those who have set abstractions above humanity, and we call attention to the profound wisdom of the great Indian poet, because it may strengthen those who wish to see a rich humanity here, and who have more love for humanity than for the triumph of some one logical abstraction, which is arid to the heart, because it demands the subjection to it or exile of all the spiritual immortals whose interblending makes rich our lives.

Krishnamurti

HE HAS HAD a claque of charlatans about him since he was a boy, announcing him as an avatar, and it says much for an inherent sweetness and simplicity of character that he has emerged with that sweetness and simplicity from the most horrible chorus of wonder-seekers and devotees who ever encompassed a child with their chattering and folly. Probably driven in upon himself as a refuge he sought for something simple and lovely and sweet in his heart, something altogether different from the church which was being organised for him, and the bishops who were being nominated as his apostles, and the worshippers who waited in expectation of wonders and miracles.

Kahlil Gibran as well as Tagore has expressed the mystical faith of Asia much better than Krishnamurti, but there is an engaging, boyish innocence in his poems, though I cannot find in them a wisdom or beauty which would lift them beyond the average expression of spiritual life.

Kahlil Gibran

I DO NOT THINK the East has spoken with so beautiful a voice since the *Gitanjali* of Rabindranath Tagore as in *The Prophet* of Kahlil Gibran, who is artist as well as poet. Rodin said of him: "He is the William Blake of the twentieth century". Two of the drawings are specially moving, one a lovely drooping figure of a girl, the arms outstretched as in crucifixion with the hands nailed to the hearts of two other figures.

I have not seen for years a book more beautiful in its thought, and when reading it I understand better than ever before what Socrates meant in the *Banquet* when he spoke of the beauty of thought, which exercises a deeper enchantment than the beauty of form. To the mother he cries:

> Your children are not your children,
> They are the sons and daughters of Life's longing for itself.
> You may give them your love but not your thoughts,
> For they have their own thoughts.
> You may house their bodies but not their souls.
> Their souls dwell in the house of to-morrow, which you
>   cannot visit, not even in your dreams.

He asks of the dweller in the house, has he beauty there—

Or have you only comfort, that stealthy thing that enters the
house a guest, and then becomes a host and then a master?

I could quote from every page, and from every page I
could find some beautiful and liberating thought. How profound is that irony of Gibran's about the lovers of freedom
"who wear their freedom as a yoke and a handcuff". Have we
not seen here souls more chained to their idea of freedom
than a prisoner is limited in his cell? The most terrible chains
are those that gnaw at the soul. I wonder has the East many
more poets to reveal to us? If Europe is to have a new renaissance comparable with that which came from the wedding
of Christianity with the Greek and Latin culture it must, I
think, come from a second wedding of Christianity with the
culture of the East. Our own words to each other bring us
no surprise. It is only when a voice comes from India or
China or Arabia that we get the thrill of strangeness from the
beauty, and we feel that it might inspire another of the great
cultural passions of humanity.

Gandhi

I AM FILLED with wonder as I read his life, not wonder at
such a character as Gandhi, for many men as spiritual and
selfless could be named, but wonder that so exalted teaching,
making so profound a demand on the spiritual nature, could
have affected so many millions. Tagore and Gandhi are the
two great personalities in India, both men exerting an extraordinary influence on the thought of their countrymen. It is
safe to say that men of like character and genius would in any
country in Europe be but the idols of small groups, their
teaching would be too high to appeal to the multitude. This
may be because civilisation in India antedates European

civilisation by thousands of years, and the culture of the people has been more religious and less secular than with us in Europe, so that an appeal for the use of spiritual rather than material forces fell on ears more sensitive by long usage to such appeals than ours. When Gandhi was asked by a missionary what books influenced him most he named first the New Testament, and he makes the most revolutionary teaching of Christ, the forgiveness of enemies, the non-resistance to force, powerful to affect multitudes who are not Christian. I cannot recall in European history any popular political movement of such dimensions as the non-co-operative movement created by Gandhi where there was such a superb reliance on spiritual law to justify and sustain it. While Europe had mobilised forty million men for slaughter India had mobilised millions for passive resistance. I confess while I wonder and admire I am filled with doubts, and speculate upon this holding up of the passions natural to average humanity. If it does not achieve its object, if it is not victorious, must there be a reaction? Must the pent-up forces fly to the other extreme, and would we see reliance on force following the failure of passive resistance? Gandhi had a nature too profound not to be aware of this danger. He said at his trial, "I knew I was playing with fire", and he took upon himself the responsibility for the outrages which occurred when the intensity of sacrifice translated itself, as all intense passions are liable to do, into another frenzy as intense, when human nature, unable to hold itself longer at the spiritual pole, relaxed its control, and the energy fled to the material pole and animated the passional nature. Lao-Tse said, "Nobody can remain for ever standing on tip-toe", and the leader who makes extraordinary demands on his followers, who asks them to exercise an unusual moral restraint, must take into account the tendency in human nature to reaction, and ask himself, "If I fail in my purpose what will become of the forces I have roused?" Energy is

indestructible, and human energy, like light, heat, electricity, which can be translated into each other, is no less
indestructible and no less capable of transformation. If a
secure resting-place is not found at one pole of the nature
the energy flies to another centre and takes new forms.

Why should there be reaction? Because there was passion
in the moral force movement, and all movements of passion
inevitably create their own opposites. Tagore uses the gentleness of intellect where Gandhi uses the gentleness of will.
Tagore dreads an intellectual and spiritual penury following
this passionate absorption in one idea. I feel temperamentally
more sympathetic with those who aim at the richest and
most varied intellectual life than with the puritanical concentration on one idea exalted above all others.

George Bernard Shaw

SHAW IS the best-known literary man in the world, a unique
personality, the last veritable saint we produced in Ireland. Though the elder saints might consider his doctrines
dubiously, he is none the less the ascetic prophet of our
generation, his mission being to quicken or vitalise the
torpid mental body of humanity by shooting into it the
electrifying shafts of his wit. He has faced the world, and
has never been anything but himself. From first to last
he has kept inviolate the character of his personality, the
nationality of his own spirit, if we may call it so; and this
while mixing with all kinds of men, dreading no contact,
fearing no submersion of himself, confident that, whatever
flood might rise, the boat of his soul steered by so expert a
captain would float and not go under. The theatre before
Shaw in England and America was a place for unintellectual
amusement for well-to-do people after a heavy dinner. He
made it as impossible for anybody to feel somnolent at a

theatre as it would be watching the most sensational of melodramas. After melodrama one relapses into coma, but after seeing a play by Shaw one becomes wider awake than ever before. It is impossible to remain intellectually torpid after receiving these electrifying shocks. We all desire life and to have it more abundantly, and no writer in our time has communicated intellectual vitality more in his writing. He has not the beautiful art of some of his contemporaries, nor is he as profound as others, but in sustained intellectual vitality there is none to match him, a most valiant man of letters and, on the whole, the most genuinely loved literary character of his time. Even in the most indignant protests he arouses, there is secret admiration. It will be some time perhaps before Ireland recognises that he is the last saint sent out of the Island of Saints to impart vitality to the intellectually torpid nations. He has not altogether forgotten the land of his birth and shot a few arrows in our direction. But he is our gift to the world which has annexed him, and we can only take from him what he gives to everybody.

Alice Stopford Green

THERE ARE SOME PEOPLE, a rare tribe, who excite admiration and affection in us, because we feel they are disinterested. They have so freed themselves from entanglement with the personal that they find their happiness in service to country, devotion to noble causes, to science for the sake of truth, to scholarship because it preserves a heritage of culture in which there is something precious, which ought not to be allowed to perish. The nation is to them what self or the family are to others less spiritually evolved. They suffer an anguish from what is ignoble in their nation which others would suffer from some misfortune affecting themselves. Alice Stopford Green was of that noble tribe. I had with her a friendship extending over twenty years and came to know her enthusiasms and the spirit in which she laboured for her country. She laboured to preserve the precious things in nationality, which are too often forgotten and trampled on in political controversy. Revolutionaries will squander in a few years a sentiment which was a slow growth through centuries, the creation of poets and scholars. They will seize the sentiment, divert it from its natural objects to give strength to some crude and violent agitation in which all that gave birth to a nation and justified it, its idealism, is ignored. These precious things in tradition, in literature, in the arts, which are in the sacred love of the best men and women for their country, Alice Stopford Green set herself to explore and preserve. She endowed Irish scholarship. It is due to her that it is no longer necessary for an Irish scholar to become an exile in some European university to gain an exact knowledge of the ancient language and literature of his country. The most famous of her books, which she entitled *The Making of Ireland and Its Undoing*, fascinated Irish readers to a fresh interest in their own history. The effect of her history was like the cleaning of an ancient wall-painting which had been blurred by age or obscured by dark varnishes and dust so that what was painted was invisible. But after its cleansing one could see mediaeval scholars and craftsmen at their work. What was empty to the imagination became rich and filled up with vivid life.

She was a noble representative of the Anglo-Irish, of those who were descendants of settlers, but who became so much in love with the country that they gave their hearts to the Dark Rose as passionately as any of the Gaelic singers. She was a good friend. No trouble was too great for her to take if it could help others to do their best work. She transferred her home from London to Dublin at an age when most men and women shrink from change or from initiating new

labours. In these last Irish years of her life her industry was
incessant. She would tire out people half her age by her
sustained intellectual vitality. In one of the most beautiful of
Alice Milligan's poems there is a picture of a grey-haired
lady, her veil blown by the wind, at an ancient castle speaking to a crowd. That was Mrs. Green, her affection for
Ireland like a fire illuminating mind and speech. Until quite
lately, when her age lay heavy upon her, she had a clear-
carven kind of speech which it was a delight to listen to, and
a delightful sense of humour. She was often a genuine artist
in conversation, and could depict a character or an incident
as well as George Moore. If not altogether devoid of malice
at times, it was that playful malice natural to the humorist,
not the malice of a spiteful nature. She would tell her stories
with a perfect psychic understanding which is rare in people
who are reminiscent. If she had written her memories of the
many famous people of her time with whom she was intimate
it would have outlasted her histories but would have given
material for future historians. We shall never have those
reminiscences. But it is to be hoped that some of her more
intimate friends who knew her in her various phases as friend
of scholars, historian, Irish patriot, will make for the next
generation some portrait sketches in words of one of the
most noble, generous and disinterested of Irish women of
her time.

America and the Americans

I SEE AS THE BOAT comes into New York harbour a gigantic
mass of heaven-assailing architecture. It breaks the skyline
as huge cliffs might do. Within the city the impression
deepens. Forever new comrades rise up beside the elder
giants; they tower up in new, beautiful and wonderful lines.
What will New York seem after another half-century?

Already it appears the most ancient, ancient of cities, because here alone does an actual architecture soar above the dreams imaginative artists have conceived of the Towers of Babel. At night the highest lights seem hardly larger than stars, and one set there without knowing where he was might imagine the stars also were points of light continuing that aerial architecture up to infinity. Chicago is hardly less impressive: a darker, fiercer, more tumultuous jumble of lofty buildings, and a surging humanity. City after city seems to be going their way, raising man-made cliffs from the flat American plains. Architecture is the great contemporary American art. The civilisation is in that first stage where, as Flinders Petrie said in his *Revolutions of Civilisation*, there is a mastery over the plastic arts, because there is a physical vitality equal to any labour. The railway stations, even, are awe-inspiring. Entering the Grand Central or Pennsylvania stations one almost feels the head should be bared and speech be in whispers, so like do they seem in their vastness to temples of the mysteries but for the crowds which hurry about at their secular business. The material foundations of a mighty civilisation are being laid everywhere.

What am I to say of the people? As I met them they overflowed with kindness. I find it difficult to imagine a kinder people. Haughty to those who do not like them, but lavish in their goodwill to all who meet them with unaffected liking. It is easy to like them. They are young in their minds. It is rarely one meets age in thought or emotion. But because there is youth in their nature one must not assume that their youth is not as competent as the age and experience of the ancestor continent. The evidence of competence lies everywhere about. They were no bunglers who built those great cities, whatever graft may have gone to their making. They look outward rather than inward. The activity is so tremendous that people are called away from central depths to surfaces. There they achieve marvellous things and are

delighted as children at what they do. They are a little
doubtful about it also. They ask you what you think, and
listen to see whether you have an intuition of anything better
still which is to come out of them. They are evolving a
beauty and elegance of their own. The women have almost
standardised good taste in dress. It is rare to see a woman
who offends the artist's sense in colour and form. I wish I
could commend the art with which so many redden their
lips with fierce colour. Even lovely girls yield to this hideous
fashion. It is the mass mood of youth for the moment. It will
probably vanish in another year or two. The girls are so
naturally charming that they do not need the arts of the
demi-mondaine, who must conceal the withering of her
freshness. They almost all have an intellectual eagerness. It
yet remains to be seen what this eagerness of American
women for ideas tends to, what discovery for themselves or
for life. I feel at present their eagerness is like bubbles under
water, trying to rise, to come to their own natural air. So
they may move to the creation of a new feminine type, perhaps hermaphrodite psychically, fusing the intellectual and
the emotional.

The American man is less effervescent but, I think, with
strong elements of romanticism and idealism, even in those
powerful masters of industry. All are lavishly generous. They
have discovered the economic applications of that spiritual
law which gives to the giver: so that whoever pours out to
others what is in them to give, whatever there is of love or
beauty or imagination or intellect, are themselves perpetually
being fed from within. The spendthrift nation is the prosperous nation. While one notices with delight this instinctive lavishing of what is earned, a doubt arises whether the
natural resources of the country are not being too lavishly
squandered also. It is right to spend what one earns. But is it
right to mine the lands, as too many farmers do, taking from
the earth its stored-up fertility and restoring nothing to it,

cutting down the forests, draining the oil wells, and in a thousand other ways leaving to their children an inheritance of Nature somewhat exhausted, as a woman by too much child-bearing?

What is arising or to arise in the States? I think of it as some mood of planetary consciousness. I cannot get a more precise word. Intuition and reason alike prompt me to say this. In the ancient world where travel was difficult, danger-ous and expensive the material basis for such a planetary consciousness was not in existence. The cultures of China, India, Egypt turned inward and brooded on themselves. Within the last century only has a nervous system interlock-ing the planet been evolved. The characters of European and Asiatic were formed in elder centuries, and they change but little from their intense self-concentration in the new era. Biologically the American people are made up from fiery particles of life jetted from many human fountains. The biological ancestors of the people in the States are European, Asiatic, African, with some survival of the aboriginal Ameri-can. Nature will find in this multitude the materials to blend, to make a more complex mentality than any known before, with wide-reaching affinities in the subconscious. I notice, too, that the writers who form the spiritual germ-cell of American culture manifest in their writings something like a cosmic consciousness. I do not say this planetary outlook or consciousness is universal. It exists rather in a few minds. The ordinary man may not understand, indeed he is first repelled by, the thoughts that move the mightier of his kind, but the same elements are in his being, and finally he reels after the shepherds who call. A planetary consciousness I surmise will grow up through centuries in this astonishing people, warring with its contrary idea, which also has its own meaning and just basis. Our human faculties are burnished by their struggle with opposites in ourselves. And it is no less true of the ideas which become dominant in great civilisations. I imagine centuries in which in the higher minds in the States a noble sense of world duty, a world consciousness, will struggle with mass mentality and gradually pervade it, to establish there, and in the world, perhaps, the idea that all humanity are children of one King, or at least to make so noble an idea part of the heritage of those who come after, until, finally, as it must in the ages, it becomes the dominant idea in world consciousness.

A Journalist

EVERYTHING IN HIS PAPERS was keyed up far beyond concert pitch. The slightest news was shouted so that other planets almost might hear it. There never was any human mechanism so devised for drawing humanity from the depths where it obscurely dreamed and whirling it to the surfaces of things. What could the soul of the average man do but come out of the murky depths of its unconsciousness when a brass band was playing as loudly as brass could at the gates of the senses? The effect of this rowdy journalism, with its tom-toms beating all the while, is to bring consciousness out of its depths, so that finally nothing seems to exist except sensations, wars, murders, politics, graft, comic stuff, sob stuff, all the ostensible visible realities which might be featured and headlined, attacked or defended. The horns of Elfland sound no more on ears deafened by this clamour. In half a century the America which, with Emerson and his spiritual kinsmen, had been brooding on the over-soul, or was stern, Puritan and religious, was made vivid, modern, superficial, drunken psychically by excitements. Of all the agencies which helped to bring about this change from subjective to objective, Hearst was the last and greatest. It must not be assumed that all journalism in America is of that character. There are great papers, as ably edited as any in

Europe, and many intellectual journalists. But the popular Press does in effect cause the soul to reel away more and more from depths to surfaces, and finally when a man looks inside himself he finds nothing, but outside himself there is this rich, noisy variety show, so that eyes and ears and all the senses grow more and more intent on the visible, audible and sensational.

I think America is unconsciously desirous of beauty more than of anything else, and if a great imaginative writer or poet were born there, he would be able to sway America as Byron once ruled the emotional life of Europe. They would reel back from surfaces to depths if those depths were populated for them with images of beauty. This yellow journalism is strangely idealistic. The reformer in America, however he may mislike the methods of Hearst, must admit that many reforms were brought about by this man, who knew that his countrymen were reeking with idealism, and only needed to be led against abuses or graft by having them pointed out. He became the terror of the grafters. The average man felt Hearst was champion of his rights as Jefferson was. There was this impulse in his journalism: whereas our sensational dailies seem to have neither heart nor soul, and would sacrifice nothing for an ideal, Hearst was continually risking his great properties by his audacities on behalf of some crusade or other. Winkler presents him as half genius, half charlatan, the genius using the methods of the charlatan, but never losing altogether its own idealism.

Dietician

IT IS ONE of the worst diseases which can fall upon a man, the disease of worrying about his food or drink. The utterance I remember which was most filled with human vanity and extreme self-satisfaction, came from a man after a vegetarian lecture in which the lecturer, with the ego-mania common to his type, told his audience for an hour what he himself ate. The owner of the voice, who had checked off the items, found out one thing to boast about over the lecturer, and at the end of the lecture that puffed-up voice chirped out, "I never take salt".

POLITICS
OF
TIME
AND
ETERNITY

POLITICS
OF
TIME
AND
ETERNITY

The Nation and Beauty

A NATION EXISTS primarily because of its own imagination of itself. It is a spirit created by the poets, historians, musicians, by the utterances of great men, the artists in life. The mysterious element of beauty, of a peculiar beauty, exists in every nation and is the root cause of the love felt for it by the citizens, just as the existence of spirit, the most mysterious and impalpable thing, is the fountain of the manifold activities of the body. Let the spirit go, and the body soon decays. The national counterpart of this truth was stated in the phrase, "When vision ceases the people perish". Whatever contributes to the sustaining of vision, imagination, beauty in a people is of prime importance in national life. Let beauty fade, and in some mysterious way public spirit, sacrifice, enthusiasm also vanish from society. The foundations of its moral have been obstructed.

If we destroyed in Ireland our National Gallery, our Abbey Theatre, our Feis Ceoil, and our poetic and imaginative literature, the agencies by which that mysterious element of beauty filters into national consciousness, we are certain that in fifty years the nation would be corrupt or dead. All that was best in its humanity would have deserted it and gone to countries where there was still a wealth of idealism in society to make living endurable. It is a very small price a nation has to pay to keep its soul alive. What infinitesimal part of the national revenues go to sustain the agencies we have referred to? The spirit which brought about national independence was a spirit created by the artists in life, by the poets, the musicians, the architects, and, in some way, those who struggled for freedom were inspired and sustained by thoughts or images created by the artists in life and associated with the national being. Those who create national ideals need certain things to sustain their own enthusiasms. There must be some provision, how-ever slight, made for art, music, architecture and literature, or the spirit is stifled. Even the materialist should know by now the economic importance of the element of art or beauty in the things in which he is specially interested.

Must Ireland's Beauty Perish?

WE ARE CONTINUALLY priding ourselves upon our spirit-ual and religious nature. We have not the slightest belief in the reality of a spiritual nature which does not create beauty, does not seek after beauty, and which is not distressed by what is ugly. Great religions can be accepted in a hoggish spirit. That is, men profess belief with the utmost passion, and at the same time do not care what ugliness is in their houses or outside them, what cesspools are in their yards, what manure-heaps lie close to their homes. We have a country ravishing in its natural beauty. It is yet almost uncorrupted. It might be made endlessly attractive to visitors, for it may be doubted whether anywhere in Europe there is lovelier or more romantic scenery. Though we think that beauty is its own excuse for being, it has, for the French, Italians, and Swiss, very great economic advantages, and their countries get very many millions of pounds brought into them every year, simply because Nature is lovely and is kept uncontaminated, and art has conspired with Nature. It is not enough to have clean hotels. The visitor must not be offended and irritated by the beauty he came to see being degraded by ugly hoardings. Things have not gone so far that way in Ireland that we could not save our country. It is possible that, in spite of all the National Trust can do, in England the disease has gone too far.

Is there a lovely spot anywhere by lake, river or sea? The mere fact that lovers of beauty go there brings sooner or later the architects of the unbeautiful to the same place to desecrate it, and it begins to break out in a leprosy of mean bungalows for week-enders or flaring advertisements. The exploiters and destroyers of natural loveliness, on a national scale, act as putrefactive germs do in a body, causing it to break out in horrible blotches, pimples and abscesses. Travellers through England can see this disease everywhere. Whether they travel by train or motor the roadsides and fields are made hideous by hoardings screaming out in the gaudiest colours about the sausages of this manufacturer, or the pills of that, or about drinks, tobacco, underclothing, soap, hats and boots. We see the most degraded-looking beings drinking somebody's whisky or swallowing somebody else's meat extract with leers supposed to indicate their sensual gratification. The fact that the most beautiful spots are chosen by the cheap builder or the wayside advertiser may be regarded as manifesting in a dark or inverted manner the attraction of beauty, though they come but to destroy, or to prove the truth of the poet's bitter line:

. . . each man kills the thing he loves.

Man has a power of creating ugliness which no other animal can approach to. It is the dark or obverse side of his power of creating beauty. Every higher faculty in man has its dark or demoniac side, and the problem is how to prevent people who have lost the feeling for beauty offending sense and soul in those who have it still. There is hardly a country road in the United States or Great Britain where the divine imagination is not made obscene by some trades-man screaming at us. The law which imprisons the drunkard or the robber or the blasphemer never seems to have con-sidered there should be any limitation placed on the freedom of men to make the world as ugly as they can. A man found blaspheming in a fit of rage for a minute or two is subject to certain penalties. But an advertisement can blaspheme against beauty for years and the State thinks nothing of it. Yet Beauty is one of the names of God in all the religions, and the deepest of all our spiritual aspirations is that our eyes might see the King in His Beauty.

We are inviting the world to come and see our lakes, mountains, our romantic scenery. But will they come if their vision of beauty is obstructed by the maniacs screaming out in scarlet and yellow the merits of their pills and sausages? We may be quite certain that where the tourist goes the advertisements, placards and posters will go. What can be done to protect our as yet almost undefiled country-side?

Ireland, so far, has an almost unspoiled countryside. We should try to keep it unspoiled. This can be done without in any way hindering economic development or imposing financial hardships on those who wish to build factories. There are innumerable ways and places in which merchants and manufacturers can call attention to their goods. They do not complain that they cannot advertise their pills beside the altar in a church as a restriction on trade, and they have no more right to complain if the aesthetic conscience declares the setting up of hoardings amid beautiful scenery is another form of blasphemy just as likely to be offensive to the divine eyes. If those enthusiasts who tried to blow up the monument to King William had been animated merely by a passion for beauty and a hatred of the ugly, instead of political hatreds, one would almost be inclined to have sympathy for their activities. George Bernard Shaw, after Easter Week, had the passion of the artist when he cried regretfully, "Oh! if I had the control of the artillery how I would have beautified my native city!" Heine, in one of the most beautiful of his poems, spoke of lovers of beauty and poets like himself as Knights of the Holy Ghost. Of that honourable company we have had but few knight-errants. We are not generally in favour of law-breakers or violent methods, but we believe that when a hideous hoarding is set up amid beautiful scenery, if a companionship of lovers of beauty went out with hatchets or petrol at night and hewed down or burnt down that ugliness, the law might condemn the doers, but they would have the warm sympathy of every cultivated person, every lover of beauty, every person with a soul or a civic sense. It is not merely the religious folk or the moralists whose feelings should be protected. The lovers of beauty have just as much right, for they suffer just as much as the religious or the moralist when their feelings are outraged, and ugliness in any shape comes in the last analysis from some obscenity of the soul, the thing against which religion and morality are alike allied.

Censorship

YOU CANNOT MAKE a literature out of undiluted sweetness any more than you can have light in a picture without equal and contrasted shade. Take away that dark tree in the foreground of Turner's painting of Lake Avernus in our

National Gallery and that ethereal distance behind it will at once become dull and lightless. Now, to prohibit frankness in literature and expect literature still to be vital would be as foolish as the expectation that Turner could create that ethereal delicacy of manifolded mountains without his dark pine trees massed against the light. There can be no height of wisdom in any nature which has not vision of an equal and contrasted depth. Nor can any wisdom be effectively passed on to others unless the writer has freedom to report so much as he considers necessary of his descents into the inferno of human life. He must not be restricted merely to sweetness and light; for the soul must not be the slave of light. Its virtue is to stand between light and dark, seeing both and making its choice, and giving its allegiance to the nobler of its own free will. You cannot make people noble by legislations or prohibitions. You are only sweeping the dirt under the couch or into dark corners where it cannot be seen.

There is, we might say, a necessity for the exposition of the depths, because what is unknown and unfathomed cannot be overcome. It was after the descent into Hades that there came light to the spirits in that prison, and this may symbolically illustrate the necessity for a realism about human life, the sounding of its depths from which so many cowardly natures shrink, as if the revelation of these constituted a crime, whereas it is only when the truth about gross natures is revealed that any transfiguration of these becomes possible. We should wish for our literature, which has had so noble a renaissance in our time, that it should be as wise and profound as any, and not be debarred by limitations imposed by timid and mediocre intelligences from a fearless approach to any aspect of life.

We know how delicate the mechanism of the body is. A tiny clot lodged somewhere in the brain and after that the body may live, but in a paralysed state, incapable of athletic motion. The mechanism of the soul is no less delicate. Some prohibition on its liberty may paralyse the expression of genius. A dramatist may find it impossible to give point to his work because he is prohibited from dealing with characters or incidents by foolish sentimentalists or fanatics who think that exposition of character or incident constitutes the crime against taste, whereas whatever may be evil in literature arises solely out of an ignoble attitude of mind on the part of the writer. There is a censorship over drama in Great Britain, and what did it bring the theatre there? Genius denied, freedom almost deserted the theatre and the theatre of commerce arose. Very soon, because what was really profound was impossible, public taste, contaminated by the theatre of commerce, got out of tune with great drama, and Shakespeare, played in every German town, is hardly heard in his own country. In Ireland we had no censorship over the theatre except what was dictated by the inherent taste of author and playgoers, and in a quarter of a century we produced the most vital dramatic literature in Europe. But if we had a censorship of timid people thinking of the young girl, who has no business to be in the theatre at all, we can imagine how they would have been terrified at masterpieces which have made our literature famous. We would have had hacking and cutting and censorship of character and incident, and a paralysis would have set in. It needs a true wisdom to comprehend the truth in the statement of Plotinus, that the scurrilous person, however we mislike him, is an essential ingredient of the drama.

> Take away the low characters and the power of the drama is gone: these are part and parcel of it.

It is not the revealing of the depths to which human nature can sink which is its crime, but the base spirit in which those depths are sounded. Any abyss in human nature may be revealed if the revealing lantern be dropped from the heights. The greatest masters of literature have always claimed freedom to deal with any aspect of life, and we owe to that unfrightened intelligence, that penetrating vision and all-exploring genius unforgettable wisdom about human nature. Tolstoi could go into a brothel in Moscow and depict with that terrible realism of his its squalor, the mute despair of the lost souls inhabiting it, their indifference to reproof or scorn, and yet transfigure the whole scene for us by his genius when he told how the accent of pity in a single voice woke up the whole sisterhood from their lethargy, so that they sat up in their beds with staring eyes, recalling to him that vision in Ezekiel of the valley of dry bones which was clothed and called into life by the Breath of the Spirit.

We are not concerned about proposals directed against the baser kind of journalism, the commerce of the specialists in murder, divorce, scandal and pornography. We have no defence of that commerce to offer. The prohibition of it will not be fought by us, for we do not see that by its prohibition any appetite for truth or wisdom is starved. The vulgarity of such journalism in our opinion is a greater evil than its gloating over sensation, over perversities and abnormalities. It is a real peril in a country where there are vast numbers of semi-illiterates, who can be roused to help in the denunciation of books which they never read, and so create the impression of a mass movement, whose triumph would be to place genius in servitude to mediocrity, to give the control of literature to those who have themselves produced nothing of worth or beauty or profundity. Just as in our economic life the producers, farmers and manufacturers are of more importance than the distributors, because they are the only creators of wealth; so in literature, drama and the arts the creative spirit alone is valuable, and it is by this creative spirit alone, acting in freedom, a national culture becomes profound and vital. We have stated the problem and it is for our legislators to find a solution.

The One-Dimensional Mind

OUR WORST DIFFICULTIES in Ireland are not material, but psychological. Our natural resources are such that but for these psychological difficulties our credit would be equal to securing loans to the amount necessary to enable us to pay for past wreckage and make provision for future reconstruction. But during the past years of conflict too many characters have been hardened, beaten by the Hammer of Thor into some mould or shape where they cling to one idea to the almost complete exclusion of any other idea. Some lost kinsmen in the conflict, and their hearts are hot with hatred. With others again the soul was born while the Russian Revolution was in the ascendant, and a wild image of it was stamped on them and remains with them. Some had a truly noble aspiration for national freedom, and the defeat of that dream has made life bitter for them, and they cannot bring themselves to accept freedom in another form than that they had imagined. Others again have chained their souls to one idea by a vow. All these constitute at present a class of irreconcilables or impossibles, more numerous than ever before in Ireland.

The one-dimensional mind obsessed by a single idea or passion can never comprehend the nation truly or be of service to it, for the national being is manifold, rich, intricate and of many dimensions. The first service anybody can render to his or her nation is to study and comprehend something of the infinite variety of its cultural, social and economic life, as well as its political consciousness. We have met people who talk to us of a Republic, but go no further, and the word as they use it is an opaque symbol, because we cannot see through it to the beauty of any civilisation to which it must inevitably lead. It is not enough to fling a word at us when what the word implies is not explained in terms of a culture, a civilisation or a social order. To fight for a Republic or Kingdom or Empire in the abstract is like fighting for the abstract idea of religion, for this might signify anything—Christianity, Brahmanism, Islam, snake or serpent worship. It saves the necessity for thinking certainly, but those who fling words at us which are not explained must not expect intellectual people to be impressed, or indeed to be anything but bored.

Any idiot with petrol and a match can set fire to a house. It needs trained architects, masons and carpenters to build a house. The latter class of technical competents is rare. The former are numerous. We certainly cannot accept fighting ability as synonymous with creative statesmanship or as even indicating a capacity for it. Of itself it shows nothing more than courage, which is a fine quality. But one fine quality in a man does not imply necessarily that all the other fine qualities are present in the nature. There are still people who seem to think because a man is a brave volunteer ready to risk his life he is thereby a statesman and should if possible be a deputy. There are quite a number still in political power for no other reason than fighting ability, and their political incompetence is becoming recognised. The same blundering judgment in regard to political or administrative ability would be manifest if our revolutionaries came into power.

There is much to be said for the intellectual rivalry of idealists in a country, because they spur each other on to create nobler and more alluring images of life, and the richer and more varied our intellectual life is the stronger is the national being. This richness and variety does not weaken the nation, for where it is evident the whole country feels national pride. Our revolutionaries have done little or nothing to so enrich the nation. They cling to symbols which are unexplained, and they cling so passionately to them, and will not hear of any other ideas, that they have become in effect the Shylocks of politics and economics who would let their nation bleed to death rather than compromise on what they think is due to them by reason of their imaginary bond with society. A nation is not a divine revelation. There are no fixed or immutable ideas connected with it as there are with an isosceles triangle. It has not its basis in race or national frontiers, as a glance at the European map or the reading of European history will show. A nation arises because a number of people come to an agreement about government. The agreement may be due to acceptance of a common culture, to identity of character or religion, or economic interests; and no exact science can be formulated with regard to it. The nations which have come nearest to the ideal of our intransigeants are those whose politicals have allured their countrymen by creating images of lovable or desirable life which they have joined with them in creating. It is the only path for our political extremists to follow. They may allure us by a superior beauty, but they will never allure us by a one-dimensional mentality with its argument of physical force.

Light in Dark Places

IF HALF THE MONEY and energy devoted to providing Ireland with bombs had gone into supplying books and training people to read them, we might still have all our problems, but we should at least have created an atmosphere more favourable to their peaceful solution. We have not the smallest doubt that when the Irish realise it is only by the cultivation of their natural intelligence they can make their way in life, they will cultivate it and will delight in the use of their natural endowment of intellect and imagination. People used to jeer at China and its Mandarins, who were an aristocracy of learning. But they are not jeering now so much, as they are learning more about that marvellous civilisation which endured for so many thousand years and produced some of the greatest literature, art, architecture the world has known.

It was not a revolutionary, but Louis XIV, the most absolute of monarchs, who said: "No man who is badly informed can avoid reasoning badly. I believe that whoever is rightly instructed, and rightly persuaded of all the facts, would never do anything else but what he ought." Not a few of us in Ireland find it simpler to invent or imagine facts instead of investigating them.

The aristocracies of the past, though democracy has brought many just charges against them, did develop among themselves, because of their superior education, a culture which manifested itself in beautiful buildings, in patronage of the arts, and we might say that whatever is memorable in Europe, the noble buildings, the sculpture, paintings, furniture and tapestries which delight the traveller, were possible because of the patronage by religious or landed aristocracies of the intellectuals of their time. When new aristocracies based on leadership in commerce and industry arose, the intellectuals of science benefited by their patronage as the intellectuals of culture were benefited by the patronage of the aristocracies which preceded them.

The old Anglo-Irish aristocracies built beautiful houses, and the country is filled with monuments to their taste. Economically they were found to be too heavy a burden on the people, who revolted against them, and their culture, which was genuine enough, was purely an aristocratic culture and did not overflow into the common life. We have to spread culture widely and commonly so that our Irish democracy may leave memorials of its own existence behind it. Any regulations which will help to force our people to develop their intellect by study and education will assist in this. Five years ago the word to the young Irishman was:

"Get to your rifle". To-day the word should be: "Get to your books". Literature and science are the mirrors in which we may discover what our aptitudes and capacities are.

We have bad stained-glass and statues in our churches because there is no authority in matters of taste to indicate what is poor and what is truly beautiful. The book-shops are filled with cheap and bad literature. Our country towns have few libraries or centres of culture. Our rural industries are without repute because we are so backward in the application of science in production. The arts are without patrons, and we doubt whether a single literary man in Ireland could make the income of an agricultural labourer by royalties on sales of his books among his own countrymen, however famous he may be abroad. A great and generous Irishman before the war wanted to endow the capital city of his country with a gallery of masterpieces, and he was assailed with abuse by the uncultivated in Ireland, and the best of his scouted gift was seized by the trustees of the National Gallery in London and placed in the greatest collection of paintings in the world. Another great and unselfish Irishman devoted his life and his fortune to organising the Irish farmers, and ignorant Irish ingrates, as a reward for his services to his country, burned down the house he had built.

Books alone will not solve our problem. But they are the easiest way of making a beginning, and without them there is no hope of a solution. Their real value lies less in the formal knowledge which their study imparts than in their power to develop a sense of proportion and create a temper in which differences can be discussed without acrimony and with a resolute determination to see facts in their true perspective. "It makes all the difference in the world", it has been said, "whether we put Truth in the first place or the second place." Our present controversies are waged by all sides on the principle that Truth comes second to party needs, and until we have found a better way the triumph of either set of combatants is not likely to advance the true interests of the nation.

Imagination and the Ideal State

A LACK OF CORRESPONDENCE between imaginative theory and objective fact does not dispose of the imagination of the ideal State as a folly.

Human energy always operates through the image which is most present in consciousness. It may be the image of a pretty woman, of an industry, a business, a civilisation, but whatever image is most present to the man, for that he works. It is so with nations. Let the statesmen and reformers present clear images of objects to be attained, let these be images of desirable and attainable life, and the country will direct its energies to realise these objects.

The power of imagination in national life might be the subject of a great book. It is the despised faculty among the vast mass of people, who do not realise how much their whole life is ordered by imagination, a spell cast on them by some enchanter who raised up in their hearts the image of a nation, a civilisation or social order.

What is imagination? Something latent in the spirit of man takes form. There is, as yet, nothing, or but little, in the external world in harmony with it. But it may be a divine idea in the Platonic sense. It may be as much of destiny as the imagination may lay hold of. It may be that the Divine mind has some far-off divine event to which it would shepherd humanity, and in great national crises, when the whole being is stirred, when the existence of the nation itself is in peril, it summons up all the forces ponderable and imponderable in its being, and the conflict becomes as much spiritual as material. Then the archetypal conception of the nation, all we would have it, all it may become, takes possession of our minds. If we had not grandiose conceptions we would not undertake great labours or make great sacrifices. That national imagination becomes real to the spirit while the national struggle lasts. It is to the nation what "the Kingdom of Heaven" was to the first Christians, something apprehended in the imagination but which had yet to find its counterpart in the world. That imagination, spiritual or national, is the most powerful thing in human affairs. Intangible itself, it moves bodies. Invisible itself, it changes visible civilisations. The temples of old gods become ruins and desolate when the imagination is withdrawn from them. When imagination withers the world becomes stagnant.

Cities ～

TOLSTOI SAID, "The town influence is our greatest danger. Towns are the places where mankind has begun to rot."

It is true, but a truth which will never secure practical recognition until the Golden Age returns. Cities are an experience which humanity must again and again pass through for the quickening of mind until the mind has acquired a momentum which will serve to sustain it in Nature. The mind of man at present is like a lamp which requires continual replenishing. There are but few who have found in themselves the Ever-Burning Lamp, which illuminates alike the city and the wilderness. Wordsworth and Thoreau used that lamp now and again. But even Thoreau found "a little languor in the afternoons", and Wordsworth, in spite of his vision of a spirit in Nature, grew dull. There is still a use for cities.

The City States

FEW INTELLECTUAL OCCUPATIONS are so fascinating as to trace back to origins the ideas of civilisation and government which are the substance of our minds. We find ourselves asking every now and then—did humanity take a wrong turning here?

The fountainhead of European civilisation lies in Greece. It is true that other streams have been tributary to that river of intellectual, aesthetic and political ideas which arose in the tiny Hellenic communities. But it was there the stream began. Beyond that there is only myth and surmise. The statesmen who to-day talk about democracy, oligarchies, despotism are intellectually talking Greek. These little city states began to grapple with the problems of government which still engage the great nation states and empires, and the rulers and statesmen of the Greek communities which flourished over two thousand years ago are in a sense still ancestor statesmen of our own political systems.

What brought about the intensive cultivation of human faculties which existed in these little city states, so that their art, their literature, drama, poetry and philosophy are still potent sources of inspiration? There never since was anything like this intensive cultivation of human life, never so rich a harvest of ideas from the cultivation of so small a population. Was there a wrong turning when the city states became an empire? Is it possible for us to evolve in our great nation states communities equal to those which flourished with but little more territory than an Irish county? The modern state has swollen, indeed, from the Greek ideal, which was that it should not contain more citizens than could be influenced by the voice of a single orator. If the orators were great men they rapidly brought their hearers into their own intellectual household. There was personal contact, and that quickens ever so much more than the cold print in which we for the most part make acquaintance with our national chiefs. Communication in the modern world tends more and more to be by way of artifice and less and less direct. Does life lose by this? Did the invention of printing lead us into the shallows and out of the deeps?

We do not really know whether it was a good thing fundamentally for humanity for the city state to develop into the great nation state, whether our mechanical inventions are good for life, whether even the invention of money was a good thing for the individual, that invention which made international trade possible and lessened the self-sufficiency of communities and the variety of occupation in the country. Of course, a magnificent defence can be made for all these things, but if we ask ourselves seriously has the quality of human life become better because of them, we must confess that we do not know, and there are many really profound minds which would gladly exchange their lot in this age of mechanical development if they could by any magic be a contemporary of Pericles, Aeschylus or Sophocles before the era of electric light, railways, steamships, printing or daily newspapers, and would feel that they had exchanged a mechanical order for a truly civilised society. Perhaps it was not so shining to the Greeks as it appears to us. Time may have washed away all but the precious metals and jewels of their life. The good life of the Greeks was urban, and since then all civilisation has been on a few square miles of stone, brick and mortar. There is a repute greater than that of Solon or Cleisthenes now waiting for the statesman who can create a rural civilisation, who will make it possible for as high a quality of life to be attained in the country as in the city.

Peace ◡

WE SHOULD DESIRE the greatest richness and variety in human life, and try to create a spirit which will balance its diversities rather than try to obliterate them. Pericles praised the Athenians of his time for this, that they listened gladly to others and did not turn sour faces on those who disagreed with them. That is the kind of spirit which should prevail in Europe, and indeed all over the world, a delight in differences of culture, in civilisations, feeling that all these contribute to enrich world culture in a way that a uniformity of life and a standardisation on whatever level of prosperity never would. In Nature diversities are balanced by some all-inclusive law in which night and day, heat and cold, centrifugal and centripetal, and all the opposites have their place. We trust far more to a profound sentiment for world peace arising among its peoples, to the awakening of a planetary consciousness, in a feeling for universal brotherhood than to any mechanisms, such as the rationalisation of industry, or universal free trade. As that world consciousness awakes it will create its own organisation, which will not be, we think, to obliterate differences but to balance them, and to see that justice is done by courts where international disputes can be adjudicated on and their judgments enforced.

Complexities

THE INDIVIDUAL MAN is a very complex creature. We remember hearing a man, his voice choked with sincere emotion, speak about pity, forgiveness and universal brotherhood, and heard the same man a quarter of an hour after, his voice hoarse with equally sincere emotion, swear that he would crush some scoundrel, take the law of him and grind him to poverty. It was not hypocrisy, but simply sincere out-pourings from the two poles of the man's dual nature not yet harmonised. If the individual is so complex, able to pray fervently, "Give peace in our time, O Lord": able also to cheer soldiers going to battle, or even to enlist himself, how are we to harmonise the infinitely more complex life of nations where the passions have created organisations for their own manifestation?

Whitehead and Religion

I FIND MYSELF much more in harmony with Whitehead when he treats of religion as something contemporary than when he begins to discuss origins. Religion, he says, so far as it receives external impression in human history exhibits four sides of itself, ritual, emotion, belief, rational-isation. He says these factors emerged in the inverse order of the depth of their religious importance. First came ritual, then emotion, then belief, then rationalisation. Now I doubt if enough is known about the origin of religion to trace it back to ritual, which, he says, is the primitive outcome of superfluous energy and leisure. It exemplifies the tendency of living bodies to repeat their own actions. Thus the actions necessary in hunting or other pursuits are repeated for their own sakes. Their repetition repeats the joy of action and the emotion of success. Emotion waits on ritual and ritual, he says, is repeated and elaborated for the sake of its attendant emotions. This is all very dubious in its relation to the origin of religion. The evolution of feeling associated, let us say, with a hunters' dance into a religious emotion is not made clear. It is just as probable, indeed I think far more prob-able, that the soul in its solitariness at the very beginning of thought began to wonder about life, and to speculate and to communicate its wonder and its thoughts to others. That is, it sprang up directly because of a natural need of the soul rather than as a by-product of some other activity. I think it would be truer to say that ritual arises because of religious feeling rather than the reverse. The truth is that all these speculations arise simply because some people do not believe in God, they do not find it natural that there should be a relation between the spirit in man and the spirit of the universe, and to explain how religions arose they have to imagine some transformation of material activities into psychic. If there is any truth in religion now, as Whitehead thinks there is, that relation between soul and Deity should have been present from the very first. Whitehead does say what I think is profoundly true when he says, "Religion is what the individual does with his own solitariness", and "If you are never solitary, you are never religious". I think if he had been obsessed with this idea when he began to speculate on the origin of religion what he wrote would be more intelligible.

A Centenary

NOBODY WHO WALKED about Dublin last week could have failed to be impressed by the evidence everywhere of the magnitude and profundity of feeling evoked by the centenary of Catholic Emancipation. What was most moving was the manifestation of religious faith in streets inhabited by the poor, where from many thousands of houses fluttered the white and golden flags. The princes of the Church in Ireland may rightly feel proud thinking of these great gatherings of their faithful, the evidence of loyalty and devotion, which were everywhere present. The memory of long persecutions endured without being overcome by them are the most precious memories for Church or nation, for they are the proof and test of character. It is easy to be fair-weather followers of religions in States which are in the ascendant; to be on the side of the most powerful, where privilege and place and profit follow ostentatious adhesion. The test of character of faith and loyalty to the Spirit or to the nation comes when to be faithful or loyal means that our material prosperity, or even life, are imperilled. The Church and people who can look back through centuries and find how multitudes stood the tests of penal laws may rightly be proud. Even those of different faiths should share that pride because of our common humanity and the proof that there is a heroic character in the nation.

In another way those celebrations, attended by such devout multitudes, in our capital city and over Ireland, are of profound interest, for they are evidence that in our modern world, in spite of secular and external activities into which men are sucked, in spite of the hard business of life which seems to demand almost all their attention, there is still underlying all that a widespread allegiance to the Spirit, to the Invisible, the Intangible, to a divine order not present to the sense, but which is apprehended and believed in by reason of some still uncorrupted spiritual atom in the soul. While there is that uncorrupted spiritual atom there is always the possibility of beauty, art, poetry, music, the lovelier things in life being born. Rationalism has never created beauty. Now that those dark cycles of persecution lie in a past that only centenarians can remember; now that there is religious freedom, we may hope that the energies which in the past were so absorbed in resistance may become creative, and the spiritual nature may manifest in literature, poetry, music, painting, architecture, as it has done elsewhere; that they will not be content with the cheap and commonplace, but will seek for a deeper initiation into beauty in their culture and civilisation. In the long run what is most beautiful wins allegiance. There is a great sentiment in our people to be moulded and directed. Religion is the high culture of the average man, and especially of the poor, who do not often have opportunity to read the great master-pieces of secular literature. By religion they have contact with eternal and universal ideas; and, while they hold to these with faith, there is the seed of a fire which can be blown to a flame by great teachers, and almost any miracle is possible in society.

This Miraculous World

IT IS REPORTED from Calcutta that the most famous of Indian scientists, Sir Jagadis Bose, has demonstrated the existence of a pulsating heart in trees and plants following upon his discovery of the possession by plants of a muscular tissue. It is now almost a generation since by marvellously delicate instruments he demonstrated the existence of a life current in metals, and showed how the current could be killed and reanimated, how it was affected by narcotics and by their antidotes. A few years ago he showed the sensitive-ness of plants, how a little mimosa plant could perceive a cloud coming up in the sky that the human eye hardly noticed. It will take a long time before these discoveries will affect our ethical sense so that we shall have a society for the prevention of cruelty to plants, and our sensation-loving Press will be able to horrify us by reporting a shocking case of cruelty to a cauliflower. The vast majority of scientific generalisations affect society but little unless they are em-bodied in some invention. We know that in every pin-point of space there is an image of the universe of light brought by waves or rays so that the eye can echo that compression of infinitude. Through wireless and broadcasting we have become practically certain that every pin-point of space is capable of holding within it an echo reverberation of the whole universe of sound, that a voice crying here goes round the world, for it may be caught up anywhere there is an instrument delicate enough. Our ears, as yet, have not the range of our eyes and cannot bring to consciousness that universe of sound as the eye brings to consciousness the universe of light. Perhaps the ear will become more sensitive in our further evolution. But it is astonishing how little this miraculous Nature science reveals to us affects our normal consciousness. We walk about with our being insensitive to the miracle our intellect is convinced of, and the intellect soon gives up the effort to civilise the whole nature and we relapse after the first wonder of hearing some new discovery into a normal unwondering commonplace. The theory of evolution was probably the scientific generalisation which most rapidly affected human consciousness. We began at once to talk about the struggle for existence and the survival of the fittest, and made these generalisations the excuse for pushing other people out of our way and for trampling upon weak nationalities. There were popularisers of that now almost obsolete Darwinian doctrine. But what genius will popularise the new and infinitely more exciting vision of Nature revealed to us by later scientists, who will make the universe suddenly appear living and spiritual to us as it really is, and not inanimate and material as our gross senses made us think? Someone will do it. We hope it will be an Irishman, a Berkeley of the twentieth century.

Reason and Intuition

ANATOLE FRANCE in the preface to the fourth series of *Life and Letters* writes: "This sacred and salutary truth lies at the bottom of all religions, that there is a safer guide for man than his reason, and that we must listen to the heart when it speaks".

Now the heart is for ever telling us of its clairvoyance, its penetrating power, it assures us of the hearts of others by some transcendental process superior to reason. Philosophers who set out to convince us by reason have never aroused convictions so deep, so widespread, as the founders of religions who rarely if ever reason, but who reveal, or assert truths, relying on the intuition of those who listened to them. Of the spirit a wise man said: "It is understood by those who do not understand it. It is not understood by those who do understand it." It may be necessary to interpret this paradox. It is this spirit which comprehends spirit, without thought. The intellect must ever deal in symbol or fantasy, and its most complete analysis still must be misapprehension, because it is symbol, not reality. It would seem that some intuition of Anatole France prompted him to suggest a faculty in man superior to the reason which assured him he could never get out of himself. It is very important. If we cannot get out of ourselves, then criticism has no objective truth. All that I say, that you say, that anybody says, is personal opinion, and its truth or falsity can never be brought to any objective test. I think we can get out of ourselves, or, to put it more truly, we can enlarge the boundaries of consciousness to take in and comprehend truly the feelings of others and can make them our own. When St. Paul spoke about becoming partakers of the Divine Nature, he seems to suggest that some transcendental enlargement of the boundaries of our being would enable us to assimilate and make part of oneself the Divine Nature and its laws.

Have we a real power of extension of ourselves into the thoughts and feelings of others, or the germ of such a power? I believe we have such a power and we use it more often than people dream. It may be rare by deliberate experiment to read the thoughts of others, as Gilbert Murray seems to have the power to do at times. But without any self-consciousness of the process I think there is a continuous reflection of the universe of life about us in our own life. The broken water surface reflects only broken images, and our minds are too agitated to permit of so clear a mirroring of another nature in our own nature that we could not fail to recognise another self in ourselves. But none the less, though the surface consciousness denies the subconsciousness or— shall we use Anatole France's term ?—the heart, it is perpetually receiving true impressions or is acting on them in defiance of reason.

Suffering

HOW ARE WE TO PROVE the existence of the soul? Some deny it is an entity and hold that it is the offspring of the blind amours of energy and substance. If there be nothing else in its ancestry than what it received from that parentage, it could not prevail against them. The soul, if it be an entity, must be self-moving. Balzac, in the most beautiful of his short stories, *Christ in Flanders*, said the will in man was nearest to what religious people call the soul. It is, I think, true that we never feel anything real in ourselves, unless at moments when the will in us is so concentrated that it can hold itself within its own being and stay itself against the stream of things. To be able to deny the clamour of emotions and desires, the apparitions of Nature, the appetites of the body, to compel them to be silent, or remote, to experience this power is to experience soul, an entity, self-moving, acting by its own inherent vitality. There are few who cultivate the will with this intensity except the saints and the ascetics who try never for an instant of their waking life to relax that unwavering concentration of the soul upon Deity. It is true men and women have suffered as much for love, or for country, or for some cause as the saints and ascetics have suffered to draw their souls nigh to God. But these have not left such intimate records of the intensifying of the will as the saints and ascetics have left.

Endurance

MEN HAVE SUFFERED so greatly for all causes, good and evil, that their endurance proves nothing except the power that is in the soul. It is this power in the psyche to sustain itself against all external government, still to persist, still to defy, obeying only the orders of the spiritual captain, which is the wonder in the records of endurance by the heroes, the saints and the ascetics.

The Two Certainties

THERE ARE TWO certainties for the soul: one is Earth and the other Heaven, and when the soul is contented with the first or absorbed by the Spirit, there is something for it to rest on. Most of us live in a mid-world between these two where there may be beauty, but there is a poison in its beauty. It is all fluctuating; the ever-changing desiring psyche is crucified between the two spheres, and has no certainty about anything. I am drawn to those who are certain and contented with either Heaven or Earth.

Religion and Fear

I OFTEN DOUBT if the barbarities in Eastern lands which we shudder at are in reality half so cruel, if they mean so much anguish, as the threat of after-torture means to those who believe in the power of another to inflict it. It wounds the spirit to the heart: its consciousness of its own immortality becomes entwined with the terror of as long enduring pain. It is a lie which the all-compassionate Father-Spirit never breathed into the ears of his children.

The Intruder

THE METHODS by which men and women try to shelter themselves from their souls are innumerable. If the superficial mind is for a moment unoccupied, a gentle tap makes it aware of the majestic outcast calling on it to be up and doing, playing its part in the cosmic purpose, and the prospect is so terrifying that the mind immediately occupies itself with bridge, or ping-pong, or crossword puzzles, and closes all relations with the unwelcome intruder. After a time the soul will give up attendance on the body as a bad job, and the body can then play ping-pong, whist, crossword puzzles, the decoding of limericks, and rest after such labours in peace, without any soul annoying it at all.

Hell's Pavement

THE TRAGEDIES in high souls are brought about less by a conflict between their virtues and their vices than by a conflict of the virtues among themselves. A man aiming at the highest will be beset by the beautiful, pleading face of some one of his good qualities which plays the part of a devil to drag him away from the highest. The devil appears in the form of wife and family, or in the mask of pity for beauty, or in the guise of philanthropy. Any of the virtues may enshrine the spirit for the moment and the others may unite to dethrone it. If we could track back the path of descent of many utterly lost and miserable souls, we would find often at the first stair of the descent into Hell some one of those beautiful, piteous, angelic faces calling for succour.

Human Nature

WE ARE CONSTANTLY being reminded how perilous is the adventure of civilisation, how the galleon sails over seas which are ungovernable, how the crew itself may become as ungovernable as the sea. The geologists tell us of sunken continents, and even in our time the occult forces in Nature break out in fires, upheavals and subsidences. Our own human nature is but partly charted and governable, and we might speculate on the conception of humanity formed by higher than human intelligences who were able to watch humanity in its wars and revolutions. The great religions, the great cultures, and the State are perpetually trying to reclaim what is elemental, unintelligible and untamed in human nature, and bring it under the domain of law.

Religion and Science

SOME WOULD HAVE RELIGION AND SCIENCE kept in water-tight compartments until they develop so that religion has no relation to the universe we see and science has no bearing on the psychic nature of man. It is much better to have the discussion so that the introverts and the extroverts of truth, both seeking sincerely for it, may not become unintelligible to each other. If we are ever to get at truth it must be by establishing an intellectual harmony between what is within us and what is without. The more the scientist knows about religion the subtler is his exploration of Nature likely to be. The more the religious know about science the more likely are they to make their doctrine appear a true interpretation of the universe.

Primitives

WE HEAR every now and then of unlettered peasants and primitives who have a wisdom which commands respect from the learned, and no doubt a more profound psychology will discover that absolute purity of mind brings with it its own vision, that the nature is thereby made sensitive to respond to messages and currents that flow through more material natures without quickening even an intuition.

Conversions

IT IS FUTILE to expect national conversions swift as St. Paul's. Only the highest genius gets a sudden illumination, or the empty and ignorant get blown by a gust of wind. The vast mass of people evolve slowly, and it is well for a nation that it is so, or its brilliance would bring it to a speedy termination, like a candle burning at both ends.

Symbols

THE SEERS and philosophers of the past mounted on each other's shoulders. None can say, so ancient are the beginnings, who first charted the invisible heavens, mid-world, heaven-world, or created symbols, gods and divine beings, populating with imaginative light that darkness which falls upon us when we close our eyes and the external world is shut out. These symbols created by the philosophers, seers and poets of the past have become familiar to us. When we turn our backs on the external world we cling to the ancient symbols, which are like stairs up which we mount to survey the world invisible. The unrevealed heaven, hell, the invisible, become real to us by intensities of feeling which rise beyond what is normal in life so that we interpret the invisible, the unmanifest, by the peaks of emotion or imagination, what is known becoming the interpreter of the unknown.

Foolishness

I HAVE ALWAYS ASSUMED that a beautiful foolishness is not altogether unpleasing to the Divine mind which has imagined the kitten chasing its own tail, and the pranks of puppies and marmosets and the flippant wanderings of butterflies as well as the moral colonies of ants and bees with their insistence on hard work and their stern dismissal of the drones. There are human beings who delight us less by their wisdom than their wit, or their gaiety, or a kind of lovely irresponsibility. They make us gay while the Marthas only make us comfortable and we are ever so much more grateful to the people who fill us with gaiety, the comfort of the mind, than we are to the people who fill our bodies with good cooking, though we would be sulky enough if the cooking was bad.

The Eternal Feminine

I REMEMBER READING a translation of a poem by a Chinese lady written five hundred years before Christ, and it was to the effect that the men came after breakfast and they talked politics all day long. The moon rose over the garden and found them still talking. "I", she said, with the self-confidence of a modern suffragette, "could have settled the whole matter with a word, but they will not listen to me. I am only a woman, fit to look after the garden and flowers and mind the baby." How near we feel to the dear creature. She might have been born in our still young century. The prattle in a famous idyll of Theocritus of the Syracusan ladies discussing their husbands and their clothes before going to the temple, gave us reason to suppose that these have been favourite subjects of conversation between women since humanity first appeared on the globe, and they have never got any deeper into it for all the discussion since prehistoric days. Such idylls, with no more profound mentality, and with no better art, will, doubtless, be written a hundred thousand years hence. We see no curve of ascent or descent in thought when we compare ancient with modern humanity.

Boxers ⟨ℓ⟩

DEMPSEY AND TUNNEY divided between them close on three hundred thousand pounds as their reward for a brief tussle in the prize-ring and a few weeks of hard physical training. One might make the ironical commentary on our civilisation that there are no men of genius, however exalted, now living on the earth who could by the nobility of their minds in open controversy with each other reap such a reward as these men do for physical fitness. A public controversy between men of genius on any high matter would never attract to any stadium such a crowd ready to pay such high prices for the excitement of a contest. But it is probably a sound instinct in humanity which maintains its interest in physical endurance, courage and indifference to pain. The vast mass of people in our civilisation except when war forces them to undergo military training tend to develop physical flabbiness in their urban employments, and the flabbier they get the more excitedly do they contemplate the trained gladiators embodying in themselves primitive strength and endurance. For this reason the prize-ring and the football match attract their thousands of spectators, and it is possible that a voice in every heart whispers to those who watch, "You ought to be strong and swift like these".

It is easy enough to denounce these conflicts as brutal, and so they are, but humanity, however at the time it may be engrossed in other things, is not going to lose or forget any of its powers, and it maintains its interest in the athlete and the fighter with some intuition, perhaps, that its own final perfection will involve superb, much-enduring bodies as well as hearts and minds that embrace the universe. The endurance of the prize-fighter is an astonishment to the flabby civilised man, and perhaps the fight awakens some physical conscience, has even moral consequences which offset the other evils of such an exhibition.

Women and Civilisation

THE BUSINESS of women is really to civilise men. No doubt men would have remained in cave dwellings if women had not insisted on proper apartments. Women did not like men to look like wild beasts, and they spun and wove and embroidered garments and put the semblance of external civilisation upon their savages. But we have lost almost all traces of aesthetic character in our national life. We have no distinctive national dress for men or women, nothing like the national character men and women preserve with so much pride in their clothing in other countries. Our women, so far back as Bishop Berkeley, began to look outside Ireland for fashion, and he interjected an inquiry in his famous *Querist*, whether they could not use Irish material, devise dresses, embroider them and make themselves as beautiful to look on as if they got all their dresses from London or

Paris. We beseech of Irishwomen to ponder over their function in national life. To our mind women never appear more unlovely than when they are hysterically urging on men to fight and kill each other; and never more noble than when they are inspiring men to create a humane society. We would like to see women in Ireland urging on the young men to make the world about them worth living in, to build halls in every village, to try in some practical fashion to realise their own dreams of an Irish civilisation.

The Social Skin

GEOLOGISTS HAVE SPECULATED much on how many million years were necessary to put a skin of cold rock and clay upon our planet, confining within those walls the wild fires and forces which even now break out in earthquake and eruption. There are in humanity passions like those slowly tamed forces pent beneath the ribs of rock. The purpose of civilisation is to put a moral skin upon those passions and subdue them to law. It is a labour of long centuries. If the skin is broken by war, or civil conflict, if the moral compact lose power and prestige, it is at once seen how much of human nature is still savage, and how much of the harmony in society was due to the consciousness that force existed in the form of law and its agents ready to overpower anti-social activities.

New Powers

IN THE EIGHTEENTH CENTURY literature and science were coming to be very great powers indeed, and through them the autocratic rule over soul and body exercised by prelate or prince was soon to suffer further domination than prince and prelate had inflicted on each other.

   With Voltaire the literature of Europe became free. It was to duck and deprecate no more, to fear no more Bastilles or exile. Soon all the wrongs inflicted on literature and science by the old autocracies would be revenged, the philosophers would put kings in prison, cut off their heads even, while those who survived had their claws pared. They became, as Frederick said to himself, "lame and cracked lions". Not a king in Europe would dare now to have a controversy with a great writer. Even the last autocrat in Russia did not dare to interfere with Tolstoi. Europe had made Tolstoi more powerful than the Czar, as it made Voltaire in his time its intellectual king. What one now wonders is what new powers will arise to supersede the intellectuals. Will it be the Communists, who discipline literature so sternly in Russia, or the Fascists, who discipline the Press so sternly in Italy? Are Communist and Fascist portents of the same thing, the machine which is to kill the soul? It is certain there will be new rulers. What will they be?

The Greatest European

THERE WERE NO OBSTACLES preventing the union of States in North America. They were caught young and trained in the way they should go. The nationalities in Europe are old and have got so fixed that it is possible the only way in which the United States of Europe can be brought about will be by the emergence of some conqueror of the Napoleon or Caesar type who would bring them all by force under one Government. It would, doubtless, be very unpleasant for a century or so, but it is possible that the great-grandchildren of those dragged into a European confederation might look back on the conqueror who made so great a State as the greatest European who ever existed.

Dictators ⟶

THE AVERAGE MAN generally knows that he knows nothing about either economics or politics or world affairs, and he does not believe his neighbours know any more than he knows himself, but he believes there are people who do know, and, when the strong man appears, the people—who in the mass are feminine—adore him. The reaction towards democracy will set in again when the first strong men are succeeded by incompetents, and the people will discover that they are as wise as their ruler and will despise him and make themselves rulers once more.

Rivalries

THE POLITICAL LIFE of a country is always benefited by the rivalry of ideals, so long as the game is played, and the conflict is kept on the plane of reason and imagination. If attempts are made to win by force they merit the condemnation given in Scripture to those who try to win their goal, not entering by the strait gate, but climbing over the wall like thieves and robbers. Whatever is true or practical or beautiful in a policy inevitably affects those who are first opposed to it, and they are forced to make it their own.

The Dublin Record Office

LAST YEAR when certain political vintages had gone to the heads of young Irishmen, they were prepared to offer any public building as a sacrifice to the deity of the vintage. One noble building and a great deal of Irish history went as near to heaven as a high explosive could lift it, but the sacrifice was not accepted because scattered leaves of history rejected by heaven were found on many roofs and in many back gardens.

Intensities

IT IS NATURAL ENOUGH when war is being waged that passions should proclaim themselves as everlasting. If they did not seem so men would not risk life or take life. But human nature passes away from its intensities because life would be burned up if they persisted. After conflict a time comes when, whatever the lips utter, the storm in the inner nature has subsided, and it is possible then for magnanimity to be met by good humour, if not by affection. Magnanimity has profound political results. It affects first of all the on-lookers, the mass of citizens, who act the part of the Chorus in Greek drama, awarding praise or blame, delivering moral judgments, and through them the protagonists or actors are again influenced.

The Pack

AS THE IMAGINATIVE LIFE dwindles in intensity we balance the loss by becoming more social. For the soul that once contained multitudes we substitute the external crowd. As civilisation establishes itself the psychology of the crowd, the opinions shared in common with many, replace the meditation of the solitaries who originally created national cultures. The tendency is to think in packs, and the solitary who persists in thinking for himself is regarded by the pack as the enemy of society, though in truth he is the last remaining spark of true life in it.

The pack are the inheritors of what once were truths.

How could an idea once be really true and not be true now?—
I hear a puzzled or irritated query. What I mean is that ideas
are only true and good for us when they are identical with
character, when they inform the whole nature. Then they
are creative. They manifest in conduct, in art, in architecture, in poetry. A change takes place when the idea establishes itself as an externality which people accept because of
what it once created. It is on the surface but not any longer
in the depths. It does not animate the whole being, and it
brings about nothing but external harmonies of opinion, and
society holding to correct opinions is like that famous tea-
party of respectables which sat "all silent and all damned!"
Ireland is smothered with ideas which have become exter-
nally accepted and which create no longer because they have
descended from spirit to matter, from the creative phase to
the mechanistic. I do not believe in the inevitability of the
Spenglerian sequences, of original creative culture, external
civilisation or mechanism and death. That only happens to
those who will not think for themselves, who are satisfied to
become inheritors only. The spirit in man can be as vital and
creative to-day or to-morrow as it was yesterday. Therefore
we should cherish the aristocratic intellect which will not
follow the pack but goes on imaginative adventures. We
should mistrust any culture which has ceased to be creative
but is only opinionative. I do not yet know whether the
Gaelic is a vital culture or merely an external drapery as
misleading as the pelt of a lion disguising an ancient and
decrepit sheep. I hope it is the first. I am suspicious about it
because it has a pack cry. The creative soul makes its own
garments. Let the soul but speak and the symbols it uses
become sacred as any invented in the past.

The Aftermath of the War Mood

AFTER EVERY PERIOD of excitement there is reaction. The cold fit follows the hot fit. For a year we existed in a delirium of political idealism, in which economic considerations were waved aside as indicating materialism of spirit, though the national soul and body politic must always be dependent on each other, for there can be no high culture, no civilisation, without an economic basis. In that delirium railways were wrecked, bridges destroyed and houses burned. If the economic ruin of Ireland was not to be made complete, an army had to be created; and armies in active operation are the most expensive of national luxuries or necessities. The cold fit has succeeded the hot fit: and, in this psychic chill, people have begun to realise that national expenditure has gone far beyond national revenue; that a national debt has been incurred, and that everything must be paid for, railways, bridges, houses and army. No nation can escape payment of its debts unless its people are prepared to endure greater extremities of misery than would be entailed by acceptance of the obligation. It is no wonder that the word "economy" should now be heard on every side.

Now, an armed minority in a country, menacing the Government, has exactly the same ruinous effect on its finance as competition in armaments between great States. These think of possible risks and build against each other in the air, on the seas and under the seas. On land they call up and train ever more men, and the cost mounts up and up until the burden becomes intolerable to life, and the threat of internal revolution is added to the foreign menace. No Government after passing through a year of ruinous conflict can lightly risk a renewal of such a struggle. Individuals may take risks which the State cannot take. The individual may sacrifice himself and all he possesses, enduring suffering and poverty for a cause he deems noble. It is his right, while he only sacrifices himself. Such nobilities are rarely possible for the rulers of States, for too weighty destinies hang on their action, and that is why the idealists generally denounce the statesmen, who may sacrifice themselves, but may not without a clear mandate sacrifice the nation, the millions whose interests they were put into power to defend. So while a menace persists they must continue to provide against it, increasing taxation, borrowing and burdening the State with debt, heading to the gulf in which nations are drowned when they cannot raise more money from their own citizens and are destitute of credit abroad. So services necessary to civilisation are starved, and poverty, ignorance and despair beset the people.

We see quite clearly it is to such a *finale* militant Republicans are herding the people of this country, and it is quite possible that they do not foresee the logical consequences of their policy. We assume in all sincerity that they are militant through love of country, and we ask them is there not a better path to take than one which ends inevitably in such wretchedness. There are always two paths for men to take to a national ideal. The higher human faculties of imagination and intellect may be used to draw their countrymen to their side. There is the way of physical force for those who prefer to live in the bodily plane. We believe no cause, however intrinsically noble in itself, but will lead to the degradation of the finer attributes of humanity if it involves the people in a prolonged conflict. All parties at present exist in a state of exasperated nerves, and their mood of anger prompts them too hastily to commit themselves to declarations of irreconcilable hostility. They do not realise that the mood of warfare in Ireland is an infection caught from a warring Europe, as definitely an infection as the catching of fever in an epidemic. The nurse forgives the ravings of the fever patient, and we must forgive each other a great deal of wild talk and action. The patient recovering from fever does not think it a matter of personal pride to continue the ravings of his delirium, nor should we as a people continue the hatreds of the last passionate year.

The State

WHAT IS A NATION? Is it anything fixed by divine revelation? We know it is not. The problem is not discussed in the Scriptures. Does the existence of nationality depend on race? We know it does not. We know that the most undoubted nationalities are of the most complex race origins, including our own. Does it depend on geography, on clear natural limitations of territory? We know all over Europe that distinct nationalities exist with only artificial frontiers between theirs and adjoining states. Does it depend on language? If so, Switzerland has little right for separate existence as an independent nation; the United States has no rights; nor have the Spanish-speaking nations in America. It will be hard to find any definition of what constitutes nationality other than this: that it is an identity of consciousness or interest which has grown up in regard to certain things among a number of people, and which makes them inclined to act as a single entity in relation to other human groups. It is, we think, impossible to argue on abstract principles in regard to such a human group, which is obviously the product of an evolution in human society.

Nationality, as distinct character and culture in old civilisations, was almost unconscious as breathing. It was only as it was passing away that the self-consciousness of nationality and the desire to preserve it became a passion, and that passion expressed itself, less in an actual return to ancient habits of the ancient national individuality, than in a concentration in the idea of the State, its powers and its independence. In normal times the average citizen concerns himself but little with constitutional problems. He is interested in business, love, religion, family, culture, recreations; and the State is on the remote horizon of his mind. It is only in times of national crisis that the idea of State or nation emerges very powerfully and a man is ready to risk life, to desert family and occupation, in order to support or save these entities, which he is contented in his normal mood to let be as they are if they do not interfere too much with his own life. This attitude is, on the whole, wise, because the State exists for the individual and not the individual for the State. The latter claim is only pressed when the nation is in peril; and, when the peril is averted, the majority with relief pursue their private occupations, which may be as noble as if they had devoted themselves entirely to the service of the nation.

There never was a State of which the high idealist could not say with Omar Khayyám:

> . . . could you and I with him conspire
> To grasp this sorry scheme of things entire,
> Would we not shatter it to bits, and then
> Re-mould it nearer to the heart's desire?

But before beginning with exaltation on this work of shattering, one must have the superior image clear in the mind and a certainty that there are the materials to build the image.

Unities

WE SURMISE in some ancient civilisations a unity in the life of their people such as we can find no parallel for in our existing civilisation. The ancient Egyptian civilisation appears to our eyes to betray such a unity of its art, architecture, literature, religion and science that it might all have sprung from the plans of one mighty artist. In the civilisation of ancient Greece there is a unity somewhat similar, if less long-lived. After the Middle Ages that unity of life becomes more and more broken up. We get into an age of unrelated specialisations. No vision unites society, and the tendency is for everybody, released from the domination of the great spiritual clans, or the great national clans, to wander on a way of his own, seeking for the truth and the life, and rarely coming to a truth which has life or to a life which has beauty. The arts, literature, civilisation, the city, all have suffered some spiritual loss.

How can the unity be recreated? By vision. But then we ask sadly, how is vision to be recreated? Can it be by first kindling enthusiasm? If so, the grandiose conception of many energies working together to build the Heavenly City on Earth might awaken it. But vision cannot be so kindled, we think. It cannot be imparted. It is won in the self by sacrifice, agony, will and inspiration, and the science of the soul is but little known, and most who come to vision hardly know themselves how it is attained.

Emigration

ONE OF THE REASONS of the rural exodus about which so much has been written is the lack of intellectual life, culture, refinement, amusement and social life in too many rural districts. People put up with all this before the railway and steamship came into being to transfer humanity by the million from one country to another. We in Ireland have exported how many millions within memory of the oldest living? Some, indeed, departed because of economic conditions here, but a vast number, especially during the past quarter of a century, went simply because life seemed to be gayer elsewhere. There is probably not a parish in Ireland where letters have not been received and pondered over which came from New York, Chicago, Boston or other great cities which seem more wonderful than mythic Babylon or Nineveh to people who had gone from thatched cabins in a poor country. These reports exercise a magnetic power over the imagination, and where there is no contrary magnetism created by an intense vitality beside them, no enthusiasm devoted to making a civilisation in the native land, then the most powerful magnet attracts, and so populations diminish. It is not governments alone which can stay this ebbing of the human tide away from the area they administer. It needs a strong impulse among the people themselves, determined that their nation shall not be a failure, to offset the attractions of distant civilisations.

Drunkenness

IF YOU CAN IMPLANT disgust at drunkenness in the mind of youth, in the vast majority of cases it will remain throughout life. We could hardly imitate those Greeks who brought their children into the presence of drunken slaves in order to disgust them with intemperance, but it might be possible to use the cinema to create a similar feeling. We believe ourselves that the worst deeds done in Ireland, whether to us by Black and Tans or by our own people in their fury with each other, were done under the influence of drink. It is not really easy for a man to raise the devil in himself by his own natural resources. The ancient devil-worshippers used to pour out blood to raise the demon. The modern way is to swallow a stiff dose of alcohol.

Humanitarians

M AN'S RIGHT to ill-treat his own kind is one of the most
jealously guarded of his prerogatives, and the moment
there is reference to the high mortality among children in
our cities or the conditions of housing of the poor, a numb-
ness of feeling is evident among great numbers of people who
have a subconscious conviction that you can only relieve the
poor by taxing those who are wealthier, and their hearts do
not stretch to it. It is, perhaps, just as well to begin by supplicating kindness for cattle, dogs, birds and other creatures,
because nobody as yet has suggested that considerate treatment of these will lead on to social revolution.

There are reservations, however, even with regard to the
treatment of animals. When that most noble and chivalrous
of living journalists, Henry Nevinson, protested that he could
see nothing in the hunting of animals for sport but the satisfaction of the cruel instincts in mankind, he aroused one of
our popular instructors, who explained that the people who
hunted animals were unexcelled by any section of humanity
for their kindness to the dumb creation. One almost divined
behind the indignant words that the religious instincts of the
writer were shocked, that God was conceived of as the Great
Sportsman who had created certain creatures to be hunted
for the enjoyment of man, and that, as these creatures were
made for sport, they must be at their happiest when hunted.
An Eastern Sage suggested that habits that were evil might
best be got rid of by doing something else rather than by
direct attacks on the evil habit, and that is a policy well
worth exploration by reformers. We are not sure that there
is not something of the instinct of cruelty they condemn in
others in the gusto with which they thwack and denounce
persons who thwack and ill-treat animals.

That there are many hard and insensitive spots in the Irish

soul is incontrovertible. The business of the present writer once condemned him to drive in cars all over the country, and he was made unhappy by the number of drivers who began to whack their horse steadily from the moment the car left the hotel until it arrived at its destination. The whacking of the poor beast was an employment indulged in almost mechanically, and the moral reflection at the close of the last paragraph was made because we began, with some pleasure, imagining ourselves possessed of a whip and laying it with an unmechanical zest on the shoulders of the driver. The treatment of cattle has been exposed recently, and it seems at last that something is going to be done about it. The ashplant is to be taken out of the hands of the drovers. So long as it was only the immortal soul of the drover that was in danger because of its cruelty there was no particular stir, but when it was proved that the cattle deteriorated in value by from twopence to fourpence per lb. because of the bad treatment they received on their way to market, and that the yearly loss to Ireland ran into millions, business woke up. There is no lack of sensitiveness where money is concerned.

The Danger of Ideas

IDEAS UNDOUBTEDLY are dangerous things, far more dangerous than high-explosive shells. Indeed the latter are but the shower of stars descending after some idea had first gone up like a rocket. Without the initial energy of the idea there would have been no shells. One of the wisest of sages in the oldest and wisest of countries, China, said, "To see things in the germ, this I call intelligence". Can we discover dangerous ideas in their infancy? A clever writer during the war traced its origin to an idea of Hegel, which seemed, at the stage of publication a century ago, to involve no danger to society.

Hegel was speculating in the fashion of German philosophers about the universe, and it seemed to him that God, or the Absolute, as philosophers prefer to call the Deity, insisting on precise definitions, would never have undertaken to build up the universe except for some purpose. In the usual fashion of philosophers, he imagined Deity in his own image and supposed that Deity was educating Itself and became self-conscious seeing Its own being reflected in Its creation. This idea, however reprehensible from a theological point of view, did not seem to involve the conscription of forty million men and their slaughter of each other in any inevitable way. But mark what followed. Having this idea about the Absolute becoming self-conscious, naturally a logical mind must apply it, not merely to the whole universe, but to the little atom we call earth. The Absolute was becoming self-conscious here also in the evolution of world history. It was not through the individual this self-realisation came but through multitudes—the State, in fact. The State was the Absolute in manifestation. So far the philosopher. Then the State in Prussia realised this was exactly the philosophy of itself it wanted. Hegel was made professor of history at Berlin University. By the middle of last century there were more than two dozen professors of history in German universities all teaching the Absolutism of the State. Everything that was intelligent and belonging to the ruling classes passed through a bath of Hegelianism, and gradually the idea was popularised: and because no people talked so much about the Absolute the next stage was to suppose that in some special sense the German people were the Absolute and had a divine mission to make the world in their own image. Now, one can see how an idea which seemed harmless can involve consequences so terrible as the European war if allowed to grow. Hegel himself saw Napoleon riding through the streets of his city, and went home and said, "I have seen the World Spirit riding by". Now if Napoleon had that insight the

Chinese philosopher praised, and had seen the germ of an idea so dangerous to life in that philosopher's head, and had chopped it off, would we have had the European war with the Free State as a by-product? These are portentous questions. It occurs to one, ideas being more dangerous than prussic acid, which cannot be used with like devastating effect on multitudes, that all ideas should be discouraged. But that is impracticable. We could not even continue our present imperfect civilisation without ideas. Our civilisation is, in fact, so uncomfortable that people must, undeterred by the dangers, go on seeking for new ideas. But how am I to know if I give birth to an idea that it will not in fifty years make Europe a wilderness? It may be the very idea some young man wanted to start him on his career as a world Caesar or it may inspire some beautiful girl to become another Helen and cause the wreckage of not one Troy but a hundred cities greater than that celebrated village. Look at the effect of Griffith's generalisation in two words—*Sinn Fein*. It arrived at a high expansive power in a dozen years and was ignited, perhaps prematurely, by the concussion of the final explosion of Hegel's idea in Europe. If I preach universal brotherhood, which seems a gentle idea, it may seize hold of men's minds until there would be no liberty left in the world. We can see how the idea of liberty unrestricted shatters all idea of world or even national solidarity. We are everywhere surrounded with perils. We cannot do with ideas. Neither can we do without them. The idea, perhaps a dangerous one, occurs to me, that every idea has its antitoxin; the idea which neutralises its effect; and a college of sages might be founded to examine all new ideas to discover whether they are dangerous. They might, for example, take a group of young men for experimental purposes from some university and shut them up with some new idea for a month, making a pure culture of it as the bacteriologist in his gelatine makes a pure culture of germs in order to see what they will develop into. If the young men emerge without having fought, the idea might be passed. If it had partially good and partially bad effects, the antitoxin or contrary idea might be sought out and applied. Nature does in a fashion do this. In fact the German idea that the people exist for the State was a reaction from a French idea that the State existed for the people. But the reactions in Nature are slow, as doctors know. The body attacked by a disease too often generates the antitoxin so slowly that the person dies, so doctors at once proceed at the first symptom to inoculate the invalid with germs calculated to neutralise the deleterious substances. Could we not hasten the injections of the antitoxin to dangerous ideas in society by injecting contrary ideas? The trouble is that when people have intellectual diseases and are completely obsessed by an idea, they never want to hear of any other and offer the most stubborn resistance to the injection of the saving idea. We are suffering in Ireland from the fever of ideas without balance, and the only solution we can suggest is an intense interest in ideas, and the instant balancing of them in order to prevent wars, hunger-strikes, labour-strikes and lockouts, all having their origin in unbalanced ideas about the universe, liberty, fraternity, rights of property, rights of life, and so forth. I have doctored myself for years in the way I suggest, and, without achieving a complete cure, I can say that I no longer have intellectual fevers of the intensity I once had, and almost automatically after swallowing an idea I swallow its opposite. It has become a habit, but I find it exposes me to danger from those with one idea festering in their minds. But what idea is without its dangers? Not even mine.

MORE
CRITICISM

MORE
CRITICISM

Free Verse

I AM SURE aeronauts in their first perilous conquest of air
feel nothing equal to the delight felt in dream by those
who float over hills buoyed up by will alone, or who drop
down gently nigh the dew-wet grass withheld by will alone
from a complete fall. When we fly in dream we achieve the
unprecedented. We are always the first to soar into the high
element. We do not doubt the power will be with us always.
We have that delight in aerial dream because we are free
from mechanics. The magical will suffices as guide when we
soar, or as saviour when we sink. The dream of being free
from mechanics, of song without the thraldom of a metrical
system, has of late years allured many poets who launched
themselves on the poetic air in free verse. More often they
sank rather than flew, and were embedded deeply in the clay
of prose. When I read Whitman long ago I was intoxicated
with new wine and another like him would have made me
take ship for the New World. But even Whitman, the
pioneer, when he had not the afflatus, had as many poetic

disasters as the pioneers in aerial navigation. He would cry out, "Land of beef! Land of pork! Land of cotton!" in an ecstasy incomprehensible to any, except perhaps a dealer in those commodities who had made a profitable contract. He was not writing poetry. He was not even writing prose. He had, in his fall from his own heights, penetrated an obscure sub-soil beneath prose, and that is the dark hell of literature. What example allured these poets? Had they any successes? Have they really made words to sing and soar by some inner power without the aid of metric formulae, as we soar in dream without aeroplane or engine? Poets have always delighted in certain passages in the old English translation of the Bible where the wild words rise into ecstasy, and there is a melody which cannot be measured by accent or quantity. Who is there who has not chanted to himself the exultant verses beginning:

> Lift up your heads, O ye gates.

There are many other passages, with a graver music, but all with a winged elation prose never attains. Walt Whitman was the first considerable poet to attempt sustained flight in song, discarding traditional metrical formulae. Is Whitman's poetry ever song? Yes, at times. But he had no sustained mastery over the power that lifted the lines occasionally and made them soar to the sense even as the lines of Shelley soar and sing. Without this rare afflatus *Leaves of Grass* fails as song, however exciting in idea, however thrilling as emotion. But does not this sing to the sense and imagination?

> Come, lovely and soothing Death,
> Undulate round the world, serenely arriving, arriving,
> In the day, in the night, to all, to each,
> Sooner or later, delicate Death.

That, and all that is after written in the *Chant of Death*, suggests the possibility of a new poetry with a beautiful, ever-varied music like the curves of water flowing up the sands, or the curves of birds in flight, always lovely, yet never quite the same curve. The form into which a poet casts his thought reacts on the imagination, which half unconsciously fits itself for the form, and the besetting sin is declamation, the asserting of things rather than the expression of them, being oratorical rather than poetical, to be fluent rather than concentrated. There has been no austere master writing in free verse, distilling and redistilling words and thought until nothing but pure gold remains. In all the *Leaves of Grass* we doubt if there are more than three hundred lines where the miracle is wrought, which satisfy us as song, though otherwise imagination may be excited and the heart be full as we read.

There are many things beautiful to the mind written in free verse, but the angel who presides over hearing shakes its head and murmurs, "No, it does not remind me of the music of the spheres", just as the angel who presides over vision refuses to accept the art of the Cubists as symbolic of Platonic or any other abstract ideas. I speak of the angels who preside over the senses, because in the deeps of hearing, in the deeps of seeing, there is an aesthete who relates sound and vision to some transcendental perfection of its own; and along with mere intellectual comprehension there is an intuition which declares, "This is delicate and beautiful. That is ugly and harsh". We may never know more until we are in Paradise, and the divine image in us, purified of dross, becomes conscious of its ancestry in the Fountain of Beauty. Until then we can only guess at beauty. Nobody can utter infallible judgments. There can be no exactitude over the arts as there is in mathematics. When I say this is lovely as thought or sound I am saying something I can never prove. The nearest we can come to certitude is general agreement among cultivated people interested in the arts.

Free verse was devised that the poet might have greater

freedom in form, that rhythm and music might change endlessly with changing mood. But too many have used this
form to say what might as well have been said in prose.
Though it seems easier to write, it is really more difficult to
succeed with free verse than with accented poetry. The poets
who threw away rhyme and regular beat, in their desire for
freedom, too often discarded assonance, contrast of vowel
and consonant, tone, harmony, all that makes for beauty of
sound. Rhyme and regular stress can indeed go, but if quality
of sound goes then art is gone, and what pleasure is there in
reading verse where there is no quality of sound; such music
as delights us in:

A shielded scutcheon blush'd with blood of queens and kings.

To write poetry, whether one uses traditional metrics or
free-verse forms, is to essay the highest spiritual adventures,
and every word should be weighed as if the space it occupies
was more valuable than diamonds, and not a line be allowed
to pass that is not like a living thing shapely enough to keep
companionship with the creatures of melody created by the
great masters. One may not succeed in this, but it is in this
mood one should write poetry.

The Secret of Verbal Music

WHENEVER POETRY falls into the hands of the prosodists
the poet feels a little uneasy, for the prosodist is like
a man of science measuring the works of the Creator. The
poet, as he writes, is, we believe, unconscious of these
measurements, as most of us are unconscious that we balance
ourselves as we walk along. We learned how to balance ourselves in childhood—it is now instinctive. So it is possible
there are many poets who know nothing of the rules of
prosody and who yet by inspiration make their poems to

suggest flowers. We know one quite famous poet who did not know anything about scansion and who did not know what spondees, iambics, anapaests or dactyls were. Yet his verses sang as well as his contemporaries'. The wild words fly up to the poet's brain in composition, and metrical marvels are wrought which are well worth investigating, though if the resulting pattern of sound had been present to the poet's imagination beforehand he could not have written at all because it would have seemed too complicated. A work truly fascinating to poets, as well as to their readers, might be made by taking some fifty or hundred of the loveliest verses in the language and subjecting them to minute analysis so that assonance, contrast of vowel and consonant, pattern, tone, stress, all that goes to make a quality of sound might be made clear as far as possible. The study of accent by itself is a little mechanical. What is important in the technique of verse is the means by which a quality of sound is maintained, the quality which the angel of hearing loves to caress and murmur over and over. Now we are but little helped to this discovery by even the strictest examination of metrics, accent or quantity, for the writer of verse may obey all the rules and yet not write a musical line. The secret of verbal music is to be found in some relation of vowels and consonants to each other, either in the harmonies they make or in the contrasts by which they make each other to vibrate, as orange in a picture makes any blue in it to shine. The harmonies are easily discoverable but the contraries in sound are not yet tabulated, and until this is done the secret of verbal music will elude the scientist.

A Gaelic Literature

WILL THERE BE a new literature in Gaelic? That is worth discussing. Love can draw upon such endless supplies of blindness we need not fear that any element of reason which creeps into our meditation would discourage a single enthusiast. The enthusiasts are certain there will be a literature. But I wonder was it for that purpose Nature blinded them with love, and made some go to prison rather than write their names in English upon their apple-carts? No literature is of value unless it includes works by real thinkers and many men of genius. Now if a man of genius can choose whether he will write in a language spoken by three million people, few of whom have acquired a habit of reading, or in a language spoken by nearly two hundred million people, including his own countrymen, what language will he choose? The poet, the story-teller, the historian, the man of science, all desire readers and that they might have them most abundantly. If they be men of genius they will desire to devote all their lives to their work, and will hope to live by it. What life would there be for a man of genius writing in Gaelic? He must be stoical as Epictetus, take vows of poverty and forswear as many comforts as Thoreau at Walden. Is it likely men of genius will give up the hope all genius has of imparting its own imagination to myriads? I admit a man of genius will write in the language in which he can express himself most perfectly, and a great poet knowing Gaelic well and English badly would undoubtedly write in Gaelic whether he starved or not. But everyone in Ireland will know English intimately, and there will be the choice. What will it be? Nature did not think it worth while blinding me with love, or perhaps it left me blind. Hence I have to ask these questions.

A second consideration is whether Gaelic has evolved

sufficiently to make it equal to mirroring the modern mind with all its psychological subleties, its economic and scientific complexities. Yeats, who had written some beautiful tales, using the full resources of English, rewrote some of them in a dialect akin to that used by Lady Gregory and other writers, a dialect based on peasant speech. The revised tales had beauty, as with all Yeats writes, but the delicacies of sentiment in the earlier versions were omitted, the quarter-tones and the half-tones, because the dialect was not equal to expressing delicate shades of mood and feeling. Would there be a similar difficulty in trying to make Gaelic, a language anciently fashioned by poets and story-tellers and later modified by peasants, a medium for expression by the modern man with all his complex interests? I could not answer the question myself, and I referred it to two high authorities. One assured me that Gaelic was equal to anything, and the other high authority confirmed my worst doubts. They had both edited Gaelic texts and both have high repute.

The heroic enthusiast will not be troubled by my perplexities and questionings. Nature has gifted him with a faith which has already removed one mountain and he is ready to confront a whole range of mountains, and it is such an astonishing universe in which we exist that he may be right. I have walked round my mountain, and as a result of my survey suggest the purpose for which Nature fitted the modern Gael with enthusiasm might possibly be to bring the Irish to-day into contact with Gaelic literature and tradition, so that the Gaelic spirit might incarnate in a world language and affect not merely Irish but world sentiment. Gaelic literature is the great almost untapped reservoir in Europe of primitive natural imagination and beauty.

As that extraordinary bardic literature, so much richer in imagination than the ballad poetry which influenced Scott, becomes more widely known, may we not hope Irish writers of genius will see in its legendary heroes and demigods the noblest symbols for the expression of their own emotions? That bardic literature was written at a time when little was prized except the elemental virtues, and the study of it excites the spirit in an age of complex thought, when people are praised for scientific attainment or intellect or other things which are only good or bad as they are associated with fine or ignoble character. We feel when reading many of the ancient tales that we are travelling in the realms of gold, and discover it with all the breathless excitement with which Keats imagined his adventurers gazing on the Pacific "silent upon a peak in Darien". But because I desire by these speculations or questionings to evoke the ideas of Gaelic enthusiasts about the future evolution of their own language let none declare I am opposed to Gaelic. I am only filled with a spirit of reasonable scientific inquiry, and poke my pen into a nest of wild bees not to destroy the bees but to see what will happen.

The Reading of Poetry

IN JAPAN the picture-lover deals delicately with art. He does not crowd his walls with pictures, making his house like a gallery, but displays them slowly, one after another. He will hang one picture in a room for a week, and then it is withdrawn and another picture takes its place. It is the only scrap of knowledge I have about Japanese character, and it pleases me. I hope it is true. I feel that just as a biologist could construct a whole animal from a fragment of bone, so could I, by brooding upon this single custom, deduce the whole character of Japanese civilisation.

The surest way of becoming blind to art is to walk about national galleries, and the houses of great collectors, stopping for a moment before each picture. We think we have seen the picture in that moment, but we have never seen a picture until we have seen through it and have recreated the vision and feeling of the artist in ourselves. We cannot go into the profundities so swiftly as the trampers of galleries seem to believe possible. The artist may have brooded for weeks on his work, and what there is in it is not to be discovered at a glance.

The Japanese have discovered a ritual by which the person who looks at a picture has time to make his own the vision of the artist. He looks at one picture only for days, and it is not too long to look if the artist is truly great. I saw a Chinese landscape in a museum at Washington, and I feel I could have been shut up with that marvellous imagination of earth for a month and would not have exhausted its enchantment. But there is no similar ritual about reading poetry, which is heaped on us in volumes and anthologies, and the eye travels from line to line, from verse to verse, from page to page, just as tourists trot around the great galleries thinking they have seen when they are really blind. There is no ritual of reading poetry so that only one poem is read at a time, is brooded on until imagination and feeling are recreated or reincarnated in us. Perhaps if the poets printed their lyrics one at a time, and sold them for a penny, sixpence, or a shilling, those who read would be constrained to brood over what they read. There would not be other pages to turn to, drawing them away from a beauty they had not fully comprehended, to read just as superficially another and yet another poem.

There is in every work of genius not only what is consciously in the mind of the genius, but much that is unknown to himself. Emerson speaks of the great architect as building better than he knew, and Socrates says that in the poet there is a daemon who speaks through him truths from a profounder life than the conscious.

If we could truly get to the depth of any beauty it would

lead us into paradise. Every perception of beauty is also a perception of truth. Another poet held a flower in his hand and said of it that if he knew it to its inmost being he would know heaven and earth together. As we sink to these deeps of feeling we are in another sense recreating ourselves, raising the psyche up to the imagination of its perfection which was in the mind of the Lord. It is, I think, no less true of ourselves, than of the flowers and trees of which it is stated in Genesis that He made every flower *before* it was in the field, and every herb *before* it grew; that there is an ideal of ourselves in the Divine Imagination. It is only by intense brooding on what is beautiful we come to these depths in poetry and in ourselves, and that is why I plead for unhurried reading. Anyone who will read in this unhurried way will find beauty becoming a living thing in themselves, and they will be nearer to earth as it was before the Fall, and have some vision of the enchantment of the universe and of beauty, the reward of all who will fly from surfaces to depths. If they do so they will know that the Golden Age has never passed away but is always about us, and it is a vision which can be regained by any who will light some of the candles in the many mansions of the spirit.

Myth and Folk-Tale

THE UNWRITTEN IMAGINATIONS strangely have lasted longer than the written. Generation after generation passed on the folk-tales, and with but little essential difference, for the folk-lorists have found tales almost identical in plot among people sundered by ocean and continent, and the common fountain from which these tales came must have been welling in periods antecedent to history.

What is the explanation? Some, indeed the majority of folk-lorists, regard the folk-tales as survivals of the imaginations of primitive humanity, early exercises in the art which later gave us a Homer, a Dante and a Shakespeare. I confess I have my doubts about that scientific conception known as "primitive humanity", in spite of popular volumes in which our forebears are portrayed for us as hairy anthropoids with club, bow legs, enormous fangs and retreating foreheads. The archaeologists are every year pushing back the origins of civilisation. There is every reason now to suppose that ten thousand years ago in Egypt there were civilisation, arts, sciences of a high order, and the people who were such artists were in no way below our own time in mentality. There is an ivory carving of a woman's head supposed to be pre-glacial. As an artist I deduce from that head with its head-dress that the women of that period were pretty and fascinated the male, that they decorated their heads as they do to-day, in fact that femininity was fully developed with all its arts and graces, and it is impossible to imagine this of a single woman without believing that a civilisation existed about her. If this is true, what, then, becomes of the theory that the folk-tales are survivals of the primitive imagination of humanity?

Is it not more likely that the world has seen civilisation after civilisation appearing and disappearing times beyond calculation, and that what we know as myth and folk-tale is not primitive at all, but the decayed fragments of once mighty religions or literatures shrunk from their living rich-ness to be mere skeletons of themselves, yet with the articu-lation of the bones preserved ready for imaginative poet or story-teller to clothe them once more with life and renew their original shapeliness. Great poetry has been created out of primitive myth. The *Prometheus* of Aeschylus and the *Prometheus Unbound* of Shelley are examples. But who can say that that primitive myth was not the shrivelled residue of what was once mighty religion? The cultural history of earth shows how a folk version of one great religion may become the starting-point of another still greater.

Under the ruins of Troy lay the ruins of a still earlier city, beneath that again lay the foundations of another ancestor city. All these had their civilisations, their culture, their religion, their arts, their sciences. The civilisation decayed, the life went out of it. The red desert crept over its prey, the great religions, the great epics and tales which were the cultural life of the civilisation shrivel into folk-tales. Then something desirable in the site draws men there again. A new city grows. The folk-tales are expanded once more into great religious myths, great epics, great stories, and again there is natural decay, or a Helen may have lured her lovers to redeem her, and the tall towers are destroyed, and again the red desert crawls over the ruins, and the soul of the culture survives as myth and folk-tale. This cultural origin of myth or folk-tale seems to explain better than the primitive babbling theory the profound spiritual element we discover so often in myth and folk-tale, and which makes them a treasure-house for the poet. How comes this spiritual element? Is it that the fairy-tale was once a religious myth, and the fall of the gods into fairies, hobgoblins, leprechauns, cannot conceal their original aristocracy? Or can we say of the wildest tales what Neander said of the Gnostics, that we must remember in considering their speculations that the mind of man is made in the image of God, and therefore even in its wildest imaginations it follows an image of truth? What has been passed down through countless years may have come through such a test, and the king's son, the princess, the ogres, the witches, the good fairies may stand as symbols of powers in the spirit of man. Though we do not know them by such names, yet the adventures of the folk heroes may truly correspond to adventures of the spirit, conflicts between the bright power and the dark powers in ourselves.

Romance ～え～～つ

DURING THE YEARS some speak of as the romantic period in Irish history, I remember how slight was the interest felt in romance or drama, how these receded from the imagination. While lorries thronged with black-clad, sinister folk rushed through our thoroughfares, every rifle held for instant use, when we lay at nights brooding on the rattle of rifles and automatics, and when rumour was whispering the names of Collins and Mulcahy, it needed a real effort to interest oneself in a tale of adventure, though the Curfew almost ordered us to take to literary recreations. How could I be excited about imaginary revolutions when the ways of my own city were dark and blind with ambuscades? I began then to think that romance was the invention of civilised people living in security. I could not imagine Ulysses in his wanderings listening with patience to any such tale as Homer told of him later. When the primitive hunters fought for the sovereignty of the planet with mammoth and mastodon, with flying dragon and the giant cats, it is impossible to conceive of them listening on their home-coming to any speech of imaginative adventures. A desperate reality must inevitably kill at its birth the creatures of fantasy. It could have been only at the dawn of civilisation, when life had become secure, that romance had birth in the imagination and was not killed at its birth. Why did it spring up at all? Why is the appetite for narratives of adventure almost universal? What is the purpose of Nature in inspiring the inventor and the listener? Was it that the Divinity which planned the universe for the purposes of soul desired life to be lived intensely and dangerously, that the will was to be made harder than diamond by unending warfare with circumstance, with the monstrous creatures that prowled about the cradle of infant humanity, and with the elements, with the intent, maybe, that that diamond will, once gained, might be used by man the immortal for more divine labours?

In the cities where life is more secure, and especially among those whose work involves least physical hardships, there are hundreds of thousands, even millions, who, after work, in their leisure take up a tale where men undergo the most astonishing hardships, are beset by enemies, engage in ferocious combats, cities are overwhelmed, civilisation destroyed, wars are fought in air or underworld, and all these mild and spineless folk, whose hearts would almost stop beating at the sound of a rifle near them, sit thrilled and absorbed as they read or listen to melodrama in the theatres or the pictured melodrama of the cinema.

Is this a disease of the soul or the remedy for a disease? Is Nature, alike in the penny dreadful and epic narrative, whispering to its children, who have cushioned themselves round about with comforts which rust the will, of perils which they yet must face? Are the villains of romance only symbols of evil powers which the soul must sometime combat? Are these inventions of civilisation falling into ruins a warning to the soul that sometime it must be prepared to stand any shock, must be able to overcome by its divinely-given powers the armies of the darkness? We cannot imagine Tom, Dick and Harry made meet comrades for cherubim, seraphim and aeons and archangels and the divine aristocracy, by the tests of character involved by retailing tea and sugar or setting down in a ledger the credit transactions of a drapery warehouse. When we exile the dangerous out of our lives why does it insist on coming into the imagination? These are terrible questions to ask, and I have no answers, only the asking of other questions, and the suggestion of august possibilities. I refuse to believe that the soul made in the image of God will be permitted by That which created him to become secure, comfortable, fat-bellied, flaccid of muscle and will, and I have an intuition that until we school ourselves of our own initiative to live with intensity, to undertake great labours for the sake of the soul, that dangers not of our seeking will come upon us and our civilisation, that humanity shall be driven age after age out of the pleasant nooks, corners and crannies in which it would hide itself.

Nature is not altogether remorseless. It will give its children pleasant periods of peace, but when it sees the fires dying down and the will weak and the soul flaccid, just as the Red Herdsman of Gaelic legend took his boar-yard to beat people into madness, so Nature will toss its children into storm that they may grow to strength once more.

The Abbey Theatre

ABOUT A QUARTER of a century ago Ireland began to assert and practise its right to cultural independence, making it apparent to the world that it had a distinction, a spiritual personality of its own. That personality asserted itself in many directions. It began to drink at the fountain of its own youth, the almost forgotten fountain of Gaelic culture, and at the same time to be intensely modern, to create a literature which had enough of the universal in it to win recognition from lovers of literature in Europe and America. It was our literature more than our political activities which created outside Ireland a true image of our nationality, and brought about the recognition of a spiritual entity which should have a political body to act through. No single activity of that newly-kindled Irish personality did so much to attract attention to Ireland as the Abbey Theatre. The swift upspringing of a dramatic literature and art in a soil that seemed sterile has something mysterious about it. Thirty years ago there did not seem a people in Europe less visited by the creative fire. Then a girl of genius, Alice

Milligan, began to have premonitions of a dramatic movement, and she wrote little plays to help the infant Gaelic
League, and she went here and there, an elfish stage manager,
with a bag crammed with fragments of tapestry to be used
on the actors in order to create the illusion of the richly-
robed ancient Irish of romance. These activities excited
a poet of the time to write lines full of an affectionate
irony parodying one of her own lyrics and attribute them
to Alice:

> At Samhain of Little Plays,
> As I was in an awful stew;
> There were not dresses half enough
> And I was wondering what to do;
> There came this thought into my mind—
> Why, cut the dresses right in two!

> At Samhain of Little Plays
> I pinned the actors up with care,
> And gave to each a leg, a sleeve,
> And whispered in their ears, "Beware!
> My dears, for God and Ireland's sake,
> Remember, this side out with care!"

With Alice Milligan, with whom the brothers Fay were
co-workers, were the infant beginnings of Irish dramatic
art. At first the new Irish playwrights were unaware of the
genius for acting latent in their countrymen. They brought
over professionals from England. But all this was changed
when the brothers Fay showed they were capable of training
Irish actors to speak beautifully and act with subtlety. After
a performance in St. Teresa's Hall, at which the lovely
Cathleen ni Houlihan of Yeats was first staged, it was realised
that Irish actors were a more fitting and an infinitely better
vehicle for Irish dramatists to use than the English professionals. The foreigner could recognise in this amazing
activity the evidence of a nationality which was creative and

living, while the words or deeds of politicians made no such universal appeal. There is, we believe, not a country in Europe, from Russia in the East to Spain in the West, where some work of the new Irish dramatic school has not been translated and staged. We doubt if that genius has been recognised as fully in Ireland, where it was born, as it has been elsewhere. It has been our habit to grumble, to criticise, to accept as a matter of course brilliant writing and acting as if they were nothing, to cry out when venerable superstitions were smashed, as that of our having the finest peasantry in the world, when they really were one of the most incompetent in Europe. There was fresh observation instead of formulae, insight instead of superstition, realism and idealism wedded.

While we say this in praise, frankly we wish, for the sake of the Abbey itself, that it shall continue to live in that exasperating atmosphere in which it grew up. Nothing can be worse for an intellectual movement than a chorus of approval. Universal approbation means that the people have come to be on its own level, and it is not ahead of them, and therefore it has ceased to belong to the aristocracy of intellect and character. If it ceases to produce plays which set the pit and galleries shouting, it will then be time for it to go into limbo. We need many cultural shocks, the intellect of Ireland has lain sleeping for so many centuries that a national theatre, if it is to play a great part, must probe every problem. It must not only try to rise to the heaven of the national imagination, but it must not be afraid to turn up the sub-soil, explore the depths and abysses. There are many gentle and futile souls who are shocked by realism. But there is no depth which cannot be sounded if the plummet is dropped from a height. We do not wish for the Abbey a career all quarrels and controversies, for that would be contrary to human nature which must have plenty of jovial, lovable and desirable life to keep it sweet. But we hope it will never

lose its ancient fearlessness about public opinion, or that its
directors will ever come to hesitate about the production of
a masterpiece lest it might for a time lose some popular
favour. In the end, its audience will begin to love it for its
daring, will prefer the work which shakes them out of their
mould of mind to the work which echoes back to them their
own surface emotions. It was by such cowardice the great
drama of the Elizabethan age degenerated until there was
no poetry, no imagination, no reality, only the despicable
theatre which came to be known as the Theatre of Commerce. When the waters are not troubled there is no
angel of healing. It is only the smug who want life to stand
still and to wear its best covering and to hide not only its
high beauty, but its sores.

Yeats and William Morris

I FIND IT CURIOUS that Yeats, who so often speaks of the
virtues of passionate literature when he is generalising,
loves in fact the romances of William Morris, the least
passionate inventions in English literature, more perhaps
than any other imaginative work. He himself is endlessly
speculative, while the works of Morris are without speculation. He himself writes a poetry which at times is broken in
its intellectual coherence by the invasion of some factor
from what I might call a fourth dimension of life, while
Morris's romances have rarely more than two dimensions,
and are conceived on the flat as much almost as a tapestry. I
suppose an intellect which is so restless must be envious of a
spirit which is content with its vision. He writes of Morris:
"If some angel offered me the choice, I would choose to live
his life, poetry and all, rather than my own or any other
man's". This is so illuminating that I have speculated upon his
preference of this poet, which is the cry of one part of the

soul for a beauty it still desires, but from which it has parted by some magic of the spirit which drives the soul out of every nook, corner and cranny of life in which it would find comfort. It is rare to find any imagination dreaming contentedly in the mid-world as Morris does. If he had reached higher than the beauty of the mid-world, he must inevitably have developed a clairvoyance into the depths, which is the price we pay for vision on the heights, and all that placid beauty would have become distorted and it would have been no longer a resting-place for an imagination like that of Yeats, who is insecurely in the mid-world, which his nature really loves, because he has seen things both higher and lower than Morris ever saw.

Yeats' Controversies

CERTAINLY THERE IS NOTHING like intellectual controversy for quickening the intellect. In the earlier writing on the theatre the poet is simple, charming and confident. In the later articles, because of attacks from many quarters, he develops an inexhaustible richness of attack and defence, a subtlety and depth which are not apparent in the first articles. In fact, we see the growth of the poet's intellect evolving his philosophy of drama and theatre. His original impulses become self-conscious and explain themselves. The theatre he created has, perhaps, in getting body, lost something of soul.

The new style, with its more austere choice of words, is the last refinement of the poet's art. It is difficult to say whether the rich colour or the pale colour of the poetry pleases best. Perhaps the evolution of all poets is by way of loss, as biologists tell us that flowers of a species which appear to us most beautiful are those which have dropped some character from an original complex. One thing has not

been dropped, the passion of the artist for perfection, and
no line is passed until it is shapely as the artist can make it.
It will be strange indeed if the next generation of Irish
writers are not good craftsmen with such a master of the
guild to teach them their art.

"A Vision", by Yeats

HERE I FALL AWAY from a mind I have followed, I think,
with understanding, since I was a boy, and as he becomes remote in his thought I wonder whether he has forgotten his own early wisdom, the fear lest he should learn
"to speak a tongue men do not know". I allow myself to drift
apart because I feel to follow in the wake of Yeats' mind is
to surrender oneself to the idea of Fate and to part from the
idea of Free Will. I know how much our life is fated once
life animates the original cell, the fountain from which the
body is jetted, how much bodily conditions affect or even
determine our thought, but I still believe in Free Will and
that, to use the language of the astrologers, it is always
possible for a man to rise above his stars. Now Yeats would
have me believe that a great wheel turns ceaselessly, and that
I and all others drop into inevitable groove after groove. It
matters not my virtue to-day, my talent which I burnish, the
wheel will move me to another groove where I am predestined to look on life as that new spiritual circumstance
determines, and my will is only free to accept or rebel, but
not to alter what is fated.

The *Vision* is so concentrated, the thought which in other
writers would be expanded into volumes is here continually
reduced to bare essences, to tables of the faculties and their
interactions, that I may have missed some implication, and
there may be some way out, and it may be that in his system
we are more masters of our fate than my study of the book

has led me to suppose. As I looked at the diagrams and tables, so difficult to relate to life, I encouraged myself to explore by remembering what Neander wrote in his *Church History* when he was confronted by the task of elucidating the bewildering mythology of the Gnostics. We must remember, he said, that the mind of man is made in the image of God, and therefore even in its wildest speculations it follows an image of truth. That is, there is something in the very anatomy of the soul which prohibits its adventure into that which is utterly baseless and unrelated to life.

We live our lives in an erratic rhythm, waking and sleeping alone sure in their return, for in our lives one day never repeats exactly the rhythm of another. But let us imagine an Oversoul to humanity whose majestic motions have the inevitability of the rising and setting of constellations. Let us assume, as we well might, that that majesty in its in-breathing and out-breathing casts a light upon our own being as the sun in its phases of dawn, noon and sunset makes, changing the colours of all it illuminates. Yeats takes the Great Year of the Ancients, a cycle of Anima Mundi symbolised by the passage of the sun through the Zodiacal constellations, a period of about 26,000 years of our time, but in his system it is considered but as one year of that mightier being whose months and days, all with their own radiant vitality, influence our own evolution. One of its days may be the spiritual light of many of our generations. It moves from subjective to objective. There are cycles within cycles, action and recoil, contrasted and opposing powers, all of a bewildering complexity, and caught within this great wheel the lesser wheel of our life revolves, having phases as many as the days of a lunar month, all re-echoing the lordlier cycle and its phases. When he illustrates these phases of human life, thirty in all, by portraits of men and women, dead and living, typical of the phase, I suspect the author to be animated not only by a desire to elucidate the system, but by an impish humour. I ask myself was it insight or impishness which made him link Bernard Shaw, H. G. Wells and George Moore as typical men of the twenty-first phase, or what old lady did he discover in Mr. Galsworthy to make him unite that novelist with Queen Victoria? I am a little uncomfortable with some of my fellow prisoners in phase twenty-five. I welcome George Herbert, but am startled to find myself along with Calvin, Luther and Cardinal Newman, as no doubt the last three would be incredulous of their own affinities to associate pilgrim souls. I am inclined to think all the good qualities of Carlyle were pruned by Mr. Yeats' geometrical scissors to make him fit into his phase. But these character tellings, illustrative of the phases, will be to many the most interesting part of the book. For all its bewildering complexity the metaphysical structure he rears is coherent, and it fits into its parts with the precision of Chinese puzzle-boxes into each other. It coheres together, its parts are related logically to each other, but does it relate so well to life? Do we, when we read about the cycles and their attributions, say to ourselves, yes, so men have gone, changed from mood to mood? We can say from our reading of history that there is action and reaction, that the philosophers of one age are antithetical to those who preceded them, that the political ideas of our age must face in the next a recoil of contrary, equal and opposing forces: nay, that the very moment one power starts out for dominion over the spirit, it calls into activity an opposing power, "one lives the other's death, one dies the other's life". But as they are immortals they never truly die, and the life of the antithetical powers is like that combat of hero and demon the poet imagined so many years ago in his *Wanderings of Oisin*. Yes, we see this interaction, recoil and succession of mood in history, but are they the interaction, recoil and succession of moods Yeats sees? We have a tendency to make much of all that has affinity with our mood or our argument, and not to see or to underrate the importance of all that is not akin. I, with a different mentality from Yeats, see figures as important which are without significance to him. If I summed up the character of an age I might read black where he reads white. Doubtless every age has a distinctive character, or predominant mood, and I am not learned enough in history to oppose confidently my own reading against his. I have written round and round this extraordinary book, unable in a brief space to give the slightest idea of its packed pages, its division of the faculties of man, the Will, the Creative Genius, the Mask and the Body of Fate and their lunar gyrations, or of its division of the transcendental man, the daimoniac nature and its cycles and their relations to our being, or of the doctrines of the after-life. Almost any of its crammed pages would need a volume to elucidate its meanings. It is not a book which will affect many in our time. It is possible it may be discussed feverishly by commentators a century hence, as Blake's prophetic books—so ignored, so unintelligible a hundred years ago—are discussed by many editors in our time, and he is found to be the profoundest voice of his own age. It is possible it may come to be regarded as the greatest of Yeats' works. It is conceivable also that it may be regarded as his greatest erring from the way of his natural genius, and the lover of his poetry may lament that the most intense concentration of his intellect was given to this book rather than to dramas or lyric. Personally, I am glad it was written. I do not doubt that though the seeds of his thought do not instantly take root and fructify in my mind they will have their own growth, and later I may find myself comprehending much that is now unintelligible. So far as the mere writing is concerned, the part dealing with the Great Wheel and History is as fine as any prose he has ever written, and the verses set here and there have a fine, clear, cold and wintry beauty. The poetic intellect has devoured the poetic emotion, but through the transformation, beauty, the spirit animating both, maintains its unperturbed life.

Yeats and the Nobel Prize

IT IS A DELIGHT to cease for a while to brood on those material problems which weigh upon us so heavily, to consider another aspect of national life, more fundamental and inspiring, which is too often forgotten by those who think of the future of their race and see it coloured by that sadness which clouds their own being as they think. The rightness of the award of the Nobel Prize to William Butler Yeats will, we think, be questioned by few lovers of what is truly beautiful in literature. No poet of his generation, writing in English, has set before himself higher ideals of perfection in his art, and we cannot remember a single poem where the artist seems to have grown weary in his search for perfection. In that passionate consciousness of his which laboured to make all things beautiful there was restored to Ireland a spirit which had not existed since the *Book of Kells*. After a thousand years the passion of the artist was reborn to work upon a far higher plane. While it pleases us to think that the poet has received international recognition in such a form we are made still more happy to think that the bestowal on him of such an honour, conferred hitherto only upon those acknowledged by all to be among the greatest writers of their time, may turn the thoughts of his own countrymen to one who has evoked out of the Ireland in which he was born a greater beauty than any of his predecessors. Yeats has made the name of his country shine in imagination to the rest of the world a hundred times more than any of the political notorieties whose names are on every lip here, but who have rarely uttered a sentence which could be taken up and echoed by people in other lands and made part of their thought. It was by the literary movement of which Yeats was the foremost figure that Ireland for the first time for long centuries came to any high international repute. Everyone had heard of Ireland, of its tragic history, of its struggles for independence, just as all had heard of Poland, its unhappy history and its struggles for freedom; but what was Irish entered not at all into the high thought of the world. Even the greatest of Yeats' predecessors—Berkeley, Goldsmith, Swift and Burke—have always been regarded as important figures in English literature because no Irish tradition found a voice in them. They did not give to the world a beauty into which Irish tradition was woven, as the Indian poet, Tagore, expressed in his poetry the spirit of India, or as the ancient Greek poets and dramatists moulded and gave to humanity the myths, traditions and ideals of beauty of their wonderful civilisation.

During the greater part of last century the literature of Ireland was arid to the spirit. There was a riot of animal vitality in Lever, Lover and Carleton. The patriotic poetry, so widely read here, was read by but few who were not Irish. What, indeed, could interest others in poetry empty of those universal ideas which are a common food for the soul in all lands, and which had but little art in its fashioning? Moore alone was known and his songs sung outside Ireland, less, we believe, because of their merit, which we do not deny, than because the light texture of his art was sustained by the melodies to which they were married, and which came out of that Gaelic soul which was the fount of inspiration for Yeats and most of his Irish contemporaries. Towards the later part of last century the thoughts of young Irishmen of genius began to turn inward and backwards to Gaelic Ireland. Among those who so turned then and in our time, Ferguson, O'Grady, Synge, Lady Gregory, Hyde, Stephens, Colum, Clarke and the rest, Yeats was undoubtedly the greatest artist. He may be regarded as the pivot around which Irish literature turned from instinctive to conscious art, and in this last phase our literature began to take on quality, to grow rich and many-coloured. Through it, as through a transparency, the world received its first real revelation of what was beautiful in Irish national tradition. The deepest and most moving things in last-century Irish literature are the cries of despair, as of lost souls, which came from Mangan and others. That literature is not good for the soul, for it only multiplies images and shadows of its own despair. The literature a nation needs is a literature the people can live with, which adds beauty and delight to life and interest to character, and which reveals and interprets the nature in which they live.

Such a literature we have begun to create, and international recognition may at last bring national recognition. Being an ignorant people, we are very suspicious. We discount praise given to our own until it comes to us as echoes from other lands, and then we find to our shame we have starved our prophets and our souls together. We are still so ignorant and materialistic because of a century of bad education that the majority see nothing of value in Gaelic tradition, in poetry, drama or the arts, and they think the best gifts life has to offer are land and money, and do not know of the transfiguration of life and nature which takes place when we have absorbed into our own the spirit of great writers, or how much we lose when we are empty of these nobilities. Poet and artist give to us their own vision.

It is the function of the poet to name woods, stars, mountains, people, actions, thoughts and emotions, so that by those names they will be remembered, and the name shall recall the transfiguring mood and we, too, come into the magic circle. How many bitternesses in our public life might never have arisen if we had been told when we were young that legend of Maeve looking over the walls of her city at her enemies and crying out: "Noble and regal is their appearance". The noble nature sees beauty first and loves it. The ignoble nature sees first what is ugly and absorbs it. Many who sought El Dorado in other lands might have found the earth underfoot wonderful and alluring, and the air they breathed coloured like faery, if they had access to the thought of the greatest of their race. Nothing is more important to a nation than the images which haunt the minds of its people, for it is by these they are led to act. If they are images of violence, they will inevitably be led to act with violence. If they are images of beauty they will create beauty. It is according to the measure in which the best in literature is made available to our people that in the next generation we shall find them empty-headed, as in this, or creating the arts, the sciences, the culture and the social order which make a civilisation. The creation of a civilisation is the highest of all human enterprises. If we create so high a thing in the coming time nobody will have contributed more to the beauty of the building than William Butler Yeats.

Heavenly Geometry

FEW POETS have been so bountiful to their biographers as Yeats. The intellectual biographer of the poet will never suffer for lack of matter about which he may speculate. Indeed, to understand the poet in his later phases one must have gone into the psyche's own world, which the ancients fixed between earth and heaven, or have listened to the reveries of the dead, so remote from the normal is his thought; and the effort to interpret is made more difficult because he has invented a symbolism of his own. One would retreat from the effort but for the atmosphere of beauty which is inseparable from almost every motion of the poet's mind. I read, allured by the cold, lazy dignity of the writing in his latest book, which he calls *A Packet for Ezra Pound*. I call it lazy writing because he tells me little in detail of the circumstance in which were set these psychic experiences. Yet, it may not be laziness at all, but some enchantment upon the intellect when it enters into the dream world, so that it loses the alert waking questioning habit, and it becomes dreamlike itself, for in dream we are never inquisitive, we suffer or endure or gaze in joy or terror at the pageant of which we are part. Once we are inquisitive the pageant dissolves and we wake.

The most important part of this book is that which the poet has named *Introduction to the Great Wheel*, and in this he tells how the geometrical philosophy in his book, the *Vision*, came to be written. It is a collaboration between the dreaming consciousness of his wife and his own, with possibly other entities not of this plane of being. Yeats speaks of them as if he believed they were external to consciousness, but when we enter into the dream world there is a dramatic sundering of the Ego, and while we dream we are persuaded of the existence of many people which, when we wake, we feel were only parts of our own protean nature. I do not suggest that these philosophic entities who communicated to the poet and his wife the substance of the *Vision* may be simply some submerged part of the soul, because I am sceptical of the possibility. I merely say that he has not given me enough material to decide. There is a great deal of confusion both in the thought of the *Vision* and in this later *Introduction*, and Yeats himself is conscious of this. I do not complain about it, for all journeying into hitherto untravelled forests must be confused, and differ from travel upon beaten high roads. We shall probably come to an understanding by study of other books rather than the poet's own narrative. There are many subtle minds pursuing truth into the deeps of being, many tentative and confused, as Yeats is, but all contributing something to a psychology which will probably later become more luminous, and may make it easy for us to reach that ancestral wisdom which Keats said was in us all, so that we can drink that old wine of heaven, and come to that wisdom with ease where we now get blinded and lost in the search. I confess, while I find many things exciting in the *Vision*, I would like to rewrite it, leaving out almost all that over-precise movement of his cycles. The virtue of the soul is to be free, and Yeats' spirits condemn us all to a cyclic progression, which is like the judgment of a mad dictator willing it that men should be imprisoned in one cell after another in a great prison, from which there is no escape, and in the imprisonments there is no justice, only a kind of destiny willed by a divinity as indifferent as that Setebos brooded upon by Caliban. It is very dangerous to believe that life is becoming mechanised, for that mysterious mind within us may take the hint and dress up a complete philosophy of mechanisation for us, and if we accept it we weave our own enchantment, build our own prison cell, enter it, lock ourselves in and throw the key out of the window.

It is of much more importance to us to have experience than to have philosophies, and those who can tell us how to rise above ourselves into mid-world or heaven world are the only people in whose thought I have any profound interest. Philosophies of the universe are all very well; excellent intellectual exercises. But I know the moment I get out of that rational everyday mentality which enjoys such exercises, the moment I rise within myself and draw nigh to deep own-being, all these philosophies vanish. Plato said, "If there be any gods they certainly do not philosophise". This is my growl about the *Vision*, and the *Decline in the West*, and *Phase*, and other attempts to show how God geometrises, though when I cannot have spiritual experience I turn to them and devour their chaff and find it excellent food for the waking consciousness.

While I would like to know the core of this philosophy I

feel I must wait until I come to that intensity of being which, when we attain it, the sage Patanjali tells us, will enable us to penetrate to the essential essence of anything, and comprehend it fully merely by directing our attention to it. Then I might know in a second what otherwise must take me many years.

Yeats Rewritten

TO RE-READ *Early Poems and Stories* is to recall my first love in literature. The beauty which overcomes us while sensitiveness is yet virgin and has lost nothing of its poignancy by use, lasts through life for most of us, no matter how many after-loves we may have. Who under a spell can be critical of the enchanter? I was not then, and hardly now can I do anything but surrender myself anew to the music. I find a boy living in me still, affected almost to tears, longing to be remote and winged, flying over the waters listening only to the song of the heart:

> I would we were changed to white birds on the wandering
> foam, I and you.

Or I murmur the benediction sung over Diarmuid and Grania:

> Give to these children, new from the world,
> Silence and love,
> And the long dew-dropping hours of the night
> And the stars above.

And as of old the poetry creates such a loveliness in the heart that I feel I am breathing in a divinely created nature, air, earth, the stars, ourselves, all fondled by the Magician of the Beautiful, all rapt, all sharing in the benediction. In our first imaginative love there is complete union with the poetry, and I cannot disentangle myself from this early affection or say how much I brought to it, or how much it brought to me. I can be critical of what came later when I had gone on a way of my own and had become self-conscious, so that in everything I read I found myself less yielding, only accepting from another that which helped me on my own journey. But though I cannot be critical I feel as deeply as ever that the poetry of Yeats is the greatest spiritual gift any Irishman has made to his tribe. He is the finest artist in Irish literature, and after his verse began to find readers, there came a shrivelling of the resounding and empty rhetoric in which so many had been content to express themselves. I keep on wondering if Yeats had antedated Moore how much greater poetry we would have had from Moore, Mangan and Ferguson, because so scrupulous a craftsman had preceded them.

No poet since Keats and Shelley has so completely realised for us the stranger regions of imagination, has convinced us more of the authenticity of his vision, that the words depict things which were present to the interior sense. I feel a little sad sometimes that the later self-conscious artist could not let the earlier half-conscious artist be. It is a little disconcerting to find the images we loved tricked out in new fashion. It is as disconcerting as for a lover to find his mistress has powdered the hair or tinted the face he had come to love for its natural beauty. The poet would tell me probably that he has only taken out an original falsity that had deceived me, and now there was but truth and simplicity. But those who read now for the first time, and those who read in future, will not be disconcerted by a changing fantasy as those who have watched the artist at work. Often I have to admit that the change is better. But sometimes I feel that the change has come only because the artist has gazed too long at his work, and because of that over-intensity the words have lost their magic for him, as all

263

finite things do, through over-familiarity; and he has found other words for his thought which are not better words, but only temporarily release the artist from the ache over absolute perfection unrealised.

The poet of twenty-one may write as lovely things as the poet of forty if he has at all mastered the craft. But prose is made up of observation, reflection and conscious thought: and here experience brings fullness, depth and mastery. The later prose is much finer than the earlier. If it is not lit by so gay a colour and fancy the thought is infinitely more subtle and the phrasing more distinguished. It is after *Rosa Alchemica* the prose makes us pause to consider its message with full seriousness. Before that it may delight us with its fantasy, but I often feel the images it conveys are little more than coloured phantoms having but slight affinities with our intellectual being. It is in the *Rosa Alchemica* he first begins to relate the images of fantasy to the intellectual world. After this in all he writes he is conscious that the things seen are the shadows of the unseen, and they do not as at first exist for themselves, but for what they may symbolise. He has passed from the poetry of youth and his thought begins to take on age, wisdom and subtlety, and he writes the poetry which not merely delighted youth, but pondering age can linger over.

"October Blast"

THIS BOOK IS FULL of the anger of the soul discovering that the body does not share its immortality. While we are young we never have this anger because the body melts so at the heart's desire that we do not imagine of it that it is alien in nature. The poet in this last book cries out against that fading body as a boy might petulantly clod a cur which had followed him along the road, finding it was not a thoroughbred. Yet out of this anger comes a new pride in the soul which, though it can no longer melt the body into its dream, turns on itself without the company of the traitor, and laughs and sings and mourns over the images it makes up out of itself, building its own house out of its own substance and making its own light. Whatever the body has done to be clodded as if it were an old cur, it has not had power to darken the genius of the poet, for here it is burnished and bright as ever, and the poetry of Yeats' age is even more overcrowded with images than the poetry of his youth:

> What shall I do with this absurdity—
> O heart, O troubled heart,—this caricature,
> Decrepit age that has been tied to me
> As to a dog's tail. Never had I more
> Excited, passionate, fantastical
> Imagination, nor an ear and eye
> That more expected the impossible—
> No, not in boyhood when with rod and fly,
> Or the humbler worm, I climbed Ben Bulben's back
> And had the livelong summer day to spend.

The poet need not be angry nor think that time has defeated him when he still expects the impossible. To persist in age in the belief that the universe is magical and transcendental, that is victory, not defeat. It would be tragedy indeed if the body had clodded the soul into a decrepitude like its own. But the proud spirit goes on making its own youth out of its own time-defying substance:

> We sat under an old thorn-tree
> And talked away the night,
> Told all that had been said or done
> Since first we saw the light,
> And when we talked of growing up
> Knew that we'd halved a soul
> And fell the one in t'other's arms
> That we might make it whole;
>
> .   .   .   .   .

O what a bursting out there was
And what a blossoming,
When we had all the summer time
And she had all the spring!

The spirit of poetry in *October Blast* is as richly jewelled as
in youth, only it wears the cold bright stones rather than the
coloured stones on its embroideries. It played long ago
under the boughs of beryl and chrysoberyl; now it sings in
cold lands which give no less lovely images to the eye. The
old miraculous mastery over words is in this book as much
as in any of its predecessors, and phrases which would be the
commonplace of another's speech are set so cunningly that
they take a glow from his genius and have the strangeness of
new beauty. None of his contemporaries here or in Great
Britain or in America has his power to take the words of
common speech and make them aristocratic. It is exercised
like the prerogative of a king who can take a commoner and
knight him. Words with him have all the old power of
evoking delicate images:

Her present image floats into the mind;
What quinto-cento finger fashioned it
Hollow of cheek as though it drank the wind
And took a mess of shadows for its meat;

Lines like that are read with an admiring despair by other
poets; so unexpected, so precise in their conjuring up of
impalpable forces, so that the face we do not see haunts us like
the faces Luini painted, whose charm is not in the fashioning of the features, but allure us because some spirit-finger
seems to have put an almost invisible hollow in the cheeks
or a shadowy seduction in the lips, an enchantment over and
above what the bodily beauty can give. I am not so sure that
he has the gift of making me love his world as he had in the
earlier poetry. I wonder at it more, but love it less, because
love only comes with the contented heart and here the poet
is in transition, moody and irritable. I could love the imagina-

tion of youth which found earth a faery place and made it seem so to me. But here he is too angry with life and has not yet found a delighted content with the spiritual to which he is forced to turn because the old sweet companionship of soul and body draws nigh to its close.

Illimitable Horizons

THERE is a spirit latent in us all which believes that some-where or somehow all its desires will be met; all that seemed impossible—the impregnable walls will be stormed, the immutable powers will melt and will be our brothers and hearts' kin. Every book which convinces us for the moment of the impossible gives life to that spirit.

The Critic

I AM NOT ONE of those supercilious persons who will read nothing but the finest literature and who decline in art anything but the masterpiece. I confess I get some pleasure from almost every book I read or almost every picture show. The psyche trying to release its wings has interest for me, though but a glimmer of colour breaks through the dusk. That interest may be psychological rather than artistic, but it is a real interest. When the artist is in love with a place the love creeps in some way into the work, and there is almost always a pleasure in looking at what was done with pleasure.

A Rebel Artist

I EXPECT she will do still better when she revolts against herself.

Insurgents

WHEN I WAS YOUNG art had grown in skill, and had a group of lovely graces—drawing, colour, tone, values, chiaroscuro, light, rhythm, all handmaids in the house of art, and no picture was recognised as art in which the work of some of these deft and lovely graces was not visible. It was easy to enlist their aid. Was there anybody with the least ability—men or women—who might have made admirable bankers, barristers, doctors, business men or wives, but who had a fancy for painting, in the art schools they were taught their craft, and they learned how to draw a figure, how to light it scientifically, and the galleries were filled with competent, uninspired work, and it became a weariness to the soul to walk in a gallery and to see so much misapplied industry where there was no vision. Then there came a revolution. Young insurgents, seeing how little those technical accomplishments did to make art interesting, decided rather rashly that they were quite unnecessary, indeed a danger. They mutinied against tradition. Drawing, colour, tone, value and the rest were Jonahs on board the ship of art. Heave them overboard. Then when these were got rid of, the insurgents settled down happily to express themselves directly without any academic tradition hampering them. They used triangles, cubes, swirls, dots, spirals, growing wilder and wilder in the intoxication of freedom, and though the first exultation of revolt is over, still there are large numbers of young artists who have not the slightest intention of losing their freedom. They will not ask any of the ancient graces to help them, and so we have exhibitions like this of ——, where very clever young artists give us, by a kind of artistic shorthand, their impressions of life and Nature. They do not like Nature, but, as one confessed to me, "We cannot altogether do without it".

Derivations

I HAVE A PREJUDICE against illegitimacy in literature. When we read poems inspired obviously by Tennyson, Browning, Swinburne or Yeats, nobody except the author admires them. But in art it is almost deemed a virtue if a man obviously acknowledges his allegiance to Cézanne. The school is excused in art where in literature it is a crime. I think the same principle should apply in both, and the folk obviously inspired by Cézanne or Picasso should be sternly suppressed. If God has not given anything for a man to say out of himself, why should that man be permitted to acquire merit by saying over again what other artists have said? Of course it is a relief from academic dullness. But it is only another kind. The academies turned out an efficient kind, and the ultra-modern masters inspire an inefficient kind of dullness. That is, they conceive the defects of Picasso and Cézanne or Matisse to be their merits and bank on these. Their virtues are beyond them.

Juniors

ALTHOUGH I AM an elder, born when the academicians were at the height of their influence, and most of my tastes were formed while they were still predominant and the post-impressionists and cubists were in their cradles, I go with more cheerful expectation to exhibitions of pictures painted by juniors than I do to exhibitions of pictures painted by my contemporaries. I know I will get no shock from the last. But the young moderns stimulate me. I don't think they have any more talent than their predecessors, but they say things in a different kind of way.

Nature and Art

WHENEVER ONE is painting Nature, whose brilliance
exceeds any colour the chemist can make for us,
the first thing to learn is not to be afraid of the purest and
brightest colour, for we may be sure that the gayest colour
we can use will appear dingy if we look out of our window
at the sunlit earth.

Are the Masterpieces there?

LEONARDO ADVISED his pupils to look at the stains in old
marble or the markings on walls because there they
might get suggestions for pictures. But only the imaginative
man can get this inspiration from the discoloration of
marble. The picture is not in the marble but in the artist.
Many of ——'s pictures appear to be the result of incompetence. Here are monstrous men and women in wooden
attitudes, impossible anatomies, bodies like bladders, limbs
less articulated than the toys of children, flimsy landscapes,
tottering houses, and the very clever fellow faced with these
apparitions discovers masterpieces in them, as Leonardo in
the stains on the wall. Are the masterpieces there, or are
they the improvisations by the clever fellow? It is very
difficult to say, for the clever fellow half impresses his
fantasy upon us, as in Blake's *Memorable Fancy*, where there
were black and white demons and a serpent advancing with
all the fury of a spiritual existence, so long as the diseased
imagination was active. When the imagination subsided
there was only Nature, with the fishes playing in the gay
moonlight. When the critical imagination has stopped playing about ——, what is there? Talent, or feeble forcible

stupidity? Either the artist has vision or he has not. If he has not the vision the art is of no importance. There is some kind of murky imagination in ———. But my belief is that there has been more imagination in the articles on his painting than in the paintings themselves.

It seems to me the critics were very weary of academic art where there was competence but no imagination. The half-baked was interesting in comparison. Much more could be said about it. One would wrangle up to three in the morning over those monstrous modes. Trying to discover what was in the half-baked was an exciting task, much more exciting than trying to find what was in the fully-baked academic work, where the painter put all he had to put in, but obviously had not imagination. The half-baked picture left the problem of imagination in doubt, and too many of the clever fellows who write about modern painters gave the artist the benefit of the doubt.

Van Gogh

UNTIL THE CONFLICT over Van Gogh has died down it is not so easy to be judicial, and I hesitate to suggest that Van Gogh had a quite ordinary vision made extraordinary by intensity, perhaps by that exasperation of nerves which finally developed into madness. It is difficult to find a truly original vision in Van Gogh's work, but a fever seems to possess him while he works, and the ordinary becomes extraordinary, just as a man in a fever does not see the same people in a room as a healthy man does. That feverish execution, the suggestion of dementia in the brush-marks, give a unique character to this artist's work, and it is easy to understand how a generation satiated by the academic art, commonplace in vision and placid and uninspired in execution, should turn with excitement to Van Gogh, who saw the commonplace, but was crazy with excitement over what he saw.

Jack Yeats

THE MAN OF TALENT can only acquire merit by hard work, and it is proper, therefore, to be concerned about drawing, values, and whatever else may be so mastered, for it is in this way he who has no original genius can yet come to make us happy by his interpretation of natural beauty. The methods by which the man of genius achieves his effects are almost undecipherable; and while we may note that he is or is not an accurate draughtsman, or that he ignores or appreciates the beauty of true values, we always feel he gives us something better to think about. Now, Jack Yeats has this touch of genius which makes purely technical criticism appear trivial. No other person by taking thought could arrive at the same result. How many people in country towns have sat and yawned and spat under the blank walls of mills, and cursed the emptiness of life and departed to fill up the vacancy with strong drink? Jack Yeats comes, and the grey walls, the water and the two figures seen in his "Market Day: Evening" are full of mystery. The dark man and the woman with her dim oranges and reds seem to come out of a romantic world, and the picture bathes us in an emotion difficult to analyse. It may be that the artist appreciates tradition, that his figures unmistakably convey to us that they come out of Folk Tale and Ballad Country, and have a kinship, however remote, with the heroes and beautiful queens of antiquity. However it is, he manages to charge his figures with sentiment. That pilot of his who comes ashore looks as if he had returned from the Spanish Main, from gazing on glittering islands, from treasure-hunting, and his pockets might be stuffed with gold moidores. Remote centuries and a tribe of romantic ancestors come ashore with him. Jack Yeats can also invest the earth, bare of humanity, with poetry of its own. That little picture "A Windy Day: Galway Lake" has, for all its simplicity, a rare beauty; the pale green of the lake edges, the dark ruffled water, the grey hills, the humid sky and the black stones melt together, and in a few inches he suggests a poetic scene. The intensity of the vision of earth suggests a world of powerful people who might haunt it.

Who but Jack Yeats could invest with poetry and mystery two ugly naked old men wading out into the dark green waters? They appear as elemental as the sea or air they move in. We must not forget how harmonious and steeped in sentiment are these dim greys, greens and blues. Now we get once more original notes of colour which delight us. How attractive are the varied greys of the girl who looks at the wax figure in Grafton Street! It is really not Grafton Street save that there the artist saw something which started his imagination on a distant journey. The scene might be in Pernambuco, in Bohemia, or some remote city in Georgia. The picture called "Galway" seemed to me beautiful in colour, but I saw it on a grey day; it was in a dark part of the hall, and I could only suspect it was one of the best, with Jack Yeats' peculiar atmosphere of latent poetry bathing the figures who crouch by the water. The large picture, "After Rain", is probably the most completely wrought-out of any, but I do not feel that it gains by its size. The poetry would be as evident if it were on a much smaller canvas. The only reason I think the artist should take a large canvas is to exhibit a greater intensity than could be packed into a smaller picture. The tendency with too many artists when they increase the size of the picture is to lessen the intensity of the mood. The technical problem involved in painting on a bigger scale may be solved successfully without the picture impressing us more profoundly because of its dimensions. I

do not say that "After Rain" is too large, but it says no more
to me than many of the smaller pictures. I have often thought
it desirable that the problem of size should be discussed by
art critics. We feel at once that the figures Michael Angelo
paints on the Sistine gain by the vast dimensions of the
decoration. We could not feel that a little Watteau, however perfect, would gain if the figures were enlarged to life
size. There would be some diminution of dignity if a fine
Velasquez portrait was reduced to half life size. The early
pictures of Millais, which were his most beautiful, would
not gain by enlargement. How would the "Autumn Leaves",
the "Ophelia", or "St. Agnes' Eve" be bettered if the figures
were life size even if the painting was as perfect? But this is
too difficult a problem to raise, simply because Jack Yeats
has painted a few of his pictures on a slightly bigger scale
than the average. Probably he might answer: if he did not
paint on a larger scale every now and then the smaller
pictures would not impress us as they do.

Leonardo

I FEEL CERTAIN, because of the intellectual precision of his
art, that Leonardo was an intellectual ascetic who found
the materials for his meditation in courts rather than in
solitude, and he never ceased to be the ascetic. The precision of that art is incompatible with any passion except the
passion of the intellect. I find him not dreamer but seer.
Rossetti, Gustave Moreau, Burne-Jones are dreamers in their
art, but Leonardo has vision with alert, waking consciousness into the world which the others can enter only in
dream and who surrender themselves to be ruled by the
dream world. It is the mixture of waking and dream consciousness which is so disturbing in Leonardo, for he projects images from one into the other as painters like Moreau

or Burne-Jones never do. Take some of those wonderful heads. You will find in one, while the eyes are melting the lips are cold; in another, the eyes are scornful while the lips allure. How are we to interpret this? Is it not the art of one who has seen into two worlds, who saw the beauty of body and of spirit, and who tried to unite incompatibles which cannot live equally together because one must be the slave of the other? In these strange, beautiful faces spirit is never the master of flesh, nor has the body made the spirit its slave. They co-exist, superimposed on each other, by the magic of his art, beauties which war upon each other in life. It is the marriage of Heaven and Hell, which so many artists and poets have tried to paint. Heine sings the bridal song of that marriage in those lyrics which are half faery and half sensual. Gabriel Rossetti, Gustave Moreau and many another artist have painted on the meadows between the two worlds. But none with the mastery of Leonardo. It is because some intuition tells us that these two natures can never come together unless it be as king and slave that we find something sinister in the art. It has violated a law through an insatiable curiosity of the intellect.

We lament the fate which destroyed almost all the master's works, leaving us hardly half a dozen masterpieces and some marvellous drawings. Was the destruction of those things brought about by a wisdom which is watchful of life? If the imagination of humanity had brooded long on these alluring images would it have been betrayed into some intellectual sorcery, for we rarely know what life is behind those faces? If we could pass through them as through a gate into the soul would we find angel or demon? That sinister element, that subtlety, seems to belong more to the end of a great civilisation than to its beginning. If so aged a spirit were allowed to have an influence on the hot youth of a culture would it wither prematurely? The art of none of his contemporaries affects us in this way. Michael Angelo is in the elemental childhood of a civilisation. There is no suggestion of age in his emotion. Raphael, Titian, the Venetians, are no older than the world they live in.

Rossetti

ROSSETTI SEEMS like the single fiery-coloured cloud in an otherwise sober-coloured firmament. He seems to have overcome his contemporaries by his personality. He was not tongue-tied, as the majority of Englishmen are; and his speech, fanciful, amusing and dictatorial, must have made him dominant in the society he mixed with. When imagination appears in talk it is king and the listeners are slaves to it. We no longer regard his paintings with awe. The earlier pictures still impress us with an intensity of imagination, but some of the later pictures make the irreverent scoff, like that picture of the Blessed Damozel leaning out over the bars of Heaven—a clammy, vampirish creature, while behind her in Paradise a score of behaloed lovers are hugging and kissing each other passionately. Rossetti's conception of Paradise seems to have been a sublimated Hampstead Heath on holiday, with "'Arry" and "'Arriet" in erotic abandonment. This picture of the Blessed Damozel is at once sinister and vulgar. Probably it was the indulgence in drugs which destroyed his sense of humour and turned the ardent, generous young man into a sombre, suspicious recluse towards the close of his life. The drugs which he took may have opened some doors in the psyche which are better shut, for there is in the later art something sinister, as if creatures out of some terrible sphere, incubi or succubi, had incarnated in the forms of his imagination, and had changed their beauty so that the eyes expressed a thirst which could be allayed in no spiritual paradise; the sucked-in lips, the long throat, the serpentine fingers, all suggested that these passionate women might suddenly reveal themselves as amorous devils.

Of course, it was not so completely, and there are poems and pictures which show the true genius almost to the last. He was in painting and poetry seeking always to express psychic intensities, going in imagination beyond natural intensities in an endeavour to sustain the passional life at its summits. It is possible that the drug was called in to make more potent or more prolonged the psychic exaltations that his nature thirsted for. In his sister Christina the same temperament found an outlet in religion, which is the only straight road to fullness of being. Gabriel was in the border-land but did not cross over. He desired to bring Heaven down to Earth rather than to rise from Earth to Heaven.

Harry Clarke's Illustrations to "Faust"

CLARKE'S ILLUSTRATIONS to *Faust* are imaginative marginalia by the Irish artist pencilled about Goethe's masterpiece rather than an effort to realise it for us in the way resolute artists through last century, who were conscientious about costume and accessories, tried to realise for us the characters of Shakespeare. It was their ambition to show us the poet's characters as actual people walking upon the earth we know, and in periods of history made recognisable by the costume. For such work, bring model and costume and a competent craftsman together and the rest was easy. The theatre was illustrated rather than Shakespeare. It may be doubted whether any imaginative artist can ever be deflected in this way from his own nature by the author he proposes to illustrate. There was no change in mood in the Blake who illustrated Dante and the Blake who illustrated the unimaginative Blair. Burne-Jones was next in his paintings to break away completely from the tyranny of the author. He only selected among the images which were the natural inhabitants of his own soul some which might stand as symbols for the imaginations of others; and he made no pretence that he was trying to realise any author. It is probable that there is some one writer whose nature is close enough to the artist's to make of the artist his ideal illustrator; but it is improbable that the same artist will ever prove an ideal interpreter of two writers. Harry Clarke is probably the ideal interpreter of Edgar Allan Poe, and wherever the imagination of Goethe conjures up the macabre, the witch, the imp and the devil, Clarke will add a shudder which is congruous with the drama.

Nothing in these drawings represents anything in the visible world: all come from that dread mid-world or purgatory of the soul where forms change on the instant by evil or beautiful imagination, where the human image becomes bloated and monstrous by reason of lust or hate, the buttocks become like those of fat swine, and thoughts crawl like loathsome and puffy worms out of their cells in the skull. Shapeless things gleam with the eye of snake or hog, and in the midst of all this a faint and fragile Marguerite moves, like a helpless innocence or frightened fawn, and at other times she herself becomes sinister because of the sorcery which assails her. The peculiar imagination of the artist is at its most original in the nightmare of the Witches on the Brocken which stretches across two pages. Here the black night is loaded with corrupt monstrosities, creatures distorted by the lusts which obsess them, which bloat out belly or thighs, suck in the forehead, make the face a blur of horrid idiocy or a malignant lunacy. We shiver at the thought that creatures like these may lurk in many a brain masked from us by the divine image. But hardly anywhere is there a shape which in its shapelessness has not a terrible precision which reveals how the souls, which have lost the Light which lighteth every man who comes into the world, become blighted when that Light has gone out and nothing remains save that which made the revolt against Heaven.

Clarke's fertility of invention is endless. It is shown in a multitude of designs less elaborate than the page plates, but no less intense. Take the little drawing which illustrates that heart-rending meditation of Marguerite, who has been listening to the girls' chattering scandal about Hannah and who is all the while conscious of her own secret. Here the distraught soul looks out from a misery from which there is no escape. Long quivering hands with fingers like sharpened fires waver in the air and point to the piteous figure. The hands have eyes in them like vipers that know everything and will forgive nothing. We would like to close the eyes of the soul to shut out that piteous image. How awful, too, is the Despair, with head like a bird of prey, which holds the fainting girl in the Cathedral, while the choir chants the *Dies Irae*. It is the soul inside the body rather than the external form which is symbolised in the decoration to the scene in Auerbach's cellar, where one can almost hear grunt or whinny from creatures already become half-animal to the spiritual vision. In this and, indeed, a great many other drawings, the artist has escaped from the influence of Beardsley, who for a time seemed to obsess him. In other drawings the influence is still obvious, but weakened. Clarke does not attempt scenes at depicting which even the greatest artists might fail, such as the apparition of the Earth Spirit, and he is wise to confine himself to episodes of which he may give his psychic interpretation. There are weaknesses in some of the drawings: Faust himself is rarely anything but a decorative shadow and we cannot believe in his psychic existence. Clarke is not the artist of men and women, but the seer of the forms which their passions and imaginations assume. He is most original and successful where he is the seer into thought-forms, and least successful when he fails in that psychic clairvoyance and is tempted to depict an externality like the death of Valentine.

The Hibernian Academy, 1970

A Fantasy

THE PSYCHOLOGISTS now completely dominate Irish art. In this year's Academy there is but one landscape superficially of the type which fifty years ago would have been praised as a faithful transcript from Nature. This was the painting of a mountain valley by O'Meara. I saw some elderly men grouped about it. It was the one picture which recalled the intelligible art they admired when young. The title alone puzzled them. "Why does he call the landscape 'An Empty Mind'?" I heard one old gentleman ask querulously. He could never comprehend the audacity of the painter, the satire on the uncultured who see nothing in Nature but itself, and who see on one plane of vision only. Beside it hangs a magnificent picture by Paul Murphy, our most suggestive landscape painter. His psychology is many-dimensional. The picture is "Ben Bulben from Rosses Point". How shall I do justice to the subtlety which has indicated to us on one canvas the many avenues of mood and incident through which the artist had his vision of Nature, all of which must affect or blur that vision? It is obvious that the delightful Irish Ballet which enchanted so many at the last celebration of Tailteann had become prominent in consciousness. All over the picture whirling figures are seen in faint delicious colours, the tone to which they have dimmed in memory. A girl's face looks at us out of the lake as an apparition might be seen in a crystal. The enigmatic glance suggests that some mood of the girl had haunted or puzzled the painter while he painted the lake, and if he was to be truthful to his own mood he had to paint face and pool together. Some phantasmal trees like ancient time-beaten men growing out of the clouds did not at first explain themselves. Then I remem-

bered this was the country of Yeats' youth. It was here he
saw the trees

> Dipping and doubling landward, as though they would hasten
> away
> Like an army of old men longing for rest from the toil of the
> seas.

The artist also remembered this and the verses projected an
image into his mind, which doubles the suggestive power of
the picture. The whole landscape is a profound study of
Nature and the soul together by a great artist whose many
affinities with literature, drama and life veil as with a many-
coloured delicate mist his vision of the great mountain. This
is perhaps the finest landscape of the year, though Martin
Kavanagh's picture of green tumbling waters with dogs and
red huntsmen pursuing a flying fox over the waves runs it
close. It was natural that Kavanagh, who is sportsman as well
as artist, should dream of the hunt while he painted the
Atlantic. It is not, however, in so many dimensions of
psychological space as Murphy's picture, and the spiritual
content is not so rich, though it makes a fine pattern of
phantom horsemen, hounds and foaming waters. The portraits this year have excited controversy, especially those by
Miles Joyce. It certainly does indicate a rare moral courage
on the part of sitters to surrender their personalities to be
interpreted by this ruthless seer, who paints both face and
the content of consciousness. Here we have the Army Chief,
the stern soldierly face, which has awed so many, while
around it are set faces of the soul in various expressions of
timid apprehension or abject terror. It is a demonstration of
the law of reversed effect, and the artist means to tell us that
one can only be compelled to ruthless militarism on the
outer plane of our being by an inner terror, that timidity
that sees red ruin and the breaking up of laws when the least
disturbance takes place in society. This is powerful and

impressive portraiture. It is only the undoubted courage of the outer self which could endure such a revelation of the inner self. The distinguished soldier was seen on the opening day gazing on his own portrait in a prolonged meditation. It is rumoured that after this study of the forces at work in his subconscious mind, he reduced the estimates for the army by five hundred thousand pounds. The influence of this profound art on politics grows greater every year.

The portrait of Miss L—— with that vivacious face surrounded by serpents' heads with forked tongues spitting poison, it is rumoured, led to some disagreeable scenes, the sitter not being able to face the revelation of the seer as our greatest soldier did. That the seership is not blind to beauty is obvious from the same artist's portrait of our venerable and beloved James Stephens, where the aged head of the poet is seen surrounded by creatures of the Siodhe, gay elves, leprechauns, all in a shimmering iridescence, indicating that the poet is young in soul as those who inhabit the Country of Immortal Youth. This masterpiece has been secured for the nation by the Friends of the National Collections of Ireland. In landscape and portrait Art is still, like that Angel of the Apocalypse, with one foot on earth and one in the great deep, but in the purely psychological pictures of which there are many, the art of our age has no longer even partial dependence on a scene in Nature, or on the worn-out beauty of the human face. It insists on being altogether psychic or spiritual. It will only portray what is seen with the inner eye, the visionary forms, colours and chiaroscuro of the soul: its lights, its glooms, its dramatic symbolisms. Let us take Murrough O'Keefe's "Transition". There is the half-articulated anatomy of the psyche in a middle tone of misty violet, half submerged in a darkness which lays murky hands on it, while it seems itself to have been exiled and thrust out of light as by the Angel of the Flaming Sword. It symbolises perfectly consciousness at the instant between sleep and waking when the interior heaven is vanishing and our world is at the moment a heaviness which drags it down. We have already sharp divisions in the psychological school. There is a reaction from the psychic realism which perhaps owed its first inspiration to that now half-forgotten novel which so outraged our fathers, *Ulysses*. The artists who were first inspired to do in art what James Joyce did in literature could see nothing but the obscene creatures in the sewers of the soul, and their paintings were like nightmares. The younger men have deserted those grim alleys, crypts and subways of consciousness. They have risen from the Inferno to the Paradise of the imagination. Their colour has the lustre of the rainbow. Michael Lavelle's picture of wonder forms, "The Opening of the Divine Eye", is the masterpiece of this new art. One room in the Academy buildings has been set apart for an exhibition of the new changing pictures so popular in Paris and New York. There is a white canvas and opposite it five feet away resting on a pedestal is a black box with a projector. The visitor touches a spring and instantly the canvas is sprayed with lovely colour and form dissolving, changing and growing for about sixty seconds until the climax is reached. It is not photographic as the moving pictures in the popular theatre are. It owes nothing to Nature. All has been devised by the artist and it is in this as psychological as the picture "Transition" already referred to. One exquisite little moving picture entitled simply "A Lyric", by Paul Lenoir, delighted many. When the spring was released instantly there was a flash of blue like a sunlit sky, on the white canvas, then white blossoms, wind-blown, opened, a laughing face thrust its beauty through the blooms, the lips pouted in invitation, then a sweet malice came over the face, it covered itself with the blossoms and after that as a wind blew the blossoms apart for a moment there could be seen a flutter of flying draperies as if the girl fled from the pursuit she evoked. It was perhaps a little sentimental but it was delicious in colour, and after looking at half a dozen of these moving pictures one felt that the static art, even when in four psychological dimensions, was a little stale and that its days are numbered. The new moving art has this advantage, that once the artist has painted his film it can be reproduced endlessly, and there were over seven hundred orders for that single moving picture the "Lyric". This art certainly can reproduce dream with its movements as the earlier art could not, and I hear that Lavelle and O'Keefe are already experimenting in the new technique. I am old enough to remember the purely external art of forty years ago, and while I protested against the first experimenters in psychological painting—the experiments certainly were not very happy, as the first protesters against purely objective painting saw only, when they closed their eyes, coloured cubes and triangles and curves, an opacity through which they could not penetrate to the realm of Psyche—yet I soon discovered the possibilities of this art, and reflect with some little allowable vanity that I was its first champion. Now it has vindicated itself and the painter can adventure into the world of psychology equally with the novelist, and has, indeed, some advantages over him. In this exhibition Irish art stands on as high a level as Irish poetry and drama, and with the new technique to be exploited there are illimitable fields of adventure before the imaginative Irish mind.

The Art Patron

THE PART PLAYED by princes in the Middle Ages who were munificent and discerning patrons of the arts, is to-day played in the grand manner by wealthy Americans. Isabella Gardner made what is reputed to be the finest private collection of masterpieces in the world. Since her death that great collection of pictures and other works of art gathered by her in Fenway Court has become by her will a museum for the enjoyment of the people.

The gathering together of beautiful things and giving them to the people is as fine an object as wealth can propose to itself, and America seems more than any other country to have munificent donors, but then it is the only country in the world where there is enough wealth for such princely munificence. No doubt the widow's mites glow as brightly in the book of the recording angel as the public benefactions of the wealthy, but there is a good deal to be said in praise of those who let their light shine before men and who let it go on shining long after they are dead.

Art for Art's Sake

I THINK THE ARTIST has a secret delight in the art of creation which none who see the result only can ever share, and that is because in the art of creation, when we are manifesting ourselves to ourselves, we are following a law of life, and I am sure if I were condemned to a lonely existence and could exercise one art, then I would chose to paint pictures and would have a delight in the painting, though I was certain no other eyes than my own would see what was done. Some intuition about this was hidden in the aphorism, "Art for art's sake". I am not sure that there is not a truth in that now-neglected aphorism which has been overlooked, a truth corresponding in some way to the ethical intuition that we should love to be kind, not because of the consequences to others or the results of our actions, but because it should be the mode of our being to love.

Conscience in Reviewing

I RETURNED after an absence of some weeks to find my reviewer's cup was filled with honey. There were no less than five volumes of verse by Irish writers waiting judgment by the poet-taster. I will not be so unjust to this delicate art as to taste them all together, for poetry is like painting: with a few pictures we are enchanted, but a whole gallery blurs our sensitiveness, and we soon pass by masterpieces as if they were but wall space. A lyric may be the distillation into a few words of moods and reveries in which soul and body were melted, and if we pass from page to page in a rapid reading we do not allow the seed to blossom for us into the full bloom of imagination from which it fell.

Of Plotinus Again

WITH THE PUBLICATION of the fourth volume of his translation of Plotinus the long labours of Mr. Stephen MacKenna draw nigh to their close. Another volume and the transhipping of the precious cargo of thought from the Grecian to an English galleon will be completed and the spiritual merchandise of this noblest of mystical philosophers will be marketed in our generation. To how many in our time will the philosophy of Plotinus seem like a ladder let down from Heaven, a ladder up which they can climb, until they too can come to the Ineffable Light? The philosophers of our time no longer tell us of the Way or the Life. They are absorbed in something they think of as the Truth and, if we read them, except for whatever sharpening of our wits may have taken place, we are exactly where we were before. William James, Bergson, Croce, their predecessor Spencer, or the earlier Hegel, Kant and their contemporaries, all leave us with quickened intellects, but we are no nearer to the Spirit than before. Unless we include the too-fanciful visionary Swedenborg we have to go back to Jacob Boehme before we find a great thinker who bases his philosophy of life on spiritual experience. It is this which distinguishes Plotinus from all but a few of those who came after him. He has gone up into the Holy Mountain and come back with his face shining; and the Tables of the Law he received, though they make no direct reference to the comminglings with his God, which his disciple Porphyry records, are written by one who has had a vision.

When he writes in the Eighth Tractate on the Intellectual Beauty he is not merely the subtle logician, but the seer:

> To live at ease is There: and to these divine beings verity is mother and nurse, existence and sustenance; all that is not of process but of authentic being they see, and themselves in all: for all is Transparent; nothing dark, nothing resistant; every being is lucid to every other, in breadth and depth; light runs through light. And each of them contains all within itself, and at the same time sees all in every other, so that everywhere there is all, and all is all and each all, and infinite the glory. Each of them is great; the small is great; the sun, There, is all the stars; and every star, again, is all the stars and sun. While some one manner of being is dominant in each, all are mirrored in every other. . . . So, too, Repose is not Troubled, for there is no admixture of the unstable; and the Beauty is all beauty since it is not merely resident (as an attribute or addition) in some beautiful object. Each There walks upon no alien soil; its place is its essential self, and, as each moves, so to speak, toward what is Above, it is attended by the very ground from which it starts; there is no distinguishing between the Being and the Place.

We may compare the last sentence in this with that passage in the Dnyaneshvari where it is said:

> Without moving is the Travelling on this road. To whatsoever place one would travel that place one's own self becomes.

Our modern psychology does not concern itself with transcendental problems. With Freud and Jung and the whole tribe of the psycho-analysts it explores the crypts in the soul; but to its more heavenly chambers, those which lie nigh to the Sun of all being and are translucent to Its Light, they are blind. But it is a problem worthy of the most intense concentration of thought, just how was it that Plotinus came to write the passage quoted. Was he expounding something taught to him? Or had he ascended within himself to some tower of being, where he was smitten through and through with the Beauty of another nature and coming back could report of it? And if so, how was he able to transcend normal vision? Is it that the ascetic who makes his life pure by continuous brooding on the Divine cannot, once he has made his being crystalline, escape the flooding of that being by the Light of all Lights?

We perpetually ask ourselves such questions reading Plotinus. In Plotinus, whatever was earthly had been transmuted into a shining aether, and passion had been withdrawn from bodily things to cast itself upon the Beauty of all Beauty. Through every motion of that mind made so transparent we get vistas of a transcendental being. He has lost all that "desire for self-ownership" which is, as he says, the reason why life has hurried away from the Divine, until at last ignorance of its rank brings self-depreciation and it is surrounded by externalities before which it humbles itself. He would recall the soul to fly "to the beloved Fatherland". Oh, what a lofty speech! No one cries like that to us to-day, or if they cry they do not convince us by a superior beauty that they are inhabitants of the world to which they would allure us. We have been brought in our time into an intense objectivity by our civilisation, by science which concentrates the mind upon things outside itself. There were earlier epochs when the highest intellects were subjective in their aims. They tried to discover truth by exploration of the spirit.

Plotinus is one of the noblest of those who stayed the spiritual consciousness upon its highest levels in a contemplation of its Fountain and Original But as we read this record of lofty intellections we feel how lacking we are in experience to interpret it and make it living to this generation as it doubtless was to many who followed the same path in his own age. We have receded from that phase and we read the Enneads as we look afar at great mountains, whose beauty is made blue, or vaporous, or unsubstantial by distance. But the law of action and reaction is sure in its workings. While thought to-day is concentrated on the external a return to subjectivity is certain, and by this extraordinarily beautiful translation of Stephen MacKenna, the thought of Plotinus will be passed on in its integrity until a new cycle brings new aspirations, and Europe and America begin to seek within, rather than without, for fullness of being. If such a transfiguration of life takes place Plotinus may have many more followers than in his own age.

Masefield's "Jesus"

I DO NOT KNOW of any attempt to bring divine beings out of sacred literature into secular literature which has not failed. There is no life of Christ other than that in the Gospels in which the greatness of the character does not seem to suffer disintegration in the secular imagination, however reverent. In some mysterious way, in hardly explained circumstance, the brief gospel narrative pictures, with an extraordinary economy of words, a drama which has moved the world. It is like a sketch by some divine artist which conveys a dignity that a more elaborate art could not equal. The dignity of the drama is not maintained when the retelling is made so that other words are imputed to the Avatar than those in the sacred text. The original was like a jewel in a setting which was devised by a strange art to make brilliant the central jewel. Put it in a more elaborate setting and something is lost. That is the trouble with Masefield's play, *The Trial of Jesus*. He multiplies less precious material and the magic dies. I do not believe any but the God-inspired can depict the God-inspired. In painting no artist can set the sun in the sky. But without painting the sun the artist can show objects illuminated by its light. Art has no colours strong enough for the sun, nor the dramatist an art equal to the manipulation of a god. The highest art of the dramatist is hardly equal to the portraiture of humanity, and is not equal to what is above humanity. But the presence of a divinity might be inferred from the thoughts and actions of others just as the sun is inferred in a picture from the light and shade.

The Bible Retold

WE CONFESS we can see no reason for simplifying the Bible for the benefit of children any more than that Michael Angelo's art should be simplified for children. Children look up at the sky and stars. They do not understand it, but they are awed by that magnificence, and later may come to realise what that majesty implies. They can read the story of Joseph and his brethren, or of the Egyptian plagues, or of the children who walked in the fire in that noble version made three hundred years ago, and can be thrilled. Yes, they can even read psalm or prophecy, and, without fully understanding, can feel there is something wonderful, something which will draw them to read again and again. But we wonder what child would get any impression of beauty or wonder or magnificence from "Peter grabbed the sword", "Pharaoh was thoroughly frightened", "The plague of frogs made everybody most uncomfortable". Is the story of the Fall made impressive by this version? Jehovah spoke to them and said: "Listen, for this is very important. . . . You must leave the fruit of this tree alone, or accept the consequences, which are very terrible." The consequences of making young children read vulgar English are also terrible. This would make the *cliché* the daily bread of their souls. They would lose all sense of what is truly beautiful and noble, a sense which comes with childhood, though it may be almost unconsciously. Awe, reverence, spirituality are awakened in early years by whatever rightly may evoke them. Modern retelling has not even the beauty of a fairy tale. Nobody could guess from it why the history of that wonderful people—their heroes, prophets and saints— has moved so many hundreds of millions in so many lands and for so many centuries. The story has lost all magic. The intention may have been good, but the rationalising mind is fatal to beauty, and without beauty there is no divinity, and without divinity there is no sacred book.

Jung

CONTINUALLY I AM EXCITED by the theories of Jung and almost as often I feel myself dubious: "When the Ascetic has succeeded in repressing the evil side of his nature, he may be assured that it is flourishing below the threshold—all the more dangerous because no longer faced consciously". Now it is true that men can thrust back elements in their nature from the conscious to the subconscious and refuse to admit them into consciousness, but is it true that these always persist and have as powerful a life as before, only below the threshold of consciousness? Do they not, being denied food, get weaker and fainter in some men though in others they are fed by the body which whispers encouragement unheard by the Ego? The passage quoted suggests that it is impossible to purify the nature. It may be that I am making an assumption not justified by Jung's psychology, but there is the suggestion here and elsewhere of a mechanical balancing of powers which cannot be upset, which I am dubious about, though much that he says about the continuous movement of the *libido* between opposites is psychologically true in my experience. A second point which causes me to speculate is Jung's theory that there are layers upon layers of experience lived through by the ancestors of man even to the remote animal, and images derived from one of those remote epochs may emerge in dream. I do not deny that people in dream or vision do see images which suggest a remote genesis in past ages of the world. But one would like some attempt at explanation of the way in which such antique images have been preserved through so many generations, existing below the threshold, perhaps for a thousand or two thousand years, and at last emerging to consciousness in dream. Are the images preserved in the germ-cell, and does it carry this burden in addition to the power of building up an organism out of itself like the organism from which it was derived? When I remember the deadlock in Darwinism created by Weismann's declaration that acquired characteristics were not passed on from parent to child, or, at least, that there was not the slightest evidence that they were passed on, one wonders how the image in the dreams referred to in this volume of a pagan sacrifice and of Hathor the Cow Goddess were preserved through so many generations to re-emerge in a dream. Were they a psychic inheritance? This lays a very heavy burden on the germ-cell already burdened with a million obligations. Is it not possible that in dream man occasionally comes in contact with another nature, let us call it *anima mundi*, and images in that *anima mundi* evoked by something in the character of the dreamer, by some psychic affinity, are drawn to him and he becomes conscious of these forms?

Psychologists

THE ROOT IDEA in Adler's *Psychology*, that there is in every individual the organic consciousness of a need, of some specific inferiority which has to be compensated, was expressed more nobly by Emerson when he said: "I the imperfect adore my own perfect". But Emerson was a man of wide culture, and the trouble about so many modern psychologists like Freud and Adler is that they do not seem, for all their experience of life, to have a wide culture. They find in themselves some mood which obsesses them, and then interpret the whole of life by it. We get the impression from Adler of a clever little soul having become self-conscious of a mood in itself, making this mood fundamental in life. We can imagine a whole succession of psychologists each obsessed by a single mood, it may be an erotic mood, or the sense of inferiority, or fear, or ambition, or some other mood, but out of this the psychologist will build a philosophy, and there will be enough people obsessed by the same mood to give him thousands of adherents. It may be doubted whether there is any dominant passion in life. It is possible our passions are nearly all interchangeable and capable of translation one into another, just as science tells us electricity, heat, magnetism, etc., are, and the sex impulse may become something entirely different in the man of genius, an emotion which cannot be interpreted by tracing it back to any sexual root. The current that runs through the copper wire will act in one way there, and in an altogether different fashion in an open field of action.

293

Sinclair Lewis's "Elmer Gantry"

WHAT HAS HAPPENED to religion in America? In the most backward districts in Ireland, among the most ignorant, as indeed in the most backward districts in Europe, in chapel or church, the spiritual dignity of religion is maintained by a ritual, by long centuries of spiritual culture behind the priest. There is some common element of dignity in the service in great cathedrals and the service in a little chapel in some remote mountain valley. It is true that in Europe no longer is that profound faith which once existed. The unity of spiritual culture which existed in the ages of Aquinas and Dante has been broken up into sects, but something august and ancestral still broods behind almost all of these sects, and they are rarely without some dignity and reticence of their own. The religion Sinclair Lewis depicts has neither dignity nor reticence. It is in open competition with the sensations of theatre, cinema or dance hall, and while it attacks it employs as sensational methods as any of them. It is not at all necessary to assume that all who adopt these sensation methods are humbugs or charlatans, as most of Sinclair Lewis's characters are. But we may assume that, adopted with whatever sincerity, the methods described by Lewis have their correspondences in real life, that the spirit of Christianity has passed away from itself in wide areas in the New World, that in many sects it is culturally hardly on a higher level than a popular music-hall or a Hollywood film. I read somewhere a myth how Apollo, driven from the God-world, lived among the swineherds. Divinity in exile in America has been herding with the Barnums. How did what was so majestic in Europe become so squalid in the New World? Is it that the general culture in America was not the daughter of religion as it was in Europe? In Europe the arts proceeded from religion. Poetry, music, painting, architecture were all God-nurtured. Dante, the poet, is hardly less sacred than Aquinas, or Fra Angelico, the artist, than St. Francis. The poets, artists and musicians who followed Dante, Michael Angelo and Palestrina have gone on strange adventures, they have kept strange company, but even with the greatest of the heretics and sceptics there is some intellectual link connecting them with an aristocratic ancestry.

The secular literature of the States has almost lost affinities with the past. Its moods are without spiritual ancestry, and as the secular culture became more secular the mood of the people reeled further and further away from the spiritual, and at last the aristocratic language of religion became so remote from the mentality of the average man that, if he was to be interested at all, religion had to talk in a kind of slang, do its turn in the pulpit just as the acrobat does his turn on the stage. The re-conquest of America for the spirit is an adventure that the most heroic might contemplate with misgiving. The only way of recalling the soul to beauty is by the creation of beauty.

Middleton Murry and Religion

I VERY MUCH PREFER Mr. Murry writing about literature to Mr. Murry writing about religion. He is in love with Jesus. Yes. But I doubt whether he has spiritual scholarship to enable him to understand the Scriptures; words and meanings having too often receded from their contemporary significance until hardly any but scholars of the vastest learning could hope to elucidate them. This does not mean that the unscholarly reader of Scripture cannot brood over ethic, precept and example and find the most precious things. But when a Life of Jesus is attempted we ask something more. Mr. Murry rationalises the story and divests it of the supernatural, and, indeed, the spiritual. He says of Jesus in his preface: "There are many to whom he was above all a supernatural being—a God. I cannot share that belief because I do not know what it means." He may not share the belief and yet be justified in writing a book, but he is not justified in writing a book when he says simply he does not understand what the conception men have held about Jesus for nigh two thousand years means. A man who does not understand, out of some spiritual experience of his own or by intellectual pondering, that all the threads of the universe may be drawn through a single soul, had better not try to write about an Avatar of the Spirit. He lacks the necessary modicum of spiritual experience and the intellectual subtlety which is needed. Mr. Murry's Jesus is the hero of an ethical romance. It is a beautiful romance. It could hardly be without beauty with so marvellous an original. But the Scriptures were translated by incomparable stylists, and when any try to retell that story we feel at once the drop in the melody of the sentences and the intensity of the utterance. Even when passages of beauty are quoted, the effect is rather like setting diamonds in putty. Writers like J. Middleton Murry and the author of *By an Unknown Disciple* are so anxious to remove the miraculous, that they discard the beauty and, indeed, the essential miraculous element which made humanity turn to the Scriptures. They have got the idea that it was the ethic alone which drew men to the Sacred Books, and if everything else was discarded that ethic would shine out in pure beauty and attract men still more. But in reality the soul of man seeks not only an ethic, but a truth, and it clung to the Scriptures because it felt there was a truth in the almost incomprehensible, transcendental or spiritual element, and if that is eliminated the magical power they have over the soul departs for the great majority. An ethic has not virtue apart from other things. It is but fantasy if it be not wise at the same time. There is no pure ethic apart from that Being, and to exclude what is called the supernatural is to shut off the soul from its proper nature. If Mr. Murry does not believe in that nature, then his ethic should be based on biology. To shut out nature and supernature is to leave ethic suspended in vacuum.

The Hen in Eagle's Feathers

I READ RECENTLY some blank verse by Robert Graves which started me on a speculation about the fitness of the verse form for certain kinds of meditation or narrative. The poetic form fell most definitely into matter with Robert Browning. He had genius, but often, when he writes in verse, he reminds me of birds like the ostrich, fallen out of the air, which can no longer fly but retain a plumage more ornamental than useful. It would be untrue to say that Browning never soared above earth, but in *Sludge the Medium*, in *Bishop Blougram's Apology* and in many another monologue his Pegasus is earth-bound, drawing the clay and stones of the soul, and one wonders why a winged creature was put to such a task. Only an odd line reminds us that the verse form was originally the fiery chariot in which the soul went up to heaven:

> Just when we are safest, there's a sunset touch,
> A fancy from a flower-bell, someone's death,
> A chorus ending from Euripides,
> And that's enough for fifty hopes and fears.

Did Browning write his *Blougram* and his *Sludge* in verse form only because he was accustomed to it? Had it become a convention of spiritual utterance with him so that he could not feel how unfit it was to marry musical form to prose meditation, however subtle? Ever since, poets have been clothing in metrics matter which, it seems to me, is incon-

297

gruous with the form. It is ludicrous to me when so real a poet as Robert Graves puts into iambics an imaginary letter from one soldier to another.

I ask, should not officers in the British or any other Army of our times be made to speak in prose, as undoubtedly they do? I will be told that nobody speaks in verse, and that this would rule out the use of metrics altogether. But no. The heart in love, in imagination, in meditation mounts at times to an ecstasy where its being has become musical. Carlyle quotes a German mystic, who said: "If we think deeply we think musically". The pattern of sound, the recurrent beat of verse echo that inner music. In all languages where poetry has been written there has been pattern, rhythm, echo, measure or recurrent beat, and what would be unreal if it was merely the speech of lip or brain becomes most sincere when we feel it the expression of intense spiritual or emotional life. We need not discuss the psychology of this, whether when the inner nature subdues the outer nature, whenever flesh is melted into soul, the soul imposes on the body some image or echo of itself, as a ray of the Logos, of the Mind which made music and harmony in the universe. We need not enter upon difficult or unprovable speculation. It is certain that metrics as a mode of speech correspond to something in the soul. But if we say this we are impelled to deny the fitness of verse as utterance of any feeling, imagination or reverie which has not originated in the magic fountain. To clothe thought, however subtle, memories or perception, however vivid, in a verse form is to clothe them with artifice, to be somewhat insincere and pretentious. Yeats is contemporary with us, and nobody feels it unnatural that he should suddenly remember the enchantment of earth, that his heart should be quickened, or that his words should echo the music of intense feeling.

I will arise and go now and go to Innisfree.

We cannot think it artificial that Wordsworth should cry out:

> Will no one tell me what she sings?
> Perhaps the plaintive numbers flow
> For old, unhappy, far-off things,
> And battles long ago,

or that Shelley's *Hymn of Pan* should be compact of assonance, alliteration and rhyme, as if he were choked up with a sweetness of feeling, so that the ecstatic sound must repeat itself, must dwell upon its own echoes to convey its intensity. But what business has Blougram or Sludge, or Graves' British officer, to speak in measured cadence when that cadence is not a natural echo of the mood?

Much of Browning and of modern poetry is intellectually fascinating, but the emotion is not of the substance which begets music in speech, and to clothe it in verse form is to offend the sense of what is fitting, like dressing up some plain prosy good fellow with romantic attire of bygone ages. Shakespeare makes Titania speak in beautiful verse because it is fitting, but Bottom talks good prose. The great artist had an instinct what emotions echoed the starry dance and what emotions were earthbound and must plod in other fashion. Should not the artists now cast off rhyme and measured beat where it appears artificial, just as the artists after West cast off the classical convention in the painting of battle-pieces? Perhaps the Free Verse form exists for that no-man's-land between the ecstasy of pure poetry and prose, a form which can pass into music, measured beat, rhyme or regular stress when the emotion is so intense that it cannot express itself without them. I dislike all pretence, all clothing of thought in unnatural forms. The verse form is only natural when the soul speaks, when there is a momentary domination of the external by a power which belongs to the inner being. But no prosaic thought can expect us to be anything but scornful when it forgets the honest stride which is natural to it or comes mincing along on iambics or on any other kind of feet. I swear a vendetta against any emotion which does not wear the garments proper to it.

De Quincey and Poetical Prose

POETRY AND PROSE every now and then fall in love with each other. Each tries to include in itself some freedom or beauty which it envies in the other. The poet, hampered in his syntax by rhyme, stress, quantity or accent, will make his ideal the writing of poetry in which not a single sentence will appear to have been distorted from the natural order of speech by some exigency of the metre. The writer of prose, conscious of its wonderful range and the variety of rhythm possible, dreams of a prose musical and beautiful and concentrated as any verse could be. There are passages in the old English translation of the Bible where the miracle is achieved, but there the spiritual content was provided by the Hebrew poets and only the technical feat of embodying their intensity in a grave, musical and impassioned prose fell to the translators. The old English version of the Bible is really a co-operation between great poets in one language and great prose writers in another language. But has a fine poet ever written anything in prose which achieves the intensity of his best poetry? Mr. Yeats has written most distinguished prose, but he knows by an instinct that prose embodies the content of the waking consciousness, and when the dream consciousness with its intensities takes possession of him he uses the vehicle of verse. He has never, Shelley has never, Swinburne has never, in prose, even at its best, equalled the beauty of their poetry at its best. If you feel and think profoundly, you feel and think musically, and it is not artifice but Nature which prompts the measured beat, echo or assonance. In poetry the spirit of man seems to ascend towards its fountain in the Logos and to be a partaker of that divine musical nature. Can the prose-writer so ascend without forsaking his craft? I can find no theoretical argument which I can assert with full conviction, which would deny the possibility of a prose as intense, as musical, as poetry. But when prose is at its most musical, when it most approaches poetry it is almost always at its emptiest. The ear is delighted, the intellect is starved.

I can recall a passage or two in Pater which might be quoted against me, the page which he devotes to the Monna Lisa, and, indeed, sentences, "She has been a diver in deep seas and keeps their fallen day about her, and has trafficked for strange webs with eastern merchants", have a music comparable with the music of rich verse, and have also an intellectual content. But how many such passages could be cited in English prose literature? When Ruskin's prose is at its most musical it is at its intellectual emptiest. De Quincey, I think, had indulged more than any prose writer in dreams of a prose which might equal or transcend poetry, but, though there are sentences with intellectual content in his dream fugues, for the most part I find the entry into the dream consciousness has been attained at the expense of the rational which the best poetry never relinquishes. The poet is like those Eastern mystics who can pass from the waking to the dream consciousness without going asleep. He is, indeed, in the dream world but he retains his mastery of himself and controls or moulds the images of dream. When De Quincey enters the dream world he is swept away by it.

Prose has gone uninitiated into the realm of poetry without possessing the formula for control over its forces, of which the poet has the secret. De Quincey launches himself on a spiritual chaos, and its anguishes and ardours are not those the high will of the poet seeks and endures, but are imposed on him, and the soul, not master of itself, swoons towards dissolution. I cannot but think that if he had tried to write in verse, while we would not have had that reeling rhythm, that hypnotic surging of sound, he would have been master not slave of his emotion because the ordered rhythm of verse would have controlled by its spell the waves of the sea on which he was adrift. When prose seeks to attain the quality of poetry it tends to a chaos of the emotions, and the intellectual content subsides with the swelling of the music. I do not deny that the reading of such prose is a luxury which gives us pleasure if partaken of sparingly as we might breathe incense. But to breathe nothing but incense! How we recoil from the thought! We can read poetry for hours as if it was a natural nourishment of the soul. I sometimes suspect, too, with De Quincey that words, the pigments he used so lavishly, were used to eke out inspiration. In fact, that he was sometimes pretentious and suggests adventures which were never psychically experienced. I have no doubt that under opium he had a dilation of consciousness, and that there were terrors and anguishes of feeling, but many passages suggest that the opium he was indulging in at the moment was the opium of words. "All creatures", "all trees", "all the forests of Asia", "thousands of years", are phrases which suggest not precision of speech but verbal intoxication: the unrestrained use of superlatives by a great rhetorician. He probably forgot most of his dreams as we all do on waking, and his reeling rhetoric is the substitute. Prose has lost its own virtues in trying to surpass poetry. It has become merely a dissolute indulgence for the literary senses.

Maurois' "Byron"

THERE ARE POETS whose adventures are almost purely subjective or imaginative. These may be truly great adventures. A lonely man seated on a rock or walking in a field may be communing with mighty powers. But outwardly his life may be uneventful, so that his biographer would be in despair. He may know that the man sitting on the rock may have travelled further than Columbus; may indeed have gone into inner worlds, but the biographer can have no data. He cannot travel where that other has travelled. We may read with excitement of spirit the poetry a man has written, and yawn over his life because it was so uneventful. There are two English poets whose lives were varied and adventurous, whose lives have been written many times and, no doubt, will be written again and again. As their era recedes in time, they become the central figures in romances. These twain are Byron and Shelley. There is almost too much conflict, movement and adventure, so that in making a narrative of the adventures it is possible to obscure revelation of the imaginative or spiritual adventures, which indeed are the only ones which give value to a life.

This was the defect of André Maurois' *Ariel*, wherein Shelley, the poet, was almost completely obscured by Shelley, the man. He has not made the same mistake in his *Byron*, for he continually draws on the poetry to illuminate the narrative, finding in it the most intimate expression of the poet's feeling in regard to the women he loved. But in that he may be deceived. For a poem full of intensity may have but the faintest relation to anything in the objective life of the poet. He may look at a woman never to be seen by him again, but that transient vision may stir the imagination so that what he writes may, to those who read, seem to indicate an eternity of passion. It may do this truly, but it is something between himself and the Spirit, a revelation of the self to the self rather than a record of love for a real woman. But Byron, probably more than most poets, made the reactions of others on himself the subject of his verse, and M. Maurois may be right in relying on the poetry to illuminate the adventures of the man.

It is a serious, well-documented biography, and the narrative never fails to interest, and as we read we begin to understand a personality which has been more acclaimed and denounced than understood. I have come to believe that the deciding moments in life are those of the first contacts between soul and body, the marriage of Heaven and Earth, in which a germ is deposited, a mood, a sentiment, a thought which, however delicate, may later have a titanic growth. I find that when Byron was about five his mother entrusted his spiritual education to a melancholy young man named Patterson, who began to instil into the boy these doctrines of predestination, that some can be raised to a life of holiness, that others who are not thus saved are condemned to everlasting punishment; that this beatifying or damnation depends on the choice of God, "who has predestined some to life everlasting and others to damnation", doctrines which must be terrible to imaginative childhood. We can imagine the boy pondering about himself, whether he had the signs of grace, whether he was predestined to everlasting life or eternal torment. In such a home as his, with that tempestuous mother, the characteristics of grace in the child must have been battered about, and he might, in despair, come to believe that he was one of those predestined to damnation. Once that belief is born, then the imagination tends to seek companionship with the creatures of the Darkness which it believes to be its fate. It may brood with a sinister fascination upon the unforgivable sins, and at last see no reason why they should not be committed since heavenly destiny or eternal damnation is already decided on no matter what he does. A subtle theologian might find a way of escape from such moral dilemmas, but what escape is there for childhood? Some terrors like those I divine lay in the childhood of Byron, perhaps forgotten by himself, but translating themselves into more intellectual equivalents as the boy developed into a genius. Somewhere, I feel sure, in that forgotten boyhood lies the clue to the character of the man.

Byron himself took delight in painting his own life in the darkest colours to his respectable correspondents. He had, I am certain, an impish pleasure in shocking his publisher.

The writer exploited every phase of his rich vitality, from the cynical to the heroic. The heroic in him conquered in the end, and one wonders what there may have been in that forgotten childhood, what incredible bravery of spirit may have been born about the same time as those terrible doctrines of inevitable damnation. In the long race of life the hero, not the demon, was first to reach the goal. There are many who start with all the virtues but they lag by the way, and at the end irritabilities, despairs and hatreds are victors in the race. It is something to have left the demon behind, and to end life, as Byron ended it, with victory. It is what a man ends by being that we can judge. What are virtues which lie in a past if in the long run they had not staying power? What are past sins if in the long run the virtues outrace them? We can only hail the victor at the post.

Tolstoi

TOLSTOI WAS an extraordinarily serious person. One gets the impression, perhaps wrongly, from his books that he could not play, that the child was dead in the man. Almost all rich natures retain the power of playing at times, that is, of enjoying life without torturing themselves all the while about the wisdom or folly of what they are doing, just as the kitten enjoys chasing its own tail. Shakespeare, who can be so tragic, has a very fat laugh. He will conjure up a Bottom for us out of sheer impish enjoyment. If Tolstoi had seen a Bottom in real life he would have moralised about the tyranny of society, or what bad government or bad economics had brought about such a character. But somehow we feel we are right to laugh at and with Bottom, and not to make him the basis of a morality. Tolstoi was not without humour or wit, but it was of the grimmest kind. Never does he play from sheer delight in being alive. When I read the volume in which Aylmer Maude has gathered Tolstoi's writings on Art, I feel there is something fundamentally wrong because of that grim, unsmiling face which glowers at me all the time. Continually, as I read, I prostrate myself before a profound intelligence, and almost as continually do I find myself wondering at some incredible stupidity. It is doubtful whether any other man in the world could have secured publicity for the article on Shakespeare, whom he considers an insignificant writer, and the world worship which he receives Tolstoi regards as merely mass hallucination. Tolstoi had a power of concentration which was abnormal, but it was the concentration of one who seemed mentally short-sighted. He went too close to his subject, and, as I think, he saw it in wrong perspective. There is in what he writes the vividness and particularity of the man who looks closely at what he sees, but his short-sightedness prevents him seeing objects bathed in light and air. Mountains are not appreciated with one's nose up to them, but at a distance where their grandeur can be seen. Tolstoi assures us of his sensitiveness to art and music and literature, and we believe him. In what way is he short-sighted? He sees everything from the moral angle. We must, it is true, see life from this angle, but seeing life as we do in succession, in division, in part, as Emerson says, we must see life from many other angles also if we are to see it truly. There is a sentence in the Gospels which is full of wisdom, and if it had been hung up as a text in Tolstoi's study it might at last have rounded out that gigantic fragment of humanity to full vision. "Consider the lilies of the field. They toil not, neither do they spin, and yet I say unto you that Solomon in all his glory was not arrayed like one of these." To Tolstoi beauty was never its own excuse for being. It must toil and spin and, we might add, preach to justify its existence. Tolstoi was, first of all, a great novelist, perhaps the greatest of any; and, secondly, he was a preacher, and his criterion of art seems to be first, whether it tells its story well, and, secondly, whether it is a moral story, that is, his judgment of art and literature is conditioned psychologically by his own occupations. He makes great play with the definitions of beauty of the aesthetes and philosophers, and scoffs at those who regard beauty as a manifestation of spirit or Deity. All that is a great deal too vague for Tolstoi. He challenges the philosophers to be precise about beauty. He contrasts the varying definitions of beauty for two thousand years, and waves them aside because there is no certainty about them, and there are hosts of conflicting definitions. But he himself continually speaks of God, and he would probably be horrified if anyone used his own method of criticism, contrasting the conceptions of Deity made by men since the beginning of recorded thought and dismissing the whole idea of God because of these conflicting opinions. There are some subjects so vast that the human mind cannot come to agreement because they cannot be conceived of in fullness but only in part and in glimpses, and the essential nature of Deity, of spirit, of beauty, of truth, of life, will be guessed at by millions of men in the future as in the past, each one getting a flash of everlastingness but never the full understanding. We would like to offset Tolstoi's grim conscience by Whitman, to whom art is a mode of being. "The oration is to the orator, and comes most back to him. The poem is to the poet, and comes most back to him. The painting is to the painter, and comes most back to him." That is, the artist sings, paints or writes out of a spiritual necessity, and in the blindness of creation he is not thinking of other people at all. In the conflagration set up he illuminates his own being, the self is made clear to the self, and there is a profounder self-consciousness after creation. It may happen that the lamp he lights may give light to others,

but we are certain that nothing first-class came when the
artist's mind was fixed on his public rather than on his subject. We can agree with Tolstoi that the greatest art is
religious, and when the spiritual element is lacking the art is
inferior in substance. But I doubt the spirituality of Tolstoi
even when he talks most about religion. Spirituality is the
power of apprehending formless being or essence. When
Wordsworth feels in Nature the sense of some being inter-
fused with it, we think of his perception as spiritual. Tolstoi
rarely gives us the impression of direct apprehension of anything spiritual. When he speaks scornfully about the philosophers to whom beauty is a manifestation of spirit, or when
he shows a blindness to pure poetry in his criticism of
Shakespeare, we feel that all he says comes from a lack of
spirituality, and that feelings and moods which have moved
humanity profoundly were incomprehensible to him. The
excesses he admits in his confessions may have atrophied the
inner eye, and what happens after that we are told by Lao-Tse:
"When the spirit is lost men follow after charity and duty to
one's neighbours". That is, for living impulses which are lost
conscious duties are substituted, and how poor a thing duty
consciously done is in comparison with natural affection we
all know. Tolstoi's preaching leaves us cold, because somehow we feel this terrible old man is not in love with us.
Whitman's rhetoric warms us because we feel affection
in it.

I think Tolstoi wrong-headed, arrogant and blind in his
criticism of art and literature; but a great genius, even in his
aberrations, continually says things more profound than the
man of mere talent who is always sane, and these profound
things can be found in this which is perhaps the most wrong-
headed of all Tolstoi's writing. I feel the distinction he
makes is true when he says universal art arises when someone,
having experienced a profound emotion, feels the necessity
of transmitting it to others, while the art of the rich arises

less from the artist's inner impulse than because wealthy people demand amusement and pay well for it, and there is much that is true in what he says about the counterfeits of art which are so created. Artists and literary men should brood on all that Tolstoi says about this. As a class at present the vast majority of artists are simply parasites on the rich, and adjust their vision of life to please the rich. If one looks at almost any exhibition in London or any other capital city this is at once seen to be true. The artists did their best work for the God. Then they served the Caesars, the aristocracies, and now the oligarchies, and with every change of masters the art has been worse. A few powerful souls go alone to Nature, but ninety per cent are mere flatterers of the wealthy. Tolstoi's book may help to release some from this servitude, but it is to be hoped when they have ceased to flatter wealth they will not flatter their own ego, which is the next pitiful stage, and one from which Tolstoi for all his confessions and self-analysis was not exempt. The great artist forgets himself in his art.

Tolstoi's Diary

IF *The Private Diary of Leo Tolstoi* had been written by any other than Leo Tolstoi it would never have found a publisher. There are few profundities in it. The entries for the most part are the brevities in which a young man notes down that he drank, gambled, got in a rage, danced, flirted, was bored, tried to write, read, went to the opera, quarrelled with his friends or had a pleasant evening: only in rare moments is there intensity of feeling. There is always present with us the image of the later Tolstoi, a terrible and famous old man, who preached at us and made us hate his preaching because we felt this terrible old man did not love us, indeed despised us, and we will never accept monition from those who despise us, though they be high above us by reason of their intellect and power.

Was the Tolstoi of the diary, with his continuous yielding to impulse, simply the laboratory in which the terrible austere Tolstoi, the moralist, worked, collecting rich material for his art? If the Tolstoi of the diary had ever really become reformed, if there was no conflict between the outer and the inner man, then the voice which moved Europe would have been silent. Yeats says in one of his essays, we make great poetry out of the conflict with ourselves, and that disparity between the inner and the outer Tolstoi, I imagine, went on until the end of their lives. Probably the intransigeance of the outer self aroused the bitter contempt of the inner self, and the inner Tolstoi grew to judge the world by the frailties of the outer, and that is why we feel this terrible old man does not love us and why we do not love him for all our awe at the masterpieces.

Tolstoi and George Sand

BOTH TOLSTOI AND GEORGE SAND were frank revealers of themselves, and it is obvious that their own lives were the mine in which they worked. I think in the case of Tolstoi, where the artist was also a moralist, the digging into his own experience was very unpleasant to him. The moralist was always telling the artist that the substance of the life he was handling was decadent and corrupt. George Sand in her way was just as much of a moral idealist as Tolstoi. I doubt if she had a love affair that was not transfigured in her heart in a fashion which would have been amazing to those who only thought of her as an over-sexed woman. The moralist in her did not conflict with the artist as it did in Tolstoi. In Tolstoi the moralist was heartily ashamed of life, almost as much as Plotinus, who blushed to

think he had a body. With Tolstoi morality was almost
Buddhist though he thought it was the essence of Christianity. Morality, as I understand Tolstoi's soul, meant truly
the killing of all pleasant desires. If a desire was pleasant it
was almost certain to be evil. George Sand accepted life.
The moralist in her did not oppose. The novelist desired to
create the ideal relationship, spiritual and bodily, between
the sexes; and if the material was stubborn or crumbled she
then moved on to see what could be created out of other
human material. So far as one can see, her companions in
this quest were nearly all men of genius or real intellect. The
names of Alfred de Musset, of Chopin are as famous as her
own, but her other intimates seem almost all to have some
intellect or force of character. With Tolstoi his adventures
in life left a residue of disgust with him, and I think this
must have been because there was a good deal of the brute
in him. He was satisfying the appetite of the brute rather
than following an ideal. His old age could hardly be called
benign though he was the most famous writer of his time.
George Sand gathered from her adventures in life an immense understanding and kindness. She was Lady Bountiful
to the poor about her, the prop and stay of crowds of in-
effectual human beings. She shouldered all their burdens
cheerfully, set herself to earn enough money to supply their
needs, and at her funeral there were tears in eyes which one
may surmise wept very little over the rest of humanity. That
image of her soul, so understanding, so generous and for-
giving, which in her old age had impressed itself on her
contemporaries, could not have been created if her life,
scandalous as it seemed to the conventional, had truly been
the bad life they surmised, and I am sure her old age was
without bitterness because she had never been merely the
slave of bodily passion but had been pursuing truly in her
own fashion an ideal and one that did not appear to her own
heart ignoble as Tolstoi's own actions appeared to him. We

may be quite sure that what is essentially bad does not evolve sweetness just as we may be certain that what is essentially good does not leave a residue of bitterness and contempt for life.

The Dark Avatar

EUROPE SEEMS to be reverting to autocracy. Her Mussolinis arrogate to themselves all the authority of a Caesar. Will the obsequious begin to create around them or their successors a psychic atmosphere until gradually there grows up about them the authority which was implied in the phrase, "The divine right of kings"? Was it some high spirituality in the ancients or was it merely the slave mind which made them see a deity incarnate in heroes like Alexander and Caesar? Or did the seer first discover something transcendental in the great man, and did the slaves shout it out afterwards in mere servility or fear? The hero in the ancient world seems to have moved rapidly to a place in the pantheon of divinities. Alexander was cried out as an incarnate deity in his lifetime. We can see how our own Cuchulain began changing in legend from a little dark sad man to a dilated being with hair and eyes of many colours —a possible embodiment of Lugh, the sun-god. In our own time, whatever it may be makes an aureole round the brows of greatness, seership, imagination or servility, acts much more slowly. It is a hundred years since the death of Napoleon, and only now does the Russian novelist, Dmitri Merezhkovsky, begin the process of deification of his hero which, if Napoleon had lived two thousand years ago, would have taken place in his lifetime. It is perhaps exaggeration to say that Merezhkovsky deifies Napoleon. He belongs to too sceptical an age to have that fine faith in the divinity of greatness, but he feels something magical about Napoleon, some quality which needs a transcendental philosophy to explain it, and he recurs again and again to this in his study of the Emperor.

Is the will one of the radio-active forces of Nature? Have its emanations a penetrating power like those rays science tells us of which penetrate through wall or metals? Is it, when concentrated so that it can operate on an idea to the complete exclusion of any other idea, the supreme power in our being, and the one before which, when it is burnished, all the other faculties must yield? Was it this intensity of will which bent almost everybody who came into the presence of Napoleon? Those who hated him felt the mesmeric quality as much as those who loved him. Or must we speculate further, and surmise in this extraordinary man an avatar, a being sustained by some overshadowing power, to be a pivot round which the world turned, an instrument of super-natural justice or destiny? Merezhkovsky can see the divine incarnation, or avatar, in Jesus; all is clear in that radiance from the Oversoul. But in the entirely opposite character of Napoleon there is another intensity which seems to him supernatural, and he meditates on him, and, as I think, if he spoke out all that he believed in his heart, he would say that Napoleon went forth from the Lord for some dark divine purpose. Was Napoleon simply a sword in the hand of some invisible divinity, or was there a mission which failed because the human instrument had flaws in it? Was the mission the welding of civilisation into a unity? Was the earlier message of Christ to the nations like that first invita-tion to a feast given by the master in the scriptural parable? Was Napoleon like the iron hand which was sent out to draw people in from the highways and byways because the first message of love was rejected? Has Heaven imagined some destiny for humanity, a high brotherhood of all living? If that high invitation is ignored, are there secondary forces which come into operation to coerce, the demoniac nature trying in its own way to carry out the plan of the Divine nature? There was some element of infinity in this man: "One of my greatest ideas was the gathering together of peoples who form geographical entities, but are divided and dismembered by politics and revolution." That was but a beginning. The end was the uniting of these bodies into "a European League of Nations. A pan-European code of laws. . . . The whole population of Europe would have become as one family, and every man while he travelled abroad would still have found himself at home. *Sooner or later the nations will become united by the very force of events.*" Did he see such an end clearly at times? Did he work for it consciously? Was it by such a grandiose purpose he justified to himself the slaying of millions? Or did the purpose arise later in his mind to justify the deed? It is the virtue of Merezhkovsky's book that it makes us speculate on the soul of Napoleon, for, as he says, forty thousand volumes have been written about this man, his wars, policy, diplomacy, legislature, administration, about his ministers, marshals, brothers, sisters, wives, mistresses, but the more we learn about him the less we know him. In this book there is nothing except the soul of Napoleon to speculate about, and I confess I found it more interesting than any book on Napoleon I have read, because it tries to penetrate into the secret of the soul, while all others were overcome by the magnitude of the deeds.

The Anatomy of a Poet

THERE IS A BEING in us, a lover of fantasy, which is antagonised by the labours of the anatomist and dissector. We are, too, such warm and whole life to ourselves that we shrink from the skeleton and the sight of the bared organs when the lovely gloss of ivory and rose which covered the flesh is removed. The same antagonism is born in us if any would disclose too indiscreetly the moral or intellectual anatomy beneath the work of some poet who had imposed his fantasy on us, so that it entered our imagination like a living creature.

I suppose it is inevitable that one great writer after another must lose his power over the generations which follow him, and when at last he is thoroughly understood there is an end of him. He goes into limbo, is a name for a little while, and then there is oblivion. This psychological summing up of past poets and heroes is going on rapidly in our generation. The latest writer on Milton gives us not another appreciation of the great artist, but a moral and intellectual anatomy of the man, though with no undue emphasis on the animal.

I do not know if any previous writer on Milton had tracked the sources of his philosophy to the Kohar and Kabbalah, or to Robert Fludd, the hermetic alchemist and mystical philosopher. Hardly anyone had ever thought of Milton as a mystic, and though they knew the poet took any jewels polished by another so long as they would fit into his own gorgeous work, I doubt if any had thought of searching in the mystical byways of literature in order to find a fountain from which the poet drank. One has only to stand on the floor of Milton's Heaven to see the rebel angels with pick and shovel tearing up the divine soil for sulphur and nitre to make gunpowder, to feel the material solidity of his vision. His imagination was powerful to create the life of the fallen angels, but when he ascended to Heaven his vision was rather of the intellect than the imagination. The English imagination, so rich in the creation of human character, has hardly ever risen up into Heaven, and the nearest approach to this can be found in some of Blake's prophetic books. When the imagination is insufficiently winged and cannot follow the intellect, and the latter must go on lone journeys, it can only bring back bare and arid things from its travels. How inferior the utterances of Milton's divinities to his devils!

He belongs, as Blake said, to the Devil's Party without knowing it. It is in the intellectual conception of Milton's divinities he was indebted, according to M. Saurat, to the Kabbalists. He makes a good case.

It is possible, of course, for two thinkers to arrive at an identical conclusion about some problem of theology independently, but if the analogies persist we are justified in suspecting that one has had knowledge of the other. However it may be, Milton, interpreting the Kabbalah, attracts me no more than when I supposed he was interpreting the ideas of some Puritan divine.

Milton the thinker can never be made so attractive to us as Milton the poet, nor is the man so alluring as his imagination. He has in him something of that terrible fanaticism which makes us shrink from Tolstoi when he ceases to be the artist and becomes the grim moralist. I suspect, both with Milton and Tolstoi, that they were not indisposed to inflict on us the lashings with which they quite properly castigated themselves, and we fly like children from the teacher who approaches us whip in hand, even though he has whipped himself first to show us how to bear it. We do not suspect Milton of the excesses to which Tolstoi confessed. Indeed the purity of his life was notorious. But just as a man can be a glutton on a crust of bread as well as upon a banquet, so a single lapse, a fall in the mind even, not in the flesh, will afford the born preacher, such as Milton was, enough material for long and austere homilies. M. Saurat, indeed, suspects that out of some such fall, perhaps only in the soul, Milton built his gigantic epic, the Fall in Heaven and the Fall in Eden alike coming from the same sin. He may have found his own imagination outcast from the Spirit because of some fancy, some "sport with Amaryllis in the shade", or there may have been some real lapse bitterly reflected on, out of which came his grandiose interpretation of Heaven and Earth and the moral law which is one for both.

No writer could be more lucid than M. Saurat. He divests Milton of his poetry and shows us the moral and intellectual anatomy around which that marvellous fantasy was built, and he convinces us that these are verily the bones and internal organs of the poet's soul. I prefer them clothed, and think that I can truly know more of Milton in the mirror of himself I see in his works than in the psycho-analysis, just as we know more of a man alive than we can possibly know of him when he is dead and the anatomist discloses to our gaze the internal organs.

Swinburne

A CREATURE all cerebral excitement, with small redheaded body electrified, the use of words—beautiful or violent—his main passion; a passion to which he surrendered on any temptation, whether it was to blaspheme extravagantly some contemporary or to praise him just as extravagantly, or to do both—not at all an unusual thing. The frail body dreaming of abnormal physical adventures and endurance, committing sins in the mind of which the body was incapable, super-sensitiveness expressing itself with passionate arrogance, yet in all probability on its knees in the soul with humility and gentleness, that mood which allowed the poet to surrender his personality to his nurses.

The soul of Swinburne was a fiery crucible in which the airy elements became dissociated from the gross or solid, and he could but rarely manufacture a poetic substance which combined abstract and concrete in a living union. He was either abstract or gross; when the former he was too often unreadable; when the latter he was too often unprintable. But they were the poles in his being which vitalised each other, and without some element of the concrete the abstract nature becomes thin, unreal, almost incredible.

Plotinus says that the scurrilous clown, however we mislike him, is a necessary ingredient in the drama: "Take away the low characters and the power of the drama is gone; these are part and parcel of it". The low character in Swinburne's genius, the scurrilous clown, was chained up, and hence the monotony of his poetry. Some may quote against me Tennyson's epitaph on another poet:

> His worst he kept, his best he gave;
> My Shakespeare's curse on clown or knave
> Who will not let his ashes rest.

But if we take Iago or Lady Macbeth, or Bottom or the other villains and clowns out of Shakespeare's drama the plays would at once become devitalised, and what is true of Shakespeare's drama is true of Swinburne's work. It may be argued that it would be better to let Swinburne drop into oblivion, that it is not worth while to revitalise what is fine if it has to be paid in a resurrection of what is scurrilous. But if he is to be written about at all he must be exhibited in all truth for we do not allow the genius to be manifested by omitting the shadows which intensify its shining.

There was an imp, a scold, a blasphemer, a foiled sensualist and a very great deal of the angelic and ethereal in his make-up, the personality at least as interesting as the poetry. In another decade the veil will in all probability be lifted as completely as it is possible to unveil the personality of such a genius. That unveiling can only be of what was hitherto concealed because it might injure his reputation. It would be an ironical commentary if the lifting of the veil made his genius appear greater to posterity than it did to his contemporaries. But that, curiously, may be the result of daubing a figure round with shadow; what seemed dim in the features may shine out more than before by contrast with the added darkness.

American Culture

WHITMAN DEDICATED one of his *Leaves of Grass* to the Old World readers, hearing that they wished for something by which might be defined to them the new continent and its athletic democracy. He exhibited himself as typical of the divine average, he who was, perhaps, a thousand years ahead of that average in rich humanity. If any had gone to the States lured by Whitman's rhapsodies he would have discovered the poet almost a solitary in his own land, his chant alien to the mood of the people he lived among. His muse was in a sense the Spread Eagle, but in its noblest and loftiest form almost out of sight of those it soared over. Americans were for so many years intoxicated by the swift material development of their country, by the belief that theirs was the dominant race on the planet, that through last century one had to turn to the pages of travellers to see America for what in truth it was. Now that it has become materially dominant a new humility is arising in the best minds. Its culture can be discussed almost as dispassionately by American writers as if they were Swedish or Dutch observers. Lewis Mumford has now written a book, *The Golden Day*, which seems to me the most penetrating criticism of American culture I have yet read. The charm of the writing is such that one is tempted to read on and on and perhaps to overlook the solidity and seriousness of the thought which is dressed in such lively colours. To explain America he has to show the ancestor culture of Europe in that break-up which was beginning before the discovery of America.

The solidity of that culture began to be broken up when ingenious workmen invented clocks and began to measure time, and with other instruments to measure space—the telescope, the microscope, the theodolite, all instruments of a new order of spatial exploration, so that before Columbus'

time the geographers began to cover their maps with imaginary lines of latitude and longitude. The world in which
men lived began to open before them illimitably. Science
pursuing a knowledge of external nature became a rival in
men's imaginations of that other culture of the Kingdom of
Heaven. When America was discovered there flowed to it,
to North America especially, a preponderance of the rebels
and heretics of the ancestor culture, and no one can understand American culture to-day who does not realise the
character of the pioneers whose interests had become either
externalised or abstract, though it was only in the nineteenth
century that the multitudes who swarmed from Europe
brought most completely the dream of mere worldly success, the spirit of revolt against feudalism, the irreverence
for tradition, and made their spirit dominant in the United
States.

We can understand in a country temporarily so dominated
by externalities how Mark Twain on behalf of American
authors could write an almost unbelievable letter to Walt
Whitman on his seventieth birthday congratulating the poet
on having lived in the greatest era the world had known. In
what did the greatness of that era consist? Was it its poetry,
its art, its music? No. Mark detailed to the old poet what
happiness should be his in living in the age of the steam press,
the steamship, the railway, the electrotype, gaslight, phonograph and the sewing-machine. He did not refer to literature
at all, to art or culture or poetry. They were unnoticeable
things, much less important than the sewing-machine or the
phonograph. One would like to think it was irony, but for
once in his life Mark was serious, telling the poet of the
things which to him and those he spoke for really mattered.
But while the refugees from Europe brought in this un-
spiritual mentality, a mentality which hardened in their
struggle for mastery in the new environment, there were
Americans who applied to their own world the noblest

thought of the ancestor continent. There were Emerson, Whitman, Thoreau, a spiritual triad, who together with Melville and Hawthorne belong to the Golden Day of American literature, a day which was soon overcast and obscured. America passed swiftly from itself in that transcendental mood, and in a generation these had shrunk almost as far behind time to the American consciousness as the Red Branch cycle has from ours in Ireland.

In Emerson, in Whitman, and in Thoreau more, I think, than in any of their European contemporaries do we find the dawning of something which might be spoken of as cosmic or planetary consciousness, a mood fitting for so gigantic a nation which it may return to, but which, after these pioneers had spoken, never again inspired American genius. After these men come a lesser brood of psychologists and philosophers like William James, Henry Adams, Santayana and Dewey; novelists like Howells, Upton Sinclair, Jack London, Dreiser, Sinclair Lewis, Sherwood Anderson; poets like Carl Sandburg, Vachel Lindsay, Frost and Robinson, all men of some force and talent but no sky-touching genius, no one even who burrows so deeply as our James Joyce. Ireland with four million people has produced a literature at least as important as the United States with a hundred and ten million people. What is the cause of this? Mumford finds it in the break-up of European culture, in the life of the pioneers whose consciousness was brought to the surface in the effort to master materials; but is it not that a new race is being formed, a race which is yet young, and that the young look outside themselves, while literature demands reverie and introspection? Emerson, Thoreau, Whitman, Melville, Hawthorne—all seem to have been born with the spirit aged within them and predestined to contemplation. But the new hustling America seems to be antagonistic to reverie or meditation in which the soul discovers its own heights or depths. Hence the range of the American consciousness as revealed in contemporary literature is confined almost to the alert, waking consciousness, to the things that excite it for the moment and pass from it again and are forgotten because they have little relation to the enduring spiritual life. One might speculate about the future of American culture. It seems as if European culture in all its depth could not be transplanted, could not accompany the emigrants, that America must create its own culture and traditions. A speculation about this would be full of interest. All the great cultures of the world have started with a religion. European culture has its roots in Christianity, Chinese culture in Confucianism, Indian culture in Brahminism. Almost every great culture has its roots in the Heavenworld. But while in America superficially its people are inheritors of the spiritual culture of Europe, which was so profound, so Heaven-reaching in the age of Dante and Aquinas, in the New World it has become shallow and inspires no literature. We are witnessing in Europe in the Spenglerian sequence the downfall of a culture which once dominated its humanity, but which has now almost externalised itself and is rapidly coming to be buried in the mechanism itself created. In America their civilisation begins by the perfecting of mechanisms. What will cause a spiritual life to be born out of that? Will the inner ever become more important than the outer as it was in Europe in the birth of its spiritual culture? Must America have a prophet of its own: a Shakespeare, a Dante, a Plato, to make populous the empty mansions of the spirit? As it is, the States are more notable for prodigious external developments than for spiritual magnificence, a skyscraper is more than a poem, though one may help the spirit on its heavenly climbing and the other will bring the body but a hundred yards or so into the sky. I feel certain that so great a people will not be content with- externalities, that the poets of whom Whitman was the prophecy, the thinkers of whom Emerson was but an anticipation, must be born there. How difficult it will be for the soul to rise from that huge body, what spiritual battles must be fought, what martyrdoms be endured we may divine. But it seems incredible that so vast a continent can be left with so little soul.

Francis Thompson

CONTEMPORARIES ARE LIKE LOVERS who have intimacies for each other which none other can know. By the fact of my being contemporary I may accept as gold a literary currency which time may assay and prove to be sounding brass.

I suspect that when the time-spirit has twice blown his trumpet a great deal of the poetry which moved us as contemporaries will seem like withered leaves to our grandchildren. But I feel sure there will be enough of the timeless in Francis Thompson to keep his name among the poets so long as the language lasts.

I feel I ought to denounce the pompous, over-coloured language, his inventions of over-purpled words, but while I read there was some light reflected from these gaudy jewels of speech which made a kind of magic of their own which was communicated to me and from which I cannot yet escape, and for which I forgive what I would possibly denounce in an elder or a junior.

I do not know whether he was naturally a creature abnormally sensitive or whether an over-sensitiveness was created in him by the drugs he took. But I cannot read Thompson's poetry without feeling the affinity much of it has with De Quincey's dream fugues and opium reveries, over-wrought emotions, rhetorical pomposities created to express the perception of senses drug-dilated beyond what is natural and human. He does as De Quincey does, or as

Coleridge does, brings us into lustrous, remote regions of
life for a moment, and makes us feel for that instant that
they are some of the many mansions of the spirit and we

> Pass the gates of Luthany, tread the region Elinore.

But these are unreal worlds, however their magic affects us.
It is when the poet is spiritual he is at his greatest. In *The
Kingdom of God*, found among his papers after his death, his
vision had access to a reality more moving and profound
than any fantasy: this world and life transfigured by the
spirit.

> O world invisible, we view thee,
> O world intangible, we touch thee,
> O world unknowable, we know thee,
> Inapprehensible, we clutch thee!
>
> Does the fish soar to find the ocean,
> The eagle plunge to find the air—
> That we ask of the stars in motion
> If they have rumour of thee there?
>
> Not where the wheeling systems darken,
> And our benumbed conceiving soars!—
> The drift of pinions, would we hearken,
> Beats at our own clay-shuttered doors.
>
> The angels keep their ancient places;—
> Turn but a stone, and start a wing!
> 'Tis ye, 'tis your estrangéd faces,
> That miss the many-splendoured thing. . . .

After writing that lyric he might have felt as De Quincey
did, that the Sorrowful Sisters had but plagued his heart
until they unfolded the capabilities of his spirit. I am inclined to rank this last poem above the famous *Hound of
Heaven*, for all its magnificence, for there is in the famous
ode something of the "unperturbéd pace" which belongs to

the God, rather than of the hunted soul. There is the obvious delight of the phrase-maker in his phrases. It is not so electrically concentrated as the shorter lyric, but it will always seem marvellous to those who look upon fine phrases as a lover.

A creature of overwrought sensibility, preserving as he grew up the virgin sensitiveness of childhood, sometimes this led him, as in *The Making of Viola*, to a kind of poetic infantilism, a pretty prattle, a child's imagination of Heaven. The other pole from this infantilism was pomposity. But when the sensitiveness and dignity were blended together we had exquisite poetry.

I confess I read through the most extravagant pomposities in his poetry, expecting to find the reward of some marvellous lines. Sometimes that lustrous speech reminds me of Monticelli the painter who by some wizardry of rich, dim colour and half-defined forms created for us a beauty we feel is artificial, but which yet makes the heart ache. It is dangerous, the pursuit of magic in life or literature. It led Coleridge and De Quincey and Thompson into drug-taking. They may be likened to those people in Scripture who do not go into the soul by the strait gate but over the walls like thieves and robbers. Shakespeare has plenty of magic, but it is supported by an immense human vitality. Those others are frail spirits who could not force their way into the paradise they sought without a strength drawn momentarily from a sinister fountain. But they did reveal beauty to us strange and new, and they have given us that beauty without our having to go to the sinister fountain to enable us to share their ecstasy. They sought high things, not low things, and in the final judgment their faith or the ideal they followed may be the absolution of their sins.

The "Prometheus Bound"

THE "PROMETHEUS BOUND" OF AESCHYLUS is one of the most mysterious works of the human imagination. It has almost the awe-evoking power of a mighty scripture. We are carried away while we read it from all the accidents of human life to its fundamentals. This mind by which we think, plan and foresee, this which sets us apart from the animals, its incarnation or awakening in man seems to be the subject of the drama. But as it awakens to the use of this divine power of imagination and intellect it discovers that it is in chains at the same time. Yet it prefers the torture of self-consciousness to its ancient mindless happiness, and wills to endure, making its choice between two states. Is this the idea symbolised in the drama? It is all mysterious, and we read it as we might follow behind a curtain the motions of mighty beings who stir the curtain but never reveal themselves to us.

Poetry of Revolt

WHEN PEOPLE are in a state of revolt they are very wide awake. They have dissevered themselves from the dream consciousness, and it is out of the dream consciousness that poetry is born. Political movements and revolutionary movements rarely give birth to poetry. They are inspirers of rhetoric, which is the energy of poetry without its living soul.

Though the cause be impeccable it will not inspire poetry. The volatile spirit escapes because the political verse-writer or the revolutionary verse-writer have clearly in their minds an idea, a protest, a rage against something which is outside or beyond them, and the inspiration is limited to that idea, passion or feeling. Now a true poem seems as if it was companion to all other ideas, feelings or thoughts in the universe. It has the element of infinity in it, and it appears as if it might have been written at any time almost in the history of the world.

Coleridge

NEVER DID coloured dragon-fly emerge from a more unpromising larva. Never in poetry were the flights of such a winged and coloured creature more brief. Soon its wings wearied, and for the rest of a long life it was crawling on earth more or less brilliantly by the aid of intellect, or slobbering about through the impulse of emotion. In the same house of the soul dwelt a Bird of Faery more radiant than colibri, a subtle intellect but without rudder, and a huge sentimentality; eloquent words always at the service of intellect and emotion, but too rarely would they fly with the mystic adventurer in romance.

Mangan

WHERE MANGAN is not easily understood by English or American readers is where he is poorest as a poet. Where he is the poet of genius he is appreciated by people of any country. That he is not popular comes, we think, because of the prevailing tragic sentiment from which many recoil. But they do so in every country where tragedy is always less popular than comedy. Literature derives its sole interest from the genius of the writer. If he has not genius it does not matter from the literary point of view what his other virtues were, or for what audience he wrote exclusively. A poet becomes great because he has so much spiritual or human intensity that he becomes intelligible everywhere, not only to those who know the language but even to those who read him in translation. If he daubs himself over with local colour and has that only as a merit, he becomes unintelligible outside his own environment.

Thoreau

WITH MOST OF us the mind has not found how to become self-sustaining in Nature. After a little it becomes inactively contemplative. It has to go back to the cities, to society, to libraries, to theatres, to the academies and lecture-rooms to renew its life, to find things it can feed on. We light the internal fire by friction with other minds. But with Thoreau the peculiar quality of intelligence seemed to catch fire from Nature itself. His solitude is populous with thought. He might answer like Emerson to a question about that happy solitude: "Did you not dream some wisdom from the berries went?"

A Political Martyr

WE HAVE AN INTUITION that the soul must some time in its evolution be tempered so that it is able to withstand any shock, to front any dark power, for if it be not so tempered it will be a broken reed in the hands of the Spirit. Because of this intuition which many have, because they tremble at the thought of all they must endure, there will be readers who will follow with a straining of the heart all that Frank Gallagher writes in his book. His politics may mean nothing to them, his powers of endurance much. They will wonder when their own will would snap, what terror would overcome them, what desire would lure them away. They will measure their own soul with his, and, I think, they will be comforted in the thought that the soul can endure so much and so long. This is perhaps not the way the author would like his book to be reviewed. He is one of the apostles of self-sacrifice, and he would like any wreath his sacrifice has earned to be laid on the altar of his political ideal. I consider these records of intense suffering and lay the wreath on another altar, to the Master of Life.

Aphorisms ～

IT IS THE traditional way of the East to concentrate its wisdom in aphorisms just as it is our European sin to expand an aphorism into a volume. Kapila, Lao-Tse, Patanjali, Sankara and many another sage left us concentrated brevities. The Eastern sage gives his pupils a few aphorisms to meditate over and when they have fathomed the profundity of one the pupil is almost able to create philosophies for himself. When we meet this concentration at first it repels us, for it implies a conviction that the pupil must think at least as hard as the sage, and the European writer explains so much and is so clear that the reader has not to think at all. All he gets is ready-made opinions, whereas the brooding on the aphorisms of any of the great Eastern sages creates another with an original mind.

Respectability and Genius

RESPECTABILITY AND GENIUS are a couple who are perpetually being forced by their friends into a *mariage de convenance*, but these marriages have proved to be either sterile, or else the children almost invariably take after respectability, their mother, and not after genius, the father. Let nobody accuse me of insinuating that genius must be loose-living, that Swinburne's lyrics were alcoholic in origin, or that Coleridge's magic came out of laudanum. But I am certain genius is never respectable. It is like the spirit the Indian Sankara speaks of, which sometimes appears inexpressibly wise, and at other times quite crazy to the rational observer. Genius must be wedded to freedom, and then the marriage should be all that is desired—at least, from the point of view of posterity.

Of a Russian Novelist

HE REALLY DOES make his people live in our imagination, and every now and then some glowing sentence makes us realise that the sun shines there as immemorially alike upon the just and the unjust. Nature is lovely: "The air between the mountains and the sea is fiery and lustrous as wine." There are the old consolations for poverty. There is the sweet air, the magnetic earth, and no revolution can pull sun, moon or stars out of the sky. I am reminded by some shining sentences in the book that there are some riches of which not even the most incompetent revolutionaries can rob the soul.

Kipling

WHAT WAS MOST ENCHANTING in that old, arrogant Kipling with his superior British military fashion of judgment was the revelation every now and then of a beautiful gentleness. It appears at its best in the old lama in *Kim*, in Kim's subjecting the imp in himself in reverence, in tales like *The Brushwood Boy*, and when we came across this beautiful mood we forgave the loud and crude imperialism, the shallow arrogance of judgment like that of a half-educated British schoolboy, for we suspect one was the antitoxin of the other, the arrogance created the gentleness, just as after looking at orange we see a mist of blue. It is possible the gentleness was the spiritual reality in Kipling and it grew a crust about itself as a shelter, just as Shaw, one of the most sensitive, kindly and modest of men, beat a brass band round himself announcing his own genius when I suspect he is on his knees inside himself with humility. A writer of genius must have these contraries to heighten and intensify the interaction of faculties. A completely harmonious nature may be a lovely thing in life, but literature is not born from such natures.

Parody

THE GOOD PARODIST is one who takes the mannerisms of an author and makes a pure culture of them so that they riot in a life of their own without any harassing limitations. The ideal parody is in essence a criticism of the author, and when an author allows his mannerisms to grow, the parodist, with an exquisite sense of the absurd, is the only person who can save him from himself. There are, of course, other parodists in whose hands parody becomes "the vile art", which it was called by Matthew Arnold, who not in any justifiable mood of satire or criticism will take a beautiful poem and write a comic echo of it, so that, to those who read, what is beautiful has ever after a vulgar echo of itself in association with it. Nobody could justifiably be irritated by a parody of Tennyson's *May Queen*, but if a poem which is truly beautiful, like his *Crossing the Bar*, was parodied we would have a right to be angry, as we would be with people who chattered of trivialities through the singing of a great oratorio.

Technique ～ꝑ────○

THERE IS SUCH A THING as knowing too much about the technique of an art, because thinking too much about the technique may act as an obstacle to natural expression. The orator's mind must be fixed on his subject and if he is made too self-conscious about delivery, inflection, tone, he may become really ineffective. Audiences know whether the orator is thinking of two things, his subject or the art of speaking, and if the latter is too obvious the oratory is ineffective. It is much better to be absorbed in the subject and to leave it to Nature to do the rest.

Communism and Bernard Shaw

I FIND MYSELF affected by some fourth-dimensional concepts when I read Shaw on socialism. He has almost irrefutable three-dimensional concepts of what is justice, and he invites us all to remake society in the image he has set up. What is in my mind as I read is a fourth-dimensional instinct that justice, as Emerson said, is done now. If I drink to intoxication to-night, to-morrow will find me with a splitting head. Natural justice begins at once. Many people have a conviction that justice is another name for the root law in the universe. The Indians call it Karma. In Christianity the same intuition is expressed in the aphorism "As a man sows, so shall he reap". That is, a supernatural, infallible and inevitable justice is operating all the while, and our earthly justice is only one of the agencies it uses. While our earthly justice is inexact, not one jot or tittle of the eternal law is allowed to lapse. We seem to escape it in the three-dimensional world, but it pursues us into our souls. Its friends are agonies, remorse and an anguish of penitence. To one who holds to this idea it is not society has made this man stupid or miserable but himself. But let nobody think, because there is such a Law always operating, that he need not be concerned about poverty or misery, because people only get what they deserve and have brought on themselves, and that he may with a good conscience contemplate placidly his own fine fortune and the evil lot of others. If he does feel like that, if he has become opaque to pity and the will to action is atrophied, the Law will deal with him surely, for he has refused to become one of its agencies of mercy and forgiveness. I have intuition of such a Law always operating, and I have the intuition that the equality of incomes, which is Shaw's idea of justice, may not be its idea of justice, though I remember in Shaw's favour two statements of Eternal Justice. One is that It makes Its sun to shine alike on the just and the unjust, and the other is referred to in the parable of the man who got people to work for him in his vineyard, some all day, some for half the day, and some only for the last hours, and who paid them all the same sum, for he knew they had all to live, even if they had not had the opportunity to do a full day's work. I find these disconcerting ideas about three-dimensional and four-dimensional justice coming up in my mind reading the last book written by this amazing man, his social testament, prodigal in wit, irony and a kind of transcendental reasonableness.

Adventures in Style

THE VITALITY of these wriggling, writhing and jumping words is not human. They remind me rather of the irrepressible vitality of the cells when the soul has gone from the body and they break out in the sinister ecstasy we think of as disease or corruption. Yes, this literature is germinal, but these are not the creative cells out of which springs beautiful life, but that other breaking-out of an irrepressible vitality in the cells which we think of as disease or death. I think the law of action and reaction will operate and the oscillation will tend to normality, just as in art the cubists found they had come up against a cul-de-sac in the by-road they had adventured on, and the cleverest are returning to the main highway once more. But something has been gained. The post-impressionists, cubists and futurists made it possible for artists to have a much freer, more personal and intimate expression of their vision unhampered by academic tradition. Joyce and others as experimenters in style have enriched literature. It would be as possible to explore the heights of consciousness as the depths explored in *Ulysses*, and, indeed, that vibrationist writing seems more suitable for the expression of spiritual moods which we so rarely reach, and which are only half comprehended, than for the expression of the depths in human nature which we have sounded and comprehend only too well.

The Decree of Nature

EVERY WRITER has the past as his heritage, but how rarely does he contemplate the future or understand the strivings of those who are coming after him as they understand themselves? It is not in human nature, and the juniors must be content to find interpreters among their contemporaries and must not complain about the opacity of their elders, whose vision is ever thickening and whose mind is ever hardening after youth, not by their own wish but by the decree of nature, which toughens the organisms it begets with every year of their growth.

The elders read the classical prose of Pater, Arnold or Ruskin, and do the juniors really expect them to be delighted with the prose of Gertrude Stein, who has the smallest vocabulary of any writer of our time and who makes a few words and sentences spread over pages and pages?

We can almost imagine Miss Gertrude Stein at the age of six screaming out to her governess: "I have enough words and sentences to go on with for the remainder of my life. I can spread them over volumes. I can't learn any more words."

Joyce is the opposite of Miss Gertrude Stein, for he has a whole dictionary of obsolete words in his mind as well as contemporary slang, but is what he has to say worth saying? Has he or the other brilliant juniors anything new except a new style, and the more pains they take about their style the less do they seem to have to say? They are always working at a superficies, beating it out like the goldbeater his little ounce of gold until it covers yards with a shallow gilding that has no depth. I do not imply that there is not in this generation much that can be read with interest, but very little that can be read with pleasure.

"Pleasure!" I seem to hear one of these austere juniors cry out. "He wants to be pleased. Literary sensualist!" Yes, truly I do desire pleasure when I read. I am Epicurean. I will go into the slums of life, into the valley of their shadow if it is illuminated by the lamp of beauty, but I dislike an ugly lamp throwing light upon ugly things. I do not complain about the ugly things, but I object to the ugliness of the lamp, which is uncalled for. But here I am, an elder actually criticising my juniors, a thing for which Nature has unfitted me and my own intellectual ancestry.

The only consolation I have is the knowledge that their juniors in turn will abolish them and their pretensions, and that they will hold up piteous hands deprecating the unspeakable things the latter will be writing.

Slang

MY FRIEND Dr. Osborn Bergin tells me that many European and Asiatic languages had the same great-great-grandfather, but the children got so far away from the parent, and the grandchildren still farther away, that the great-great-grandchildren languages are as unintelligible to each other as Gaelic is to the Sassenach. I fear, unless I have an Anglo-American lexicon, that the American language will reel away even in my lifetime, in spite of the contributions to my American scholarship received from occasional visits to the cinema. I remember my confusion when an American professor wanted to know my "slant on the leadership question". I had not the slightest idea what he meant. I escaped from an exposure of my ignorance by telling him that in a highly-evolved community like the United States problems arose to which there was no parallel among primitive people like the Irish.

What is slang? The scholar's definition is "the misuse or dislocation of the serviceable right meaning of ordinary words". That definition looks too much to the past and does not think enough of the future or its needs. One speculates on the future of certain words: "boss", for example. I remember it as a child. It must be now at least fifty years old. If it survives for another fifty will its ancient ill-bred associations have fallen away from it? Will it be purified and ready for the use of the poet who may without offending us sing of some Caesar as the "laurelled boss", or may we imagine it becoming so refined that in our churches where our great-grandchildren worship they will hear prayers addressed to a "most mighty and most merciful Boss"? I get frightened at these speculations. I will indulge in them no further.

The slang of to-day may be classical speech to-morrow. I am told that the French language has become so perfect that

it is pallid or near death. It is impossible for a writer to find
new and fresh combinations of words, and the younger
French writers are deliberately filling their pages with
slang, trying to reanimate the language with new and vivid
phrases just as a tired-out man might take a stiff glass of
whiskey. Will enough of American speech come across the
Atlantic to revive the dying English language? I was aston-
ished to find how many words and phrases in Professor
Scott's glossary were already familiar to me. I thought
they were good Anglo-Irish, but as the Professor, a scholar
making a contribution to a scholarly tractate, says they are
American I can only suppose some of our exiles revisiting
Ireland had picked up enough American to dazzle their
countrymen and the American phrases became popular as
American dollars. If Seosamh O'Neill is not careful he will
find Irish people in another generation speaking neither
Gaelic nor English but American.

I found in Professor Scott's glossary the word "blurb",
which invention moves the editor of the *Tract* to cry out:
"Admirable! indispensable!" "Blurb" is a term applied to
frothy announcements or over-laudatory praise on the cover
of newly-published books. I do no know whether this word
was created out of nothing, like the universe, or whether
it had any ancestry, and evolved from some remote Aryan
original to its present exquisite fitness. It is impossible to
imagine a word for the purpose in which sound would
better fit the sense. There is something devastating about it
and, if publishers had any literary sense, which they rarely
have, the moment they met the word and knew it expressed
the mood of a continent about their own puffs of their own
books they would never "blurb" any more and the word
might then die an honourable death, yielding up its life at
the moment it killed its enemy. "Lid" for hat and "dome" are
like the child's "tassel" for tail. They arise out of some
association of ideas. But other slang phrases indicate all the

energy of a young race. A man does not get in a rage. "He throws a fit". He does not retire to his couch. He "hits the hay". The speed at which these people live might be inferred from the fact that a man does not arrive, he "hits the town". Perhaps the phrase "throw in a drink" might explain the necessity for Prohibition. It does indicate an unbridled appetite against which legislation might be necessary. America is full of sentimentalists and idealists, and this gives opportunity to the irreverent maker of slang. How devastating to the sentimentalist is the definition "sob-stuff". And the migration of poets like Ezra Pound to Europe might be explained that he fled from people who might hurt his feelings by saying, "This highbrow stuff is where I get off".

My old-world sensibilities are hurt by such words. But I understand the impatience which cries out "Shoot!" to the person who has something on his mind which he takes a long time to say. If you allow anybody to get ahead of you you "take his dust", a thing which must be repugnant to a people whose ideal is to start from Log Cabin to White House. I found in this glossary the interpretation of a number of words which were hitherto like Chinese to me. "Yep" is the equivalent of "yes", though why the transformation took place I cannot see unless young America simply felt that "yes" had had a long enough innings and it was time for a new word. But I did not find the meaning of words which surely cannot be slang as they are used in serious American writing. I find a critic referring to a new book as "snootly poetic". My glossary throws no light on "snootly", nor does it explain the word I have italicised in this sentence: "He set himself *doly* doggedly to endure". These might be noble words. They are not in my English dictionary. They ought to be in an Anglo-American dictionary as they are used by highly-educated men and not as slang. Could they have had an origin as slang and did they survive long enough to take their place in classic speech? And this leads me to speculate

338

that those who invent slang serve a useful purpose. New words and phrases are tested. If the intuition of hundreds of thousands accept them and retain them, then they are passed gradually into the association with ancient aristocratic words, and they blend with the classic languages as the daughter of a wealthy parvenu might marry into the peerage.

Sentimental Verse

I CANNOT FIX whose was the first voice, perhaps it was no big poet, only a bygone generation of verse-writers singing mildly sentimental songs:

> I'd like to leave the ingle and the thatch,
> The gossip and the sickly cups of tea,
> Just to settle under any sort of patch,
> With any sort of *men* along of me.

I seem to have heard many plaints like this of the *Pensioned Mariner*, plaints of old soldiers, old cabmen, old ploughmen, old huntsmen and endless other ancients all mildly and tearfully reminiscent by their chimney nooks. I am not moved. I do not know why. I say to myself: "You are cold and callous. Here's this old pensioner asking for sympathy. Why are you not sorry for him?" I have nothing to say. I button up the pockets of my sympathy and pass on without a twinge of conscience. I wonder am I a brute. I'll know at the Last Day. But my conscience does not trouble me now.

APHORISMS

APHORISMS [1]

WHEN A MAN attempts creative work he reveals himself most completely. If he has genius, imagination, humanity, we recognise them, for such things cannot be aped.

*

We never can be as wise and beautiful speaking to many as we can speaking to one. It is a paradox that when we speak most intimately to one only we become most universal. All great poetry I think was written first for one only, some other self of the poet, and because of the humanity which unites us all, we all understand. But standing before a crowd it is more difficult to say what is in one's heart. The sensitive soul feels how many there must be in that crowd to whom the revelation of the heart would be alien, and instinctively what is said is tempered by the knowledge.

[1] It is perhaps unfair to give these the title of aphorism. They are stray sentences, which it seemed a pity to lose, taken from some purely topical content, and were never intended to be isolated dicta.—M. G.

Poetry is a jealous mistress, and it will not give itself to the lover who will not altogether give himself to it. Those who have lost their hearts utterly to the Muse in youth may be allowed later flirtations with prose, and be forgiven when the repentant singer comes back to his first love. But there must be the period of utter abandonment first, in which the nature surrenders itself to the daemon of poetry to be moulded by it.

*

The arts are less the reflection of the age they are born in than the reaction from the age.

*

The poets of a hundred years ago conceived of themselves as prophets or seers, and they tried to create universally intelligible images in their poetry. But the poet of to-day in many cases becomes the slave of his own drifting consciousness, not the master moulding material into images of beauty, terror or pity.

*

Poetry is the spiritual essence of life.

*

Poetry creates such a loveliness in the heart that I feel I am breathing in a divinely created nature; air, earth, the stars, ourselves, all fondled by the Magician of the Beautiful; all rapt, all sharing in the benediction.

*

If zeal could produce beautiful poetry then there would be many thousands more poets.

*

There are as many earths as there are people living on it, but they are kept secret from us. We never penetrate the other worlds unless the inhabitant be a man of genius, poet, artist or philosopher who can project into our consciousness a vision of the world he lives in.

*

With every new genius a new world is discovered.

*

The poetic nature is like the weathercock on the spire, it catches the first breath of a changing wind. Tell me what the poets are saying to-day and we will know what the mass will be dreaming of in the next generation.

*

It is not easy to win a laurel wreath, but it is much more difficult to keep its leaves fresh. There are many people who wear withered leaves because they do not apply the same intensity of intellect to their art after it has won recognition. The danger of success is that after it one may continue because of a theory what was first an inspiration.

*

All true poetry is in the divine procession and moves in harmony like the choirs of the angels, and the technique of any great master never sounds a discordant note if studied beside the technique of another great master.

*

The intuitions of a poetical nature are more exciting and profound than any logical philosophy of literature could be.

*

All the aesthetics break down in trying to define what beauty is, yet the average man finds not the slightest difficulty in recognising a pretty or a beautiful woman in spite of the bewilderment of the philosophers.

*

What the lover discovers in the beloved is the beauty or poetry which is in his own being. But it may take hundreds of thousands of years before the lovers find that what they really sought was in their own souls.

*

The blindness of love with respect to persons and causes may be justified because the purposes Nature has with us might never be fulfilled if we lived by reason alone and not by faith and imagination.

*

Philosophers who set out to convince us by reason have never aroused convictions so deep, so widespread as the founders of religions who rarely if ever reason, but who reveal, or assert truths, relying on the intuition of those who listen to them.

*

In the heart of age a man may suddenly find a child in himself, and live over again with solemnity, as if it was an instant of angelic life, a moment which long ago was lived lightly and with no thought by the child, running along the sands or straying in the heart-choking magic of night.

*

It is difficult to say how much the world owes to the habit of telling children fairy stories, hero tales and legends of the Golden Age. If the child had not fallen from a childish heaven how could the grown-up man ever get imagination of a beautiful humanity yet to be born on the earth?

The human imagination is perpetually re-creating the world, and, if we imagine clearly and precisely, we create forms which presently become materialised. They become dominant first in other minds, and at last they are translated from mind to matter.

*

One of the very first symptoms of the loss of the soul is the loss of the sense of beauty.

*

I think those critics who are in love with what they call pure poetry and who cry out against the least infection from philosophy or science or politics, would bring poetry to an end, for, although the flower is beauty, the plant must seek nourishment from a thousand things, and you cannot part the flower from that which nourishes it.

*

In life the good and worthy man may be received in the best society, even if he is carelessly dressed or has a slovenly appearance. In literature there is nothing corresponding to this. The keepers of the palace are snobs, and the worthiest thought will not be received with respect if its dress is not fitting.

*

There is always some acid in the best love poetry. The highest love does not give itself so completely as many lovers declare. It always keeps something back, some consciousness of its high companionship with wisdom, beauty and the other immortals.

*

Poet and artist are always trying to enlarge their technique. As a girl becomes a little unhappy if she has to wear last

347

year's fashions, so the poet becomes a little unhappy if he is confined to metrical tradition.

*

There are hours when we are tired of high seriousness, and descend from the palace of the imagination to the kitchen and hear the housemaid gossip about the great beauty who is her mistress, and the butler tell tales about the great hero; and we like all to be reduced to the levels of the commonest humanity.

*

There is no more subtle pleasure under heaven than digging below the foundations of an intellectual, making ourselves immune to the poison of his error and enabling ourselves to enjoy his truth, of which he himself was doubtful.

*

The intellect must ever deal in symbol or fantasy, and its most complete analysis still must be misapprehension, because it is symbol, not reality. It is the spirit which comprehends spirit, without thought.

*

To many people the newspaper is a passion, strong as the passion for alcohol. The eye must always have its tipple. Deprive such men of their daily paper and they will in desperation read anything, a fragment of newspaper twenty years old or ancient advertisements. We have seen them doing this. They are like starving men who come at last to gnaw their boots.

*

Human kindness is the indispensable element in society. Where that exists autocracies, aristocracies, oligarchies and democracies may endure. Once it ceases to pervade a civilisation, that civilisation begins to break up.

*

The temptation to crack political nuts with the sledgehammer has the drawback that it grinds more often than not the kernel to powder.

*

The patriotic idealist assumes moral superiority because of his capacity for sacrifice. The humanist notes how many other things are sacrificed which may be regarded as of far more importance to humanity than the object for which the idealist strives.

*

Nationalism in every country requires a strong admixture of internationalism to prevent it becoming a stupefying drug.

*

It is only too often true in the life of nations, as well as individuals, that the dream or hope which precedes action is nobler than the realisation.

*

There is no end to the compulsions which egomania would apply to the rest of humanity to shape it in its own image and its own limitations if it was allowed free play.

*

There is incipient Caesarism lying more or less latent in every human being. Who is there, when there is disturbance in society, has not found himself with sudden rage thinking to himself how well life would go if some people could be shot?

*

A man, by persistent oppression, may weaken until he develops the slave mind. A nation will never do so. It will, through oppression, develop a fierce antagonism.

*

We are quite sure any Devil would be well content to make a treaty with the Church, leaving it a free hand in the realm of the spiritual and cultural, if he was allowed a free hand in the realm of the economic.

*

Revolutions come less because of ideas than because of circumstance. If circumstance is bad, there are always enough ideas to cause a revolution.

*

The worse our habits the more we have what is called good legislation. When there are good habits in a country the business of the state dwindles.

*

In politics, eaten bread is soon forgotten.

*

No leader, however great a personality he may be, is as important to a people as their own intellectual development.

*

There are thousands of people whose souls are so peculiarly magnetised that the needles of their being point to gold as inevitably as the needle in the compass points to the North Pole.

*

There is always decay and apathy unless there are contraries. The Devil has put it into the hearts of numberless people that the ideal thing is to have absolute peace and no change at all, and these disciples of his regard any new ideas as wicked, whereas, in truth, God is the Great Agitator, to Whose perfection stagnant and barren life is abhorrent.

*

In a sense, it is a good thing to find the opposite of all we believe stated firmly, because it is only when we know the opposites that free will can be exercised and the soul makes its choice.

*

It may be said that no truth is really ours unless the intellect has gone through great labours to make it so, that the person who is contented to receive the conclusions without following the argument will be shallow for ever.

*

We do not derive the slightest pleasure from the society of those who hold in all matters the same opinions as we do. We suffer in such society an intolerable boredom, for our own emanations are poisonous to us as they are to plants.

*

We may fight against what is wrong, but if we allow ourselves to hate, that is to ensure our spiritual defeat and our likeness to what we hate.

*

There is a law in human nature which draws us to be like what we passionately condemn.

*

The men who engage in action are those who soon begin most eagerly to desire peace. Plato was aware of this spiritual reaction against the activities of the external nature when he

351

imagined Ulysses choosing a position of great obscurity for his next life.

*

The people who do wicked things are always fools. Wickedness and folly are both forms of stupidity.

*

Reason, alas, does not remove mountains. It only tries to walk round them, and see what is on the other side.

*

The soul has to keep silent until the body is served.

*

It is as bad to starve youth of its dreams as of its porridge.

*

When the teacher has allowed himself to become a machine, it is really the wisdom of Nature which makes children grow inattentive and disorderly. If they could be forced to attention to a dead mind, their own minds would soon become dead.

*

He seemed less to be addressing an audience than allowing them to overhear some soliloquy between his own heart and himself in which he was trying to arrive at what was right and true and just.

(Of Cardinal O'Donnell)

*

Praise insensibly steals from a man his moral integrity; he grows through acclamation to an appetite for it, and afterwards he must always have an eye on the public and substitutes its judgment for that of the stern monitor within.

There can be no profound spiritual certitude except for those who have been tested; who have consciously chosen between the dark and the light.

*

A man may to-night draw nigh to Deity and become receptive in his meditation of the spirit. The next day he may be absorbed in work and in that absorption remember not at all the deep he had sounded. But was it any the less a deep because human nature could not sustain the meditation for long? A man in the duration of a heart-beat may have intuitions and moods which touch on the eternities. They are no less profound or basic because our humanity cannot hold to them always, and indeed it might not be wisdom to do so.

*

It is the unscientific who are the materialists, whose intellect is not quickened, and the divinity which is everywhere eludes their stupid gaze.

*

What profundities of speculation lie behind this quotation from Heraclitus: "Mortals are immortals; immortals are mortals; living the other's death, dying the other's life". It might be an anticipation of St. Paul's, "Ye are dead in the body", and all that follows in Corinthians on the subject of immortality.

*

It is dangerous to keep up long dialogues between immortal and mortal. Goethe made his Earth Spirit speak but a few words to Faust who evoked it, but what words of wonder and revelation they are:

> Man thou art as the spirit thou conceivest,
> Not me.

353

If our life has depths, if love has discovered its own spiritual roots, our own experience will, I think, stir us more deeply than anything in legend, anything in poetry, because we live poetry rather than read it.

*

The highest virtue is wisdom, and wisdom is the right relation of our own being to That in which we live, and move, and have our own being.

CIVICS
AND
RURAL ECONOMY

CIVICS

AND

RURAL ECONOMY

To some American Economists

THERE MAY SEEM to be something odd in a continental State like America coming to a small island like Ireland to learn from it; but the laws of human life are the same everywhere, and as we are beginning, I believe, to recover from an economic disease with which America is threatened, the method of treatment here, the policy which is being applied, will probably be applicable in every rural community. I am sorry rural America has had to travel abroad for the sake of its health. The disease of rural decay has wrought more harm in the old world than the new, and we have probably thought more over remedies here than there; but in neither the old world nor the new does there seem to be much first-class thinking on the life of the countryman. This will be apparent if we consider the quality of thought which has been devoted to the problems of the city state, or the constitution of widespread dominions, from the days of Solon and Aristotle down to the time of Alexander Hamilton, and compare it with the quality of thought which has been brought to bear on the problem of the rural community.

On the labours of the countryman depend the whole strength and health, nay, the very existence of society; yet, in almost every country, politics, economics and social reform are urban products, and the countryman gets only the crumbs which fall from the political table. It seems to be so in Canada and the States, countries which we in Europe for long regarded as mainly agricultural. It seems only yesterday to the imagination that they were colonised, and yet we find the Minister of Agriculture in Canada announcing a decline in the rural population in eastern Canada. As children sprung from the loins of diseased parents manifest at an early age the same defects in their constitution, so Canada and the States, though in their national childhood, seem already threatened by the same disease from which classic Italy perished, and whose ravages to-day make Great Britain seem to the acute diagnoser of political health like a fruit, ruddy without, but eaten away within and rotten at the core. One expects disease in old age, but not in youth. We expect young countries to sow their wild oats, to have a few revolutions before they settle down to national housekeeping; but we are not moved by these troubles, the result of excessive energy, as we are by symptoms of premature decay. No nation can be regarded as unhealthy when a virile peasantry, contented with rural employments, however discontented with other things, exists on its soil. The disease which has attacked the great industrial communities here and in America is a discontent with rural life. Nothing which has been done hitherto seems able to promote content. It is true, indeed, that science has gone out into the fields; but the labours of the chemist, the bacteriologist, and the mechanical engineer are not enough to ensure health. What is required is the art of the political thinker, the imagination which creates a social order and adjusts it to human needs.

The physician who understands the general laws of human health is of more importance to us here than the specialist. The genius of rural life has not yet appeared. We have no fundamental philosophy concerning it, but we have treasures of political wisdom dealing with humanity as a social organism in the city states or as great nationalities.

I have followed—so far as it is possible for an old-world resident—the story of agricultural population in the States; and I feel certain that, enlarged to continental dimensions and with changes in detail but not in principle, our Irish rural policy should be theirs also. They will have to fit what they have learned in Europe into their gigantic and complex national life, and I believe they will do better than Europe has done with the same ideas. They have the energy of young races, and where we are tired they are fresh. The greatest of American poets made a boast of the youth of his nation when he asked a question and answered it.

> Have the elder races halted? Do they droop and end their
>   lesson wearied over there beyond the seas?
> We take up the burden and the lesson and the task eternal,
>   pioneers, O pioneers.

I might say to the American nation, Will you do the work your race set out to do? Your task is to truly democratise civilisation and its agencies, to spread in widest commonalty culture, comfort, intelligence and happiness, and to give to the average man those things which in an earlier age were the privileges of a few. The country is the fountain of the life and health of a race. And this organisation of the country people into co-operative communities will educate them and make them citizens in the true sense of the word, that is, people continually conscious of their identity of interest with those about them. It is by this conscious sense of solidarity of interest, which only the organised co-operative community can engender in modern times, that the higher achievements of humanity become possible. Religion has created this spirit at times—witness the majestic cathedrals the Middle Ages raised to manifest their faith. Political organisation engendered the passion of citizenship in the Greek States, and the Parthenon and a host of lordly buildings crowned the hills and uplifted and filled with pride the heart of the citizen. Our big countries, our big empires and republics, for all their military strength and science, and the wealth which science has made it possible for man to win, do not create citizenship because of the loose organisation of society, because individualism is rampant, and men, failing to understand the intricacies of the vast and complex life of their country, fall back on private life and private ambitions, and leave the honour of their country and the making of laws and the application of the national revenues to a class of professional politicians, in their turn in servitude to the interests which supply party funds, and so we find corruption in high places and cynicism in the people. It is necessary for the creation of citizens, for the building up of a noble national life, that the social order should be so organised that this sense of interdependence will be constantly felt. It is also necessary for the preservation of the physical health and beauty of our race that more of our people should live in the country and fewer in the cities. I believe it would be an excellent thing for humanity if its civilisation could be based on rural industry mainly and not on urban industry. More and more men and women in our modern civilisation drift out of Nature, out of sweet air, health, strength, beauty, into the cities, where in the third generation there is a rickety population, mean in stature, feverish and depraved in character, with the image of the Devil in mind and matter more than the image of Deity. Those who go like it at first, but city life is like the roll spoken of by the prophet which was sweet in the mouth but bitter in the belly. The first generation are intoxicated by the new life, but in the third generation the cord is cut which connected them with Nature, the Great Mother, and life shrivels up, sundered from the source of life. Is there any prophet, any statesman, any leader, who will, as Moses once led the Israelites out of the Egyptian bondage, excite the human imagination and lead humanity back to Nature, to sunlight, starlight, earth breath, sweet air, beauty, gaiety and health? Is it impossible now to move humanity by great ideas, as Mahomet fired his dark hosts to forgetfulness of life, or as Peter the Hermit awakened Europe to a frenzy so that it hurried its hot chivalry across a continent to the Holy Land? Is not the earth mother of us all? Is it not from Nature we draw life? Do we not perish without sunlight and fresh air? Let us have no breath of air and in five minutes life is extinct. Yet in the cities there is a slow poisoning of life going on day by day. The lover of beauty may walk the streets of London or any big city and may look into ten thousand faces and see none that is lovely. Is not the return of man to a natural life on the earth a great enough idea to inspire humanity? Is not the idea of a civilisation amid the green trees and fields under the smokeless sky alluring? Yes, but men say there is no intellectual life—when man is surrounded by mystery and miracle, when the mysterious forces which bring to birth and life are yet undiscovered, when the earth is teeming with life and the dumb brown lips of the ridges are breathing mystery! Is not the growth of a tree from a tiny cell hidden in the earth as provocative of thought as the things men learn at the schools? Is not thought on these things more interesting than the sophistries of the newspapers? It is only in Nature and by thought on the problems of Nature that our intellect grows to any real truth and draws near to the Mighty Mind which laid the foundations of the world.

Our civilisations are a nightmare, a bad dream. They have no longer the grandeur of Babylon or Nineveh. They grow meaner and meaner as they grow more urbanised. What could be more depressing than the miles of poverty-stricken streets around the heart of any modern city? The memory lies on one "heavy as frost and deep almost as life". It is terrible to think of the children playing on the pavements, the depletion of vitality, with an artificial stimulus supplied by flaring drink-shops. The spirit grows heavy as if death lay on it while it moves amid such things. And outside these places the clouds are flying overhead, snowy and spiritual as of old, the sun is shining, the winds are blowing, the forests are murmuring leaf to leaf, the fields are green, but the magic that God made is unknown to these poor folk. Truly the creation of a rural civilisation is the greatest need of our time. It may not come in our days, but we can lay the foundations of it, preparing the way for the true prophet when he will come.

The Disappearance of the Rural Community

OUR GREAT NATIONS and widespread empires arose in a haphazard fashion out of city states and scattered tribal communities. The fusion of these into larger entities, which could act jointly for offence or defence, so much occupied the thoughts of their rulers that everything else was subordinated to it. As a result the details of our modern civilisations are all wrong. There is an intensive life at a few great political or industrial centres, and wide areas where there is stagnation and decay. Stagnation is most obvious in rural districts. It is so general that it has been often assumed that there was something inherent in rural life which made the countryman slow in mind as his own cattle. But this is not so, as I think can be shown. There is no reason why as intense, intellectual and progressive a life should not be possible in the country as in the towns. The real reason for the stagnation is that the country population is not organised. We often hear the expression "the rural community", but where do we find rural communities? There are rural populations, but that is altogether a different thing. The word "community" implies an association of people having common interests and common possessions, bound together by laws and regulations which express these common interests and ideals and define the relation of the individual to the community. Our rural populations are no more closely connected, for the most part, than the shifting sands on the sea-shore. Their life is almost entirely individualistic. There are personal friendships, of course, but few economic or social partnerships. Everybody pursues his own occupation without regard to the occupation of his neighbours. If a man emigrates it does not affect the occupation of those who farm the land all about him. They go on ploughing and digging, buying and selling, just as before. They suffer no perceptible economic loss by the departure of half a dozen men from the district. A true community would, of course, be affected by the loss of its members. A co-operative society if it loses a dozen members, the milk of their cows, their orders for fertilisers, seeds and feeding-stuffs receives serious injury to its prosperity. There is a minimum of trade below which its business cannot fall without bringing about a complete stoppage of its work and an inability to pay its employees. That is the difference between a community and an unorganised population. In the first the interests of the community make a conscious and direct appeal to the individual, and the community, in its turn, rapidly develops an interest in the prosperity of the member. In the second, the interest of the individual in the community is only sentimental, and as there is no organisation the community lets the individual slip away or disappear without comment or action. We had true rural communities in ancient Ireland, though the organisation was military rather than economic. But the members of a clan had common interests. They owned the land in common. It was a common interest to preserve it intact. It was to their interest to have a numerous membership of the clan, because it made it less liable to attack. Men were drawn by the social order out of merely personal interests into a larger life. In their organisations they were unconsciously groping, as all human organisations are, towards the final solidarity of humanity, the federation of the world.

Well, these old rural communities disappeared. The greater organisations of nation or empire regarded the smaller communities jealously in the past, and broke them up and gathered all the strings of power into capital cities. The result was a growth of the State, with a local decay of civic, patriotic or public feeling, ending in bureaucracies and State departments, where paid officials devoid of intimacy with local needs replaced the services naturally and voluntarily rendered in an earlier period. The rural population, no longer existing as a rural community, sank into stagnation. There was no longer a common interest, a social order turning their minds to larger than individual ends. Where feudalism was preserved, the feudal chief, if the feeling of *noblesse oblige* was strong, might act as a centre of progress, but where this was lacking social decay set in. The difficulty of moving the countryman, which has become traditional, is not due to the fact that he lives in the country, but to the fact that he lives in an unorganised society. If Dublin or another city wants an art gallery, or public baths, or recreation grounds, there is a machinery which can be set in motion, there are corporations and urban councils which can be approached. If public opinion is evident—and it is easy to organise public opinion in a town—the city representatives will consider the scheme, and if they approve and it is within their power as a corporation or council, they are able to levy rates to finance the art gallery, public bathhouses, recreation grounds, public gardens or whatever else. Now let us go to a country district where there is no organisation. It may be obvious to one or two people that the place is perishing and the humanity is decaying, lacking some centre of life. They want a village hall, but how is it to be obtained? They begin talking about it to this person or that. They ask these people to talk to their friends, and the ripples go out weakening and widening for months, perhaps for years. I know of districts where this has happened. There are in all probability hundreds of parishes in Ireland where some half-dozen intelligent men want co-operative societies or village halls or rural libraries. They discuss the matter with their neighbours, but find a complete ignorance on the subject. Before enthusiasm can be kindled there must be some knowledge. The countryman reads little, and it is a long and tedious business before enough people are excited to bring them to the point of appealing to some expert to come in and advise.

More changes often take place within a dozen years after a co-operative society is first started than have taken place for a century previous. I am familiar with a district—Temple-crone, in north-west Donegal. It was one of the most wretchedly poor districts in Ireland. The farmers were at the mercy of the gombeen traders and the agricultural middle-men. Then a dozen years ago a co-operative society was formed. I am sure the oldest inhabitant there will agree that more changes for the better for farmers have taken place since the co-operative society was started than he could remember in all his previous life. The reign of the gombeen man is over. The farmers control their own buying and selling. Their organisation markets for them the eggs and poultry. It procures seeds, fertilisers and domestic require-ments. It turns the members' pigs into bacon. They have a village hall and an allied women's organisation. They sell the products of the women's industry. They have a co-operative band, social gatherings and concerts. They have spread out into half a dozen parishes. They have gone southward to

Ardara with their propaganda and eastwards towards Falcarragh, and in half a dozen years in all that district, previously without organisation, there will be well-organised farmers' guilds, concentrating in themselves all the trade of their districts, having meeting-places where the opinion of the members can be taken; having a machinery, committees and executive officers to carry out whatever may be decided on, and having funds, or profits, the joint property of the community, which can be drawn upon to finance their undertakings. You see what a tremendous advantage it is to farmers in a district to have such organisations; what a lever they can pull and control! The business mind of the country must be organised to counter the business mind of the town, the political forces of the farmers must be organised to meet the organised political forces of the town—and to meet them intelligently. For lack of this political organisation our own movement is hampered in many ways. It is a trade union to promote the interests of agriculture and the business of farming which is required. And to that it should confine itself altogether, because here farmers of all politics can agree, and anything more would split them. This has been a policy adopted by French farmers with great success, and they have at present in their Parliament over three hundred deputies pledged to promote the interests of the farmers' associations. They form for this purpose an agricultural party which includes members of all parties. They can get any legislation they want since they pledged their deputies. I think legislation is the least important thing, but sometimes it becomes necessary, and trying to keep an expanding movement within the bounds prescribed by old enactments is like trying to keep a big man clothed with garments which fitted him when a boy.

But political action is the least important thing for us. The great thing for our movement to have is an ideal of its own to work towards. It is not what the State has done or can do which inspires, but the infinitely higher possibilities which arise through the voluntary co-operation of men to wring from Nature and life the utmost they can give. If farmers are to retain a surplus of wealth beyond the bare necessaries of life, if they are ever to see in rural districts any of the comforts and luxuries of the city, they must make it their steady, persistent and fundamental policy to work towards complete control over the manufacture and sale of all the produce of the countryside, its livestock, its crops, its by-products and the manufacturing businesses connected with these, so that they can act in their own interests through their own agents in distant markets, and push their produce with the energy of self-interest. I say that this policy is not against the interests of the towns, for anything which increases the wealth of farmers increases their power of consumption and makes the countryside a better market for the articles which the townsman produces.

To aim at the creation of a nobler social order in Ireland than we have had in the past might well give us all inspiration and energy, and make us feel that our movement occupies no mean place amongst those movements which are trying to regenerate our land. I would say, indeed, that all other movements, however necessary, are external and hollow compared with any movement which deals with life itself and tries to create conditions in which a higher humanity will be possible, and sets that before it as its aim.

The Creation of the Rural Community

I HAVE TALKED a long while round and round the rural community, but I have not suggested how it is to be created. I am coming to that. It really cannot be created. It is a natural growth when the right seed is planted. Co-operation is the seed. Let us take Ireland. Twenty-five years ago there was not a single co-operative society in the country. Individualism was the mode of life. Every farmer manufactured and sold as seemed best in his eyes. It was generally the worst possible way he could have chosen. Then came Sir Horace Plunkett and his colleagues, preaching co-operation. A creamery was established here, an agricultural society there, and, having planted the ideas, it was some time before the economic expert could decide whether they were planted in fertile soil.

But that question was decided many years ago. The co-operative society, started for whatever purpose originally, is an omnivorous feeder, and it exercises a magnetic influence on all agricultural activities, so that we now have societies which buy milk, manufacture and sell butter, deal in poultry and eggs, cure bacon, provide fertilisers, feeding-stuffs, seed and machinery for their members, and even cater for every requirement of the farmer's household. This magnetic power of attracting and absorbing to themselves the various rural activities which the properly constituted co-operative societies have makes them develop rapidly, until in the course of a decade or a generation there is created a real social organism, where the members buy together, manufacture together, market together; where, finally, their entire interests are bound up with the interests of the community. We cannot foretell the developments in each branch, but we can see clearly that the organised community can lay hold of discoveries and inventions which the individual farmer cannot. It is little for the co-operative society to buy expensive threshing sets and let its members have the use of them, but the individual farmer would have to save a long time before he could raise a thousand pounds. The society is a better buyer than the individual. It can buy things the individual cannot buy. It is a better producer also. The plant for a creamery is beyond the individual farmer; but our organised farmers in Ireland, small though they are, find it no trouble to erect and equip a creamery with plant costing two thousand pounds.

In the organised rural community the eggs, milk, poultry, pigs, cattle, grain and wheat produced on the farm and not consumed, or required for further agricultural production, will automatically be delivered to the co-operative business centre of the district, where the manager of the dairy will turn the milk into butter or cheese, and the skim milk will be returned to feed the community's pigs. The poultry and egg department will pack and dispatch the fowl and eggs to market. The mill will grind the corn and return it ground to the member, or there may be a co-operative bakery to which some of it may go. The pigs will be dealt with in the abattoir, sent as fresh pork to the market or be turned into bacon to feed the members. We may be certain that any intelligent rural community will try to feed itself first and will only sell the surplus. It will realise that it will be unable to buy any food half as good as the food it produces. The community will hold in common all the best machinery too expensive for the members to buy individually. The agricultural labourers will gradually become skilled mechanics, able to direct threshers, binders, diggers, cultivators and new implements we have no conception of now. They will be members of the society sharing in its profits in proportion to their wages even as the farmer will in proportion to his trade. The co-operative community will have its own carpenters, smiths, mechanics employed in its workshop at repairs or in making those things which can profitably be made locally. There may be a laundry where the washing—a heavy burden for the women—will be done; for we may be sure that every scrap of power generated will be utilised. One happy invention after another will come to lighten the labour of life.

There will be of course a village hall with a library and gymnasium, where the boys and girls will be made straight,

athletic and graceful. In the evenings, when the work of the
day is done, if we went into the village hall we would find a
dance going on perhaps or a concert. There might be a co-
operative choir or band. There would be a committee-room
where the council of the community would meet once a
week, for their enterprises would have grown, and the
business of such a parish community might easily be over
one hundred thousand pounds, and would require constant
thought. There would be no slackness on the part of the
council in attending, because their fortunes would depend
on their communal enterprises, and they would have to
consider reports from the managers and officials of the
various departments. The co-operative community would
be a busy place. In years when the society was exceptionally
prosperous and earned larger profits than usual on its trade,
we should expect to find discussions in which all the members would join as to the use to be made of these profits—
whether they should be altogether divided or what portion
of them should be devoted to some public purpose. We may
be certain that there would be animated discussions, because
a real solidarity of feeling would have arisen and a pride in
the work of the community engendered, and they would like
to be able to outdo the good work done by the neighbouring
communities.

One might like to endow the village school with a chemical
laboratory, another might want to decorate the village hall
with reproductions of famous pictures, another might suggest removing all the hedges and planting the roadsides and
lanes with gooseberry bushes, currant bushes and fruit trees,
as they do in some German communes to-day. There would
be eloquent pleadings for this or that, for an intellectual heat
would be engendered in this human hive and there would
be no more illiterates or ignoramuses. The teaching in the
village school would be altered to suit the new social order,
and the children of the community would, we may be

certain, be instructed in everything necessary for the intelligent conduct of the communal business. The spirit of rivalry between one community and another, which exists to-day between neighbouring creameries, would excite the imagination of the members, and the organised community would be as swift to act as the unorganised community is slow to act. Intelligence would be organised as well as business. The women would have their own industries, of embroidery, crochet, lace, dressmaking, weaving, spinning or whatever new industries the awakened intelligence of women may devise and lay hold of as the peculiar labour of their sex.

The business of distribution of the produce and industries of the community would be carried on by great federations, which would attend to export and sale of the products of thousands of societies. Such communities would be real social organisms. The individual would be free to do as he willed, but he would find that communal activity would be infinitely more profitable than individual activity. We would then have a real democracy carrying on its own business, and bringing about reforms without pleading to, or begging of, the State, or intriguing with or imploring the aid of political middlemen to get this, that or the other done for them. They would be self-respecting, because they would be self-helping above all things. The national councils and meetings of national federations would finally become the real Parliament of the nation, for wherever all the economic power is centred there also is centred all the political power. And no politician would dare to interfere with the organised industry of a nation.

There is nothing to prevent such communities being formed. They would be a natural growth once the seed was planted. We see such communities naturally growing up in Ireland, with perhaps a little stimulus from outside from rural reformers and social enthusiasts. If this ideal of the organised rural community is accepted there will be difficulties, of course, and enemies to be encountered. The agricultural middleman is doubtless as powerful a person proportionately on the American continent as he is in this little island. He will rage furiously. He will organise all his forces to keep the farmers in subjection, and to retain his peculiar functions of fleecing the farmer as producer and the general public as consumer. Unless you are determined to eliminate the middleman in agriculture, you will fail to effect anything worth while attempting.

I would lay down certain fundamental propositions which, I think, should be accepted without reserve as a basis of reform. First, that the farmers must be organised to have *complete control* over all the business connected with their industry. Dual control is intolerable. Agriculture will never be in a satisfactory condition if the farmer is relegated to the position of a manual worker on his land; if he is denied the right of a manufacturer to buy the raw materials of his industry on trade terms; if other people are to deal with his raw materials, his milk, cream, fruit, vegetables, livestock, grain and other produce; and if these capitalist middle agencies are to manufacture the farmers' raw material into butter, bacon or whatever else, are to do all the marketing and export, paying farmers what they please on the one hand, and charging the public as much as they can on the other hand. The existence of these middle agencies is responsible for a large proportion of the increased cost of living, which is the most acute problem of modern industrial communities. They have too much power over the farmer and are too expensive a luxury for the consumer. It would be very unbusinesslike for any country to contemplate the permanence in national life of a class whose personal interests are always leading them to fleece both producer and consumer alike.

So the first fundamental idea for reformers to get into their minds is that farmers, through their own co-operative organisations, must control the entire business connected with agriculture. There will not be so much objection to co-operative sale as to co-operative purchase by the farmers. But one is as necessary as the other. You must bear in mind, what is too often forgotten, that farmers are manufacturers, and as such are entitled to buy the raw materials for their industry at wholesale prices. Every other kind of manufacturer in the world gets trade terms when he buys. Those who buy, not to consume, but to manufacture and sell again, get their requirements at wholesale terms in every country in the world. If a publisher of books is approached by a bookseller he gives that bookseller trade terms because he buys to sell again. If you or I as private individuals want one of those books we pay the full retail price. Even the cobbler, the carpenter, the solitary artist, get trade terms. The farmer, who is as much a manufacturer as the shipbuilder, or the factory proprietor, is as much entitled to trade terms when he buys the raw materials for his industry. His seeds, fertilisers, ploughs, implements, cake, feeding-stuffs are the raw materials of his industry, which he uses to produce wheat, beef, mutton, pork or whatever else, and, in my opinion, there should be no differentiation between the farmer when he buys and any other kind of manufacturer. Is it any wonder that agriculture decays in countries where the farmers are expected to buy at retail prices and sell at wholesale prices? You must not, to save any row, sell the rights of farmers.

The second proposition I lay down is that this necessary organisation work among the farmers must be carried on by an organising body which is entirely controlled by those interested in agriculture—farmers and their friends. To ask the State or a State department to undertake this work is to ask a body influenced and often controlled by powerful capitalists and middle agencies, which it should be the aim of the organisation to eliminate. The State can, without obstruction from any quarter, give farmers a technical education in the science of farming; but let it once interfere with business, and a horde of angry interests set to work to hamper and limit by every possible means; and compromises on matters of principle, where no compromise ought to be permitted, are almost inevitable.

A Census Report

DUBLIN SO BEAUTIFUL a city to the visitor, and even to ourselves, has a dark heart to it. The West of Ireland, so enchanting to the tourist, rivals Dublin in the overcrowding of its population. In these overcrowded rooms what function of the body can be concealed? Modesty and decency are qualities which must be almost as suffocated as the people living in the rooms. Anyone who looks at the statistics, who is not content to accept tables at their face value without thinking what they imply, must be compelled to think that the unpleasant realism of latter-day Irish novelists and dramatists like O'Casey and O'Flaherty, which is so disagreeable to those whose sense of what is decent and proper has been allowed to develop unhampered in rooms which they had to themselves, must have some relation to the facts revealed in the report.

We find in Dublin that the number of persons housed in dwellings with four or more persons in one room was sixty-six thousand, and there are almost incredible overcrowdings tabulated by the statistician. One table gives the number of persons living in one-room dwellings in the Free State. We find that there were roughly nineteen thousand people living five together in one room; that there were sixteen thousand people who lived six together in one room. There were eleven thousand people living in groups of seven in one room. As we descend in the lower circles of the housing hell we find six thousand people living in rooms, each harbouring eight persons. The density of nine to a room is a misery donated to three thousand eight hundred persons. Of those persons living ten in one room the number is one thousand nine hundred, and there are a few hundreds who are crowded in elevens, twelves or "more" in one-room dwellings. It seems for these people civilisation has no particular advance from the cave dwellings of their ancestors thousands of years ago. There was probably more air in the cave than in the tenement, and it is possible the cave men and women were not made sensitive to their conditions as their descendants are, who are taught in churches and schools some ideas about human decencies which they find themselves unable to put into practice.

It is as dangerous for a child to be born in North Dublin City, No. 2 district, as it was for a soldier to be for a year in the trenches in the greatest war the world has known. There is a relation between housing conditions and health. The tables show what we expect, that people living under overcrowded conditions have shorter lives than those who are well housed, and they show also that infantile mortality increases terribly as overcrowding increases. These terrible unemotional tables bear relentless witness to the way in which Nature punishes overcrowding.

It would be foolish for us to pretend that we see how exactly this housing problem can be tackled. It has to be remembered there are many other necessary services which must be carried on, education in chief. The country is not a rich one, our Government has not been insensible to the importance of the problem, and it has done a great deal to encourage the builders. But it is obvious from this report how far many of our people are from average decency in the circumstance of their lives. The first thing to be done is to translate these cold-blooded statistical tables into realistic pictures of life. We confess we would like to see one of our latter-day novelists, who seem to have lost entirely that restriction upon realism which is known as squeamishness, writing a story about people who live seven, or nine or eleven in one room. It would probably be suppressed by our Board of Censors in that hypocritical way we have of penalising the mention of things rather than the things themselves. When somebody puts his foot through the screens and shows what is hidden away behind them, then there will be reforms, and later we may come back to idealism again, an idealism without hypocrisy.

A Dublin Street

RATHMINES ROAD, alas, is rapidly becoming a collection of architectural meannesses. We avert our eyes from these as we go into the city. They seem to be mutely crying out: there is no beauty, there is no spirit, there is no God. They are atheism in brick and concrete, and if there is any justice in the universe, those responsible ought to undergo a long and painful purification hereafter before they are allowed to have even the most distant glimpse of the Heavenly City. Dublin might be made a very beautiful city. It has many fine buildings and streets but their beauty is obviously an eyesore to some of our barbarians who, if they can lay their hands on a fine building, will try their best to discolour it with hideous advertisement. Can anybody look without disgust on the fine façade of the Rotunda which our barbarians have so desecrated with posters of cinematograph shows that it is as painful to look on as a putrefying sore? In no city where the people had civic culture would such abominations be permitted. Wherever we look in Dublin our senses are offended by civic apathy on the one side and an evil energy on the other. The station at Harcourt Street is almost smothered by a conflagration of gaudy paper set on and about it on every side. Railway companies, great national corporations as they are, ought to have the same sense of dignity as a bank or university. Imagine the noble buildings in College Green now inhabited by the Bank of Ireland under control of our railway directors! They would erect hoardings all round its pillars and we may be certain that its sky-line would be let to some brazen manufacturer of pills so that one could not even look at the heavens without feeling that our planet, at whose birth the morning stars sang to-gether, had become a stellar degenerate. We have become callous because the most beautiful view in Dublin, looking up the river from O'Connell Bridge, was desecrated for long years by a sky-line of dog-biscuits and patent foods. We were not allowed to look at the noblest sunset without these obscene manufacturers intruding their wares upon us. That abomination went when the bridge ceased to be private property, but the evil it did remains after it in an indiffer-ence on all sides to civic decency and civic amenities. At Portobello Bridge the view up the canal is obscured by a huge wooden structure on the one side, while on the other a hoarding flaunts its meretricious colours over the neglected canal bank, that canal bank that with a little care might be made so charming if trees were planted here as elsehere. We are barbarians.

Rathmines congratulates itself on its low rates, but it is begetting its own decadence by its neglect of the amenities. Its principal road used to be charming with its green spaces and trees; now it is rapidly being corroded with mean buildings. It has no breathing space. A civic sense would have endeavoured to maintain these green fields as a play-ground for children. There is no place there where child-hood can play, and neglected childhood roams about doing what damage it can to front gardens. Soon the refined inhabitants who congratulated themselves on their low rates will begin to find it an unpleasant residential area, a flitting

377

will take place and the value of house property will begin to decline. Dublin is not a rich city and the noble visions of the town-planners may take a generation to realise, but it need not permit our barbarians to make it hideous. The mere power of prohibition used with discretion and good taste would rapidly effect a change for the better at little or no expense. The Commissioners should have power to prevent anything objectionable to the senses, whether of smell, sound or sight. They do try to prevent poisonous smells which affect our bodily health. They ought also to consider our spiritual health. It cannot be any good preparation for the divine beauty we hope shall enrapture our eyes after we leave this world to have our spiritual senses deadened while we are in it.

It is bad psychology on the part of self-advertisers to be too vehement and noisy. When everybody is making a noise, nothing is heard. Where everybody is making a blatant appeal to the eye, nothing is seen. The display defeats its own purpose. The senses get hardened and opaque, and one passes by without taking any notice. We shut our eyes when there are too many sights. It is quite possible for the trader or manufacturer who must advertise his goods to make panels in the building so that the placing of the advertisement might add to, not detract from, the architecture. There ought to be good fellowship between merchants for the sake of the city, and they should consider the effect of advertisement on the appearance of the street. We are not really as a people insensitive by nature to beauty, only by lack of training. Once our city rulers set the example, we shall find the citizens beginning to catch the infection, and a pride in the beauty of the city becoming a possession of the average man here as it is a cause of pride in beautiful cities on the Continent. Civic patriotism truly arises far more from aesthetic feeling than from commercial feeling. The latter tends to disintegrate by the competitive instinct aroused.

The former tends to unite because the aesthetic spirit aims at harmony, and an orchestration of activities to create is beauty common to all. Quicken the latent sense of beauty by vigorous crusade against what is ugly and in a little we may find our wealthy merchants with something of that spirit which inspired Sir Hugh Lane. Our Commissioners have deserved well for what they have effected for the material welfare of the ratepayers. Now let them do something for our spiritual welfare. Let them save our capital city from its barbarians.

The Dublin Corporation

THE DUBLIN CORPORATION has for many years been an organism inhabited by multiple personalities like those strange psychological cases doctors write about, or the mediums at spiritualist séances through which all kinds of beings speak; now it is the Devil, having lost his sting; now it is an angel with a platitude; next, it may be a poet having lost his genius, or some other famous personalities, all having lost intelligence and common sense.

The State and Genius

THE JAPANESE GARDENERS are masters of strange horticultural secrets. They can dwarf forest trees so that they can be put in pots, and these become Peter Pans of the forest and never grow up. Great empires have exercised political arts akin to this, and subject nationalities under treatment by these political gardeners rarely grow up. The Irish national consciousness remained for centuries in a state of youth without any age in its thought. A nation luckily is not like a forest tree which remains stunted once the gardener has exercised his arts on it. A nation may escape the long arm of the gardener and renew itself by the coming into existence of new generations freed from the chemistry which stunted its predecessors, and we need not fear that the magic exercised in the past will continue its influence or that we must be permanently a Peter Pan among nations.

There is no brilliancy in the greater empires and nation states which is denied to the smaller states. Great empires do not seem to develop genius in proportion to their magnitude, and this may be because Nature never creates more than is necessary to enable an organism to function. The whale, huger by far than the minnow, has not a thousand eyes but two. Attica, no larger than Tipperary, developed political thought, arts, literature, drama and science which were the source of inspiration for Europe for centuries. So, too, many mediaeval city states, duchies or republics were rich in the arts and sciences. That was because they had to deal with every problem involved by government and civilisation, life, death, justice, culture, science and art, and human nature drew on its unfathomable resources and was equal to the occasion. But when these little states were absorbed in great nation states or empires the genius does not seem to have been absorbed. Nature created no more genius than was necessary to run the bigger organism, and the political whales have no greater range of faculties than the political herrings. They have more attention directed to them because the movements of great bodies always excite apprehension among smaller creatures. The artists of Holland are at least as good as the artists of Great Britain, Russia, and the United States. The literature produced by Irish writers in the present generation is equal in quality if not in quantity to the poetry or drama created in the great nation states. In the small states it is possible to develop something like an intensive culture of human life, and it might be argued that if the smaller states were multiplied each with their own responsibilities human nature would be equal to the demand on it, and we would have more plentiful genius and richer and more varied cultures in the world.

Criticism and Creation

WHEN PEOPLE are creating anything, when they are spending their time, their energy, their money on this, they take the trouble to think, and the levels of life are raised. The sum-total of national energy is increased in the process of creation when a good book is written, a fine play is well acted, a beautiful picture is painted, an orchestra trained, a creamery started, a mill set to work, a new factory built, a scheme for the electrification of our water-power well thought out, when an extra acre is cultivated. The sum-total of national energy is lowered by a multitude of mere critics wearing political labels as a protective colouring to hide their emptiness. Criticism which is not creative, when the critic does not make it clear that he speaks out of intimate knowledge and has himself well thought-out alternatives, is the emptiest of occupations. There is no mentality too low, no intelligence too ill-instructed for the business of criticism as we hear it too often on political platforms, or as we read it in the journals with political labels.

Culture ～～～

A NATION IS CULTIVATED only in so far as the average man, not the exceptional person, is cultivated and has knowledge of the thought, imagination and intellectual history of his nation. Where there is a general culture its effects are seen in the houses, the pictures, the home and garden and

381

the arts of life; a better taste is manifest: almost insensibly beauty enters into the household, and what is meant by a civilisation is apparent. The young men have something better to do in their leisure moments than leaning against walls or acquiring an excited muddiness of wit in public-houses. The women are better dressed, the influence of music and the arts is felt, and atom by atom the material in the soul is transmuted into the spiritual.

Wordsworth spoke of joy in widest commonalty spread, and we ought to aim at the widest diffusion of the best ideas, the best methods and models, so as to raise our average. Nobody looks with pleasure at a castle or a cathedral rising out of slums, as if there was neither *noblesse oblige* in the aristocracy nor application to the poor of the ethic of religion. Neither is it to the glory of a country that there should be a few brilliant and exceptional men, and mental darkness or ignorance among the multitude. Our politicals used to exhibit our sores to visitors, showing them round congested districts to point out the results of bad government. Too many now seem to have forgotten the existence of the sores since political capital cannot be made out of them against any but ourselves. The civic sense must awaken rapidly and our concern be about the quality of life in our country. There is really nothing else that matters but that. Governments exist for this, literature and the arts exist for this, economic enterprise exists for this, and the quality of life evolved is their justification.

THE END